83

THE
FIRST STATE DUMA

Contemporary Reminiscences

by V. A. MAKLAKOV

Translated from the Russian

by MARY BELKIN

INDIANA UNIVERSITY PUBLICATIONS

RUSSIAN AND EAST EUROPEAN SERIES, VOL. 30

DISTRIBUTED BY

INDIANA UNIVERSITY PRESS

Bloomington

THE FIRST STATE DUMA

THE FIRST
STATE DUMA

Contemporary Reminiscences

by V. A. MAKLAKOV

Translated from the Russian

by MARY BELKIN

INDIANA UNIVERSITY PUBLICATIONS

RUSSIAN AND EAST EUROPEAN SERIES, VOL. 30

DISTRIBUTED BY

INDIANA UNIVERSITY PRESS

Bloomington

Russian and East European Series
Russian and East European Institute
Indiana University
Volume 30

This book is a Translation of V. A. Maklakov, Pervaia
Gosudarstvennaia Duma, Vospominaniia Sovremennika
(Paris: Maison du Livre Etranger, 1939).

Publication of this book was made possible by grants
from the Friends of the University of Alberta and the
Advisory Committee on International Studies of Indiana
University.

All orders should be addressed to the

Indiana University Press
10th and Morton Streets
Indiana University
Bloomington, Indiana

Library of Congress Catalog Card Number: 64-63021
Printed in the United States of America

ACKNOWLEDGMENTS

The translator wishes to express her thanks to Dr. R. W. Collins and Dr. F. D. Blackley for their critical examination of the early drafts and their valuable suggestions and advice; to Dr. Walter H. Johns, through whose good offices the subsidy from the Friends of the University of Alberta was arranged; and of course to the Friends of the University of Alberta for their generous contribution. Thanks are also due to Mrs. Nancy H. Gaines for her painstaking editing of the manuscript for the press. To Dr. R. H. McNeal a very special appreciation and a debt of gratitude, for without his encouragement and assistance in the final revision and his tireless efforts in making the publishing arrangements it is doubtful that this book could have been produced.

CONTENTS

FOREWORD

For the specialist in the last decade of Imperial Russia there
is little need to explain or justify the translation of the political
studies and autobiographical works of V. A. Maklakov (Pervaia
Gosudarstvennaia Duma, Vospominaniia Sovremennika, Paris, 1939;
Vtoraia Gosudarstvennaia Duma, Vospominaniia Sovremennika, Paris,
1941; V. A. Maklakov, Vospominanii, New York, 1954; Vlast i
Obshchestvennost na Zakatie Staroi Rossii, Illiustrirovannoi Rossii,
n. p., n. d.). As a moderate liberal leader, member of the Second,
Third, and Fourth Dumas, a widely known jurist, an original, force-
ful thinker stemming from the nobility with connections in the highest
political circles (his younger brother was N. A. Maklakov, rightist
member of the Imperial Council, former provincial governor, and
Minister of the Interior from 1913 to 1915), Maklakov's analyses of
the Dumas have a unique value in the literature of the period and for
a perspective in the study of modern Russian history.

In the first place, this translation of The First State Duma and
the previously published translation of the study on the Second Duma
convey some of the invaluable atmosphere of the Duma sessions which
only a participant can offer (I remember how many facets fell into
place when in the spring of 1957 I merely observed the interior of
the Tauride Palace where the Duma met). Then, Mr. Maklakov reflects the attitude of the right-wing liberals who could not be as
nationalistic as the Octobrists. In this connection, this work on the
First Duma represents an important evaluation of the original, more
aggressive Cadet tactics in the perspective of the reform and revolutionary movement. And it drives home solidly the limitations that
right-wing liberal thought would place on the meaning and scope of
a constitutional monarchy. It clarifies the odds that constitutionalists
in the Western sense had to face in the Russian cultural scene with
its long, statist, patriarchal tradition.

Socially close to bureaucratic circles, it is not surprising that
Maklakov reflects on the traditional contrast of Duma "amateurs"
versus government specialists, or considers that a majority decision
becomes the "autocracy of the Duma majority." And he reflects
vividly a legalistic, almost bureaucratic concept of the period of
revolutionary struggle which would load all the advantages on the
side of the government. His criticism of the First Duma has some
validity if the prevailing semirevolutionary mood is deleted from the

picture (he strives to minimize its oppositional as opposed to revolutionary aspects, despite the hindsight of the second elections).
But he later carried over some of these ideas into his evaluation of
the Second Duma, after the Cadets had made serious readjustments
and government limitations became strongly reminiscent of those
with which autocracy beset the zemstvo organizations in the preceding
half-century. All of this can be instructive in the light of the attitudes
of some strata of the latter-day Soviet intelligentsia. There is a
strong affinity between some of the attitudes revealed by Maklakov
concerning control over public activity and the more blatant statist
concepts of the present-day administrative and technological leadership of the USSR.

    The need for greater flexibility and compromise by the liberal
leadership was obvious. The question is whether that was feasible
in the juncture of circumstances in the period of the first two dumas--
or for that matter natural in Russian political experience. If Maklakov
found relatively centralized structures more congenial than his liberal
colleagues, he would naturally discover more possibilities for compromise.

                                                    Alfred Levin
Stillwater, Oklahoma
September 1963

TRANSLATOR'S PREFACE

The defects of the Emancipation Act of 1861 and the subsequent progressive impoverishment of the Russian peasant had kept the agrarian population in almost constant ferment during the closing decades of the nineteenth century. Even in the most fertile sections of the country, the peasants were barely able to exist in time of plenty and when crops failed they suffered hunger and destitution. The famines of 1892 and 1897-98, aggravated by government collection of taxes and redemption dues from reserves, showed how bankrupt the agrarian system had become. Widespread disturbances were the order of the day from 1902 to 1905 in all agricultural area.

Labor was no better off. The rapid industrialization of the 1890's came to an end with the completion of the Trans-Siberian Railway, and by the turn of the century, severe unemployment was prevalent.

The conservative policy of the government took no account of the urgent needs of the nation, giving rise to a strong revolutionary opposition. There were frequent political demonstrations, particularly among students, strikes and riots among factory workers, and unrest in the armed forces. The growing public protest was silenced by harsh reprisals against the zemstvos, the press, and the universities.

The outbreak of the Russo-Japanese War sparked the agrarian, labor, and general discontent. The war was unpopular from the start, and the negligence and incompetence that contributed to the military reverses swelled the tide of indignation against the government until the authorities were unable to cope with it. A change was imperative; the corrupt, inefficient bureaucracy had to go. The clamor for a constitution was not to be denied.

The Social-Revolutionary party, concerned with the agrarian question and political terror, carried on an active campaign of propaganda. Revolutionary literature was smuggled in from abroad, and secret printing presses turned out thousands of propaganda leaflets, which were distributed among workers, students, and liberal individuals. The assassination of Pleve, Minister for Internal Affairs, was carried out by the Social-Revolutionary party as part of its program. In the fall of 1904, street demonstrations in St. Petersburg and Moscow were dispersed ruthlessly by police and Cossacks.

   The Union of Zemstvos, meeting in Moscow in November, 1904,
asked for freedom of the press, civil rights, local self-government,
and a national legislative assembly. The government ignored this request, and the zemstvos were told to mind their own business and
stay out of politics.
   The fall of Port Arthur, a blow to the government's prestige,
had disastrous internal consequences and precipitated the revolution.
The Putilov strike and the Winter Palace incident (Bloody Sunday)
outraged European and Russian opinion and resulted in a wave of
strikes, demonstrations, and protest meetings unprecedented in the
history of the country. Railways and communications were completely
immobilized. The emperor was urged to rally loyal elements of the
public by concessions before it was too late, but the March Manifesto
reiterated the tsar's determination to maintain the autocracy. However, the ministry was ordered to accept suggestions from public
organizations, and a measure of reforms was promised. News of the
annihilation of the fleet added to public indignation and aroused a
storm of protest against the bankruptcy of the administration. Resentment against existing conditions found expression in violence and
lawlessness. Concessions were necessary to restore law and order.
The country demanded an end to the war and a constitution. A joint
conference of the Zemstvos and Town Councils culminated in the sending of a deputation (Prince Trubetskoi) to the emperor, who promised
to grant a national assembly.
   In August a decree was issued instituting the consultative Bulygin
Duma; elections were to be in four stages, with strictly limited franchise. Meanwhile, negotiations with Japan ended, permitting concentration on internal affairs.
   Unrest and disorder continued throughout the country. The
Potemkin with its mutinous sailors terrorized the Black Sea. Universities became hotbeds of discontent. Peasants, stirred by the Social-
Revolutionary slogan "all land for peasants," ransacked estates.
Poland, the Baltic, Siberia, and the South were in a turmoil. Arrest
of the railway union leaders led to a rail strike, which soon became
a general strike. The socialist parties established a Soviet in St.
Petersburg on October 27. When it took over leadership of the Union
of Unions, Miliukov organized zemstvo liberals and moderate professionals into the Constitutional Democratic party, the "Cadets."
   Under pressure of circumstances and following the advice of
Witte, the emperor proclaimed the October Manifesto, granting the
nation "unshakable foundations of civic liberty, freedom from arrest
without cause, freedom of conscience, speech, assembly, and association." The government also agreed to the election of 500 representatives (property franchise) to a Duma with legislative powers,
and no law was to be passed without its approval. The tsar was not

a reformer. He did not want to grant a constitution and did so contrary to his wishes, in the hope of restoring order; but strikes, riots,
and mutinies continued.

The first flush of enthusiasm was followed by the realization
that the government promises were a long way from self-government.
Press attacks, petitions from liberal organizations, strikes, and
agrarian disorders all were proof of the discontent in the land, threatening the foundations of the existing order. Mass meetings became
the order of the day, some of them drawing 50,000 persons, and
ranged from Kiev to Tiflis and Riga.

Almost simultaneously with the October Manifesto "patriotic"
mobs began widespread pogroms--attacks on Jews, workers, students,
and the intellegentsia. Police and armed forces often stood by while
atrocities were perpetrated. In November a series of arrests of
leaders took place, among them the Central Committee of the Peasant
Union. Martial law was declared in St. Petersburg and leading members of the Soviet were arrested. The socialist parties issued a call
for a general strike, preliminary to armed insurrection. It failed in
St. Petersburg, but open conflict broke out in Moscow.

Zenzinov gives us a vivid, if somewhat biased, account of the
ten days during which a handful of revolutionaries took on the armed
might of the state. All activity in the city was at a standstill; enthusiastic meetings called for an armed uprising; barricades appeared
on Moscow's streets, blocking all main thoroughfares; all appeals to
the emperor and Witte for reinforcements were unheeded because St.
Petersburg was in the same situation. The revolutionaries were
amazed at their fabulous success. Moscow, the heart of autocratic
Russia, was dotted with barricades and held against the regular army
for more than a week. The city was beginning to show scars of battle: smashed windows, bullet-pocked walls, broken water mains.
Finally troop reinforcements arrived from St. Petersburg, and four
days later all opposition to the government was crushed.

Punitive measures were carried out by the government everywhere. Public opinion was now against the revolutionaries, and the
authorities ruthlessly suppressed any further evidence of revolt.
Whole villages were burned and peasants reduced to obedience. In
this atmosphere the elections to the First State Duma were carried
on.

The extremists of the right and the left were discredited, and
the Cadets, led by Muromtsev, emerged as the largest party, electing
179 members. Labor, led by Aladin, elected 90. A few Social-
Revolutionaries were elected, while the Social-Democrats boycotted
the elections.

During the early months of 1906, the government bolstered its
barriers against Duma encroachment. The concessions of the October

Manifesto were restated in precise form, and the Fundamental Laws, or others derived from them, were declared to be beyond the Duma's competence. The Duma's initiative was also limited in matters of finance, and the army and navy were declared to be prerogatives of the Crown. The Upper Chamber, reinforced, was to have the same legislative rights as the Duma. Witte was replaced by Goremykin, a tool of the tsar, as prime minister.

When the Duma met on May 10, 1906, Muromtsev, leader of the Cadets, was chosen as chairman, and the direction of policy was largely in the hand of the Cadets. This group was the best informed on constitutional matters, and many hoped that the solution of the country's ills was at hand. These hopes were not realized, however. The parties in the Duma were split, and matters of policy and procedure aroused much bickering and antagonism. While engaging in conflict with the established authority, the deputies had to guard against becoming engulfed in the revolutionary storm.

Transforming vast autocratic Russia into a constitutional monarchy was easy on paper. Putting it into practice was infinitely more difficult. It was necessary to "erect a bridge between the old Russia and the new," but the Cadets considered themselves not as a bridge between the nation and the established authority, but as the nation itself. Violent exception was taken to such terms as "constitution" and "autocrat." Clash of ideologies widened the gulf between the tsar and the deputies who preached the sovereignty of the people. The very existence of a constitution would have served to strengthen it. Time was on its side. Discretion counseled postponement of ideological conflicts until political circumstances were more favorable. However, the Duma was determined to force the issue, with disastrous consequences.

* * *

The original is characterized by excessive use of italics, capitals and quotation marks in reference to such terms as Autocracy, Revolution, Address, etc. Furthermore, there is considerable inconsistency in quoting from official addresses, replies and declarations, the wording being frequently altered in various parts of the book.

In the translation superfluous capitals, italics and quotation marks were eliminated and French and Latin phrases were deleted if they had no particular bearing on the material. Recurring terms-- obshchestvo, vlast, stroi, nachala--vary in the translation according to shifting connotation.

The Library of Congress system of transliteration was followed with two qualifications: no diacritical marks, and conventional spelling for names which are customarily anglicized--Tolstoy.

V. A. MAKLAKOV

V. A. Maklakov, born in 1869, was brought up in a cultured environment. His mother came from the well-to-do landowning class, while his father was a member of the intelligentsia. He received a classical education in secondary school, excelling in ancient languages. At the university he enrolled in the faculty of natural sciences.

In 1889, Maklakov, who was then in his early twenties, accompanied his father to the Paris International Exposition. The trip made a profound impression on the young man. It was the centennial of the French Revolution, and Maklakov was greatly influenced by the current evaluation, by press and public, of its achievements. The current view was that the accomplishments of the Revolution, which had begun as a liberal movement, were rooted in tradition, and, had revolution been averted, would have been achieved more gradually by constitutional authority. "Il n'y a qu'un moyen d'arreter une revolution. C'est de la faire."

While in Paris, Maklakov came in contact with the General Association of Paris Students and was enchanted by the freedom of French student life. On his return to Russia, he produced his first literary effort, an article on the Paris student association, published in Russian News.

In 1890 widespread student disorders occurred, and many students were arrested, Maklakov among them. He was soon released but was expelled from school. He went abroad and briefly visited Switzerland and France. On his return to Russia he received word from the Ministries of Internal Affairs and Education that he was barred from university for political activity. He later discovered that this was a common practice, regardless of the guilt of the accused, to impress on all the watchfulness of the government. Thanks to his father's connections, Maklakov was reinstated and enrolled in the history department in 1891.

He stayed out of student entanglements and came in contact with liberal elements of society in the club "Beseda," a zemstvo group which advocated the introduction of a constitutional order. Maklakov also made the acquaintance of Liubenkov, Tolstoy, Kliuchevski and Vinogradov. He now became interested in a legal career, and by studying extramurally he graduated in law in 1896. He made a name for himself by participating in some of the noted trials of the period.

xv

Maklakov rejected the revolutionary trend and joined the Cadet party in 1905. He became a member of the Central Committee and participated actively in the 1905 elections, although he was not a candidate. His differences with the party arose when the First Duma rejected agreement with the government and demanded its capitulation. Although Maklakov frequently opposed the party, he abstained from criticising it in the press or from the public tribune.

When the former deputies were barred from re-election to the Second Duma, Maklakov was nominated and elected as a Cadet candidate. He remained in the Duma until 1917. When the revolution broke out he emigrated to Paris where he remained until his death in 1957 in Switzerland.

Among his works are Government and Society, The First State Duma, The Second State Duma, and his autobiography, From My Recollections, published in the United States in 1954.

M. B.

THE FIRST STATE DUMA

INTRODUCTION

This book is a direct continuation of the preceding one, Vlast
i Obshchestvennost na Zakatie Staroi Rossii (Government and Society
in the Period of the Decline of Old Russia), which gives me an opportunity to say a few explanatory words about the first book, too.

When Sovremennye Zapiski (Contemporary Memoirs) began to
publish my Vospominaniia (Reminiscences) in 1928, I did not know
myself what they might turn out to be: autobiography, journalism,
or perhaps an attempt at history. Individual chapters, depending on
the subject, varied in character. Later, when I organized them into
a book that reflected my understanding of politics, the reaction was
mixed. Many of my opponents from the right and the left, even though
they did not agree with me, understood me, and their attitude was un-
biased. However, the most categorical criticism was expressed by
my own party leader, P. N. Miliukov.[1] It is not necessary to refute
his criticism, which is quite consistent. We differ on too many issues. But I shall take the opportunity to remove at least some of the
numerous misunderstandings.

P. N. Miliukov has contended that my book is harmful, that I
detest the Liberation Movement, that I oppose ideas of liberalism,
and thus it would seem that I have gone over to the camp of our former ideological opponents. Such an evaluation is a distortion of conceptions. Ideas of liberalism are actually not popular now: the
strength of state authority is defended rather than the rights of man.
The basis for this general change of ideological sympathies lies outside the Russian past. Liberal ideas, like everything else, had a
reverse side, and "dictatorships" arose wherever governments were
unable to overcome the weaknesses inherent in liberalism. Nevertheless, not only did I not reject these ideas but I claimed that, even
if we must admit that the epoch of personal freedom has come to an
end and the time for government from above has returned, and progress consists of transforming human society into a beehive or an
anthill, on which Mussolini, Hitler, and Stalin are agreed: even so,
there was no ground in twentieth century Russia for such views.
Attacks on liberalism, as such, have received their justification in
states where personal freedom reached its peak and had shown its
objectionable side. It was not so in Russia, and no wonder, since
it was a backward country. Russia still needed the experiences that

1

Many Westerners already found disappointing, such as self-activity
of the individual, defense of personal rights, and protection of the
individual against the state. This would be progress for Russia,
and the implementation of these ideas did not present the difficulties
that other European states faced after the war. Liberalism, as I
recognized in my book, had a good chance for success in Russia
since it fought for the country's needs. Where then is my difference
with liberalism?

But admitting the truth of ideas does not mean approval of all
the actions of their adherents. The ideas were both correct and
timely, but their exponents of that period could not implement them.
To accuse those who criticize their actions of betrayal of the ideas
themselves is comparable to the learned man, who, in criticism of
himself, saw disrespect for knowledge. Particularly because liberal ideas were beneficial for Russia, and the constitution might
have been her salvation, it was permissible to ask the question: why
then, did those whose destiny it was to perform this task not realize
it? They defended a just cause; they were the brains of the country;
according to their conception, they were pitted against a "régime,
rotten and condemned to destruction": yet they were vanquished.
Now they accuse the victors, just as the Austrian High Command
accused the ignoramus Napoleon of responsibility for its defeats because he did not conduct war according to rules. The politician's
skill is evaluated according to results, not according to the validity
of political grammar. If the defenders of liberalism admitted they
made errors, why was it harmful to point them out?

This problem of our errors did confront me when I thought of
the past. I am prepared to agree that in actual wartime it is not permissible to criticize either the army or the leaders, since faith in
them must not be 'undermined. This is an accepted deception to
which all submit in time of war. Armies are always unconquerable;
commanders, until they are removed, are infallible; defeats are reported as victorious "retreats to previously prepared positions."
The same thing occurred in politics. How many times after the customary Cadet blunders in the Duma did the party journalists reproach
us for not sparing them? How could they praise such blunders? Yet
praise them they did. But now circumstances are different. We are
not at war, there are no more leaders, and the halo of infallibility
is no longer of any use. The opportunity we missed will not return,
and our task will be completed by others. We have become the past.
It would be ridiculous to present as history our old "military bulle-
tins." What purpose would it serve?

Here we come to the core of the matter, the source of Miliukov's
indignation. He contends that I "made the Cadet party the chief defendant," and "placed on him, Miliukov, the chief responsibility for

the conduct of this party." He adds that my manner was aggressive and personal and so on.

Two different matters are confused here. In the first place, if such an impression of him personally were conveyed to an impartial reader, I should consider it a matter of utmost regret. I do object to the way he presented the case. The terms, "defendant," "guilty," etc., belong to different categories; you can judge and condemn failure of one's duty, but not error of judgment or lack of skill. I did not judge; I looked only for reasons and consequences. Besides, and this is most important, I did not once hint that I consider Miliukov the chief culprit, or imply that he shoulder our joint guilt. Miliukov himself introduced his personal problem into our case, and quite unnecessarily.

But since Miliukov has spoken of it, I cannot fail to reply. This is an obvious misunderstanding. I could not hold Miliukov chiefly responsible for the conduct of the party because, even though he was its leader, he was the kind who said "Je suis leur chef, donc je les suis (I am their chief, so I follow them)." There are people who are real leaders and they require certain special qualities that not all men possess. Miliukov was not a real leader of this type;[2] he tried to influence the party mood, then submitted to the majority and, having submitted, defended its tactics. This was regrettable, for he had superior knowledge and talents, but he was afraid to cut himself off from his adherents and retreated. Some people consider that this kind of conduct is the essence of democracy; but here, too, lies its weakness.[3] For even the party majority to which leaders submit is often not a majority of the party but only of its official representatives, and sometimes of a small select circle of people thinking alike. "Star Chambers" do not exist in monarchies alone.[4] In general, groups are not suitable for the role of leaders, and the variety of their composition is reflected in their decisions. All of Miliukov's influence was used in reconciling the internal differences of this group. Under these conditions, I could not hold him chiefly responsible for the conduct of the party.

If I do refer to him frequently, and according to him, "use his name in all declensions," it is not because he led the party but because he represented it most vividly in its strength and in its shortcomings. Miliukov was not a party leader but its standard-bearer. Moreover, as a journalist, he wrote in its defense more than all the other Cadets put together. His articles have remained to this day a living commentary on the actions of the party. That is why I found them more interesting than his books and so incurred his reproach for my indifference. While speaking of what I consider party mistakes, I cannot leave out of consideration his articles, to which I shall refer again later.[5]

I shall add one final word. Miliukov remained true to himself
and served his ideal tirelessly all his life; he could not be bribed
nor frightened. This earned him the respect of those who disagreed
with him. Many unjust attacks against him arouse my indignation.
But on the other hand, some of his characteristics as a politician and
polemist arouse my instinctive protest--not against him, personally,
but against the sort of politics they illustrate; he has mistakenly regarded this objection as a personal matter, which it is not. Quite
different is my attitude toward the party. I do think that, even though
it aimed at introducing a constitutional order in Russia, its unfortunate
tactics were the chief reason for its failure. I do not wish to exaggerate the significance of the party generally, but at that particular time
the Cadet party was the personification of almost all the educated and
liberal public forces. It was such an influential social force that the
course followed by the First State Duma depended on it and its mistakes could not go unpunished.

It is instructive to note that the Cadet party at first made no
pretensions to a leading role. At its Constituent Assembly, Miliukov
compared it to those "intellectual western groups who are known as
social reformers." There was much truth in this and it predetermined the party's modest role. Such parties are small in numbers.
They are the élite, the parties of the chosen few, sometimes generals
without an army. They are far from being the leaders of the country.
In the midst of a backward and therefore generally conservative population, as the Russian people were, the Cadets were the advance
guard intellectual group, few in number, advocates of a European
ideal unfamiliar to Russia. It would have been fitting for such an intellectual group to make up a program out of the latest slogans of
European theoretical thinking and it would have been quite in order
to spread these ideas.

But events imparted a different character to the Cadet party.
The assessment of the country proved to be incorrect. A favorable
political wind blew into its sails and made it "the people's party."
I recall its swift penetration by elements which not only could not
understand its program, but could not even pronounce its name.
This success caught the Cadets unprepared. If they did think of
changing their name to one more comprehensible to the people, "the
Party of Popular Freedom," they did not think of adapting their actions to their new role and of trying to understand their electors.
They did not have to reject the Cadet ideal to do this. It could remain a guiding star. But the tempo by which this ideal was to be
attained, the methods or tactics, had to correspond not to the stage
of development of the intellectual leaders, but to the level of those
on whose behalf the party acted. The country chose the party as its
defender, but it did not, as a result, itself become Cadet. Miliukov

stated at the April Convention that "following the party program
does not necessarily mean justifying the confidence of the electors."
These wise words did not meet with the approval of the majority,
and Miliukov retreated. Thus having become the representatives of
a broad popular front and spokesmen of the will of the people, the
Cadets, in contradiction to this, did not retreat from their party's
purely intellectual, factional program and tactics.

The party had the right to prefer devotion to its own radical
program to the confidence of those it represented. But then, it had
to be consistent. Having chosen such a path, the party could not pretend to govern Russia according to its will and should have declined
the role of the "party of the future" to await the arrival of its own
time. Leadership would become the lot of those who did not disdain
to come down to the level of the population's preparedness. The
Cadet leaders could have no illusions about the country's measuring
up to their level, which was far above the national standard. The
formation of less demanding parties was therefore as useful to the
Cadets as is the existence of "the radicals" to the socialists in
France. The Cadets should have supported these more moderate
constitutional parties, which had common interests with the Cadets
in desiring a constitution and a rule of law. But the Cadets tried to
monopolize liberalism; they considered that they alone were the liberal party. In 1905, when Witte appealed not to them but to the zemstvo, the Cadets sent him only their own representatives, which was
typical of their future tactics. They attacked as reactionary, parties
that developed on their right, even though such experienced, liberal
people as Shipov, Stakhovich, Guchkov, and Heiden belonged to them.
In the elections to the First Duma, they rejected agreement with such
parties as a matter of principle, and yet the Cadets had to make a
choice. Either they must observe the inviolability of their Cadet
program and then accept the fact that they were a minority and be
satisfied with urging on others; or they must agree to represent all
Russia, and then, without intellectual snobbery, coordinate their
tactics to correspond to the level of understanding and preparedness
of the mass of the people. But the Cadets, as was their custom,
wanted both at the same time.

The Cadets, of course, were truly a liberal party, but liberal
is a very broad term. In the perpetual antagonism existing between
state and individual, liberalism first and foremost defended the
rights of the individual, but it did not sacrifice the state either. The
question of where to draw the line along which it would be possible to
reach a solution is not a question of doctrine, but of fact; there is no
single solution. All depends on the circumstances, time, and the
degree and quality of the culture of the given country. The struggle
for liberalism never ceased in Russia; but the nature of liberal

goals, and the form of the struggle to attain them, varied greatly in the course of time. We should know what they were in 1905-06.

It was an exceptional period. The autocracy, which had long given Russia enlightened absolutism, oppressed her, but had also created her. At one time autocracy was the basis of the unity and might of the state. These were purchased at the price of restricted social rights, inequality of estates and classes, and systematic neglect of liberal principles. One necessitated the other. It is little wonder that the epoch of Nicholas I, when the power of the state was at its apogee, was also the epoch of the most merciless oppression of society. There was a danger that when the force holding Russia together from within should disappear, the country would disintegrate. The nonconfidence of the mass of the people in any kind of authority, the rebellious anger of the lower strata against the upper classes, and the indifference of the populace to the unity and greatness of the state and its cultured minority would all act as centrifugal tendencies. The chief task of liberalism became the transformation of Russia on a liberal basis, without permitting the triumph of revolution.

Was this possible? The attempt at a liberal transformation was successful in the 1860's. When the liberal reforms were first introduced, their chief exponents felt that the autocracy was necessary for their success. Without it, peasant reform could not have been introduced peacefully. But forty years later the situation had changed. Autocracy had not justified its existence during this period: not only did it fail to complete the reforms it started, it even retreated. Leaders of the 1890's and the 1900's came to the conclusion that in order to restore Russia to the path of the unfinished reforms, it was necessary first to destroy the autocracy. Could this be achieved without revolution? It seemed doubtful, but the liberals were not deterred by this danger. They allied themselves with the revolutionary parties against the autocracy. Why liberalism decided to follow this path, where it was threatened by danger of being crushed between the hammer and the anvil, I shall not pause to consider. Victors are not to be judged, and they were victorious. The monarchy agreed to grant a constitution, and a liberal transformation of Russia became possible, henceforth, without revolution. However, this could no longer be done by the government alone; the collaboration of society became essential. Thus agreement between society and the historical authority became the concrete task of liberalism at this time, and above all, the task of the party that personified almost all liberal society.

Its success in this task would have meant the victory of liberalism, but the party did not win. Instead it pushed Russia with increased energy to the abyss of revolutionary chaos. Why did the Cadets fail?

In the final analysis, the war pushed Russia into revolution. Without it there would have been no revolution. But if after eight years (1906-14) of "constitution, " Russia could carry on a war for three whole years, would it be too presumptuous to suppose that, had these eight years been different, Russia might have remained in the war till the end? While collaborating with society in constitutional activity, wholesome elements of the government might have grown so strong that they could have overcome the attacking microbes, such as Rasputinism, that disintegrated the government and the state. The war would then have followed a different course and might have ended differently, too. In wartime, of course, society fulfilled its obligations, but by that time it was too late. The consequences of the mistakes of 1905-06 were already making themselves felt--consequences so numerous and profound that their scope is frightening to imagine.

At present belated consolation is sought in the thought that, supposedly, no constitutional system could have been firmly established in Russia anyway. It is said the population was capable of only two extremes--"silent submission" and "merciless and senseless revolt. " There is a measure of truth in this: there was indeed such danger. That is why the party that stood for the constitution had to struggle against both "submission" and "revolt." It was not a hopeless struggle. It was true that the autocracy did not prepare Russian society for a constitution and respect for law and authority, but there were many wholesome elements in the country. If there had been only "rebels" and "yes men, " there could have been no thought of constitution at all. But even without mystic faith in the Russian soul, public spirit, communal ties and other so-called basic characteristics of the Russian spirit, there were evidences that the Russian, in certain aspects of life where he was not hindered by the government and where he was master, could be constructive and efficient. Not only as an individual, but also in social groups he had many potentialities for self-government, and this has held true from ancient times to the present.

It is true that these "doers" did not rise to great heights or concern themselves with the common welfare, but defended only their petty interests. That is why the intelligentsia branded them with the contemptuous name of "the man in the street, " though they formed the basis on which authority and government rested. The fate of the autocracy was not decided by the banquet campaigns of the progressive intelligentsia, but by these ordinary citizens, who lost faith in the autocracy and went over to the side of the constitution, incomprehensible though it was to them. The people no longer regarded the intelligentsia as their enemies and entrusted the defense of their interests to the intellectuals. Had liberalism taken the road that they understood, they could have become its staunch supporters. Because they opposed revolution, disorders, and destruction of

government, they backed the Cadet party in the election. The
party's chief strength lay in the support of the peaceful population;
all it had to do was use it wisely.

It was not the unpreparedness of the population for a constitutional order that became the obstacle to its realization, but rather
the tactics of the leaders of the intelligentsia, who self-confidently
pretended they were representing the whole nation. So long as the
war against the autocracy continued, liberalism could travel side by
side with the revolutionary parties; but when the constitution was
granted and the Duma elected, and the Cadets assumed leadership
of the Duma, their task became the reconciliation of liberalism with
the government and the defense of Russia from revolution.

Agreement between the traditional authority and liberalism
was necessary to both sides. Without the collaboration of liberal
society, the government could not have restored order in the country;
and lacking the confidence of society, it would have met strenuous
opposition even in attempting to introduce liberal reforms. Then, in
order to check the encroachment of liberalism, it would again have resorted to repressive measures from which it would have slipped un-
noticeably back to the old rut. Therefore, for the elements of the
ruling class who understood that the constitution was essential,
agreement with liberalism was a most important task. On October
18, 1905, Witte summoned Shipov to try to reach just such an agreement.

But agreement was even more necessary for liberalism. The
monarchy was still a tremendous force, materially and morally, and
its preservation was necessary to save Russia from the disintegration that revolution would bring. It was necessary to safeguard the
constitutional monarchy and maintain its prestige. Even in 1917,
when the monarchy was already discredited, Miliukov still tried to
persuade Michael to accept the throne for the salvation of Russia;
to go to the front, and at the head of faithful troops, to fight against
revolutionary St. Petersburg. This advice was then too late. But
why was agreement with the government rejected in 1906 when such
extraordinary measures were not needed, when agreement could
easily be reached in principle? Society rejected it because it did
not stop to think what it lost by doing so: immediate benefits of the
new order for the population; liberalism freed from having to please
its former allies; and the constitutional monarchy as a final form of
government rather than a bridge to revolution. A new era of budding
reforms would have begun.

Agreement of society with traditional authority did not in any
way signify capitulation to it. Should the government have taken the
wrong road, society, through the Duma, could have used its indisputable right to oppose such a course. But if both sides agreed on

the character and direction of reforms, the details, the tempo, and
the methods of overcoming difficulties could have been a matter of
concessions and negotiations. Since the government and society
were indispensable to one another, they each should have yielded
occasionally to preserve harmony. Society was not obliged to capit-
ulate to the government, but neither could it demand its capitulation.
Agreement is always a compromise involving mutual concessions.
The question of how far concessions can go is not a matter of principle but rather of fact and tact. Liberal society had to admit that
with the promulgation of the constitution, its former uncompromising
attitude toward the government lost its justification; that agreement
became possible and necessary, and on the basis of the newly granted
constitution, had to be honestly attempted.

But liberalism, insofar as it was represented by the Cadets,
set for itself a different task. It did not want agreement with the
government and aimed at immediate and complete victory over it.
By demanding the capitulation of the government, liberalism merely
succeeded in arousing it to accept the challenge and to attack and
defeat Cadet liberalism. I spoke of this also in my first book. In
my opinion, the explanation of these tactics lies in the fact that the
Cadet party was born in the atmosphere of the Liberation Movement,
so its membership consisted of liberal people, revolutionaries, constitutionalists from the zemstvo, and theoreticians of the "Union of
Unions." The conflict with the autocracy united them into a single
party, but this struggle ended on October 17. Degrees of difference
exist in every political party, but among the Cadets there were differences in principle among the component sections, and a serious
change in tactics would have split the party. A strong leader would
not have feared such a split, which would have proved beneficial for
all concerned. As two different parties, former halves of the Cadet
party could even have collaborated. But the leadership of the Cadets
was in the hands of a group in which all trends were deliberately represented. This body set as its chief aim the prevention of a party split
and preservation of its deceptive unity. The activity of the nominal
"leader" was confined to inventing ambiguous formulas behind which
party differences could be concealed, but the contradictory currents
paralyzed one another.

The tactics of the party acquired a special character, such as
is found in governments determined to retain authority at any cost.
Such a policy is readily implemented but it condemns the government
to fruitlessness, as nature condemns the individual whose chief motive in life is self-preservation. In the final analysis, Cadet tactics
proved to be of this kind.

Miliukov, of course, cannot accept such an explanation. He
sees, even now, deep political meaning in the Cadet tactics--a com-

bination of liberalism and revolution. His present Vospominaniia
(Reminiscences) attempt to prove this in every chapter, and Miliukov blames me for failing to accept this meaning.

> The old actogenarian has remained faithful to himself
> [writes Miliukov about me in Posledniia Novosti (Latest
> News), May 30, 1937], having discarded from the inter-
> pretation of events faith and enthusiasm, which comprised
> the dynamism of both revolutionary and parliamentary
> struggle. In the failure to understand that the role of
> party leaders did, indeed, consist of a series of attempts
> to introduce the former within the framework of the lat-
> ter, without extinguishing the spirit of both, lies the
> source of all the incorrect objections of Maklakov to
> party tactics, which were unavoidable if the party pro-
> gram were to be preserved.

I quoted the above extract so as not to distort its meaning,
which I fail to understand. That liberalism should have attempted
to transform its revolutionary allies into parliamentarians is clear.
But why was it necessary to "avoid extinguishing their revolutionary
spirit"? In the end it was the Cadets who extinquished their own
spirit.
    While the liberal party followed its former path because of
inertia, Miliukov justified its error by his theoretic scheme. Its
famous tactics began to correspond to the dual party composition
and the dual theoretic scheme. It refused to accept a choice between
two contradictory roads, the constitutional and the revolutionary; instead, it wanted to follow both at the same time, and sit on both
sides of the fence.
    Miliukov states in his Reminiscences:

> During this interval, a sharp struggle was going on in
> the political arena between the two rivals, both of whom
> were stronger than the newly-born constitutional move-
> ment. The Cadet party could not take the side of the
> autocracy, or of "sedition," which openly preached rev-
> olution after October 17. It is true that neither side
> needed its support, but insofar as the Cadet party re-
> mained independent, it stood in the way of both autocracy
> and revolution.[6]

It is difficult to imagine a more inaccurate presentation of conditions. The autocracy ended in 1905, so the revolution of 1906 was
not a struggle against the autocracy nor did it champion the constitu-

tional cause; rather it fought for its own revolutionary goals. No
one proposed that the Cadets support the autocracy, but they should
have sided with the constitutional monarchy against revolution, which
they refused to do.   They should have made a choice between two
realistic forces--traditional authority and revolution--but they preferred to remain on the sidelines, filled with conceit as to their importance.

And so the party that might have been the most dangerous enemy
of reaction and revolution merely proved to be useful to both; in the
decisive moment it defeated its real purpose: the peaceful transformation of the autocracy into a constitutional monarchy. It failed to
fulfill its historic destiny. The First State Duma, which is the theme
of this book, is a good illustration of this failure of the Cadet party
and its tactics.

In view of the seriousness of present-day problems, the desire
to spend time and effort on reminiscences of the distant past may seem
strange.   But history retains its fascination, and it is not wrong to
preserve its sources. People of my generation have a special right,
perhaps even a duty, to do so. The future no longer belongs to us, no
matter how much we wish for it, but we are the last living witnesses
of an interesting epoch now past, and soon we, too, will be gone. We
may prove to be useful to the historian. Our present testimony is
most valuable because, though it may contain errors and even unin-
tentional prejudice, there is no place in it for the intentional deceit
of those political "military reports" that we created.

There is another justification for reminiscences. History does
not repeat itself, but the laws of life do not change at all. We are
witnessing a common phenomenon, which unfolds on a vast scale before our eyes: how and why victors lose their victories. The victors of World War I lost in the year 1918. In France, the Front Populaire, celebrating the arrival of a new epoch, lost its victory, as
will the presently conceited totalitarian states. In my book I recall
an episode of this type: how Russian liberalism, victorious in 1906,
lost the battle in the end. And though I wish it might have been otherwise, my reminiscences are not totally unfamiliar to the contemporary
world.

Chapter One

THE ATTITUDE OF THE GOVERNMENT

TOWARD THE FIRST STATE DUMA

The particular significance of the First Duma stems from the
fact that it put liberal society into a superior position to achieve its
objectives. What were liberal leaders able to do prior to the Duma
period? They could try to implement their views at the discretion
of governors and express themselves in Aesopian language in the
press, while all their activity depended on the whims of local and
central authorities. It was not altogether a fruitless task, but it
undoubtedly was a difficult and burdensome one. Later, in the epoch
of the Liberation Movement, they gained new opportunities; and yet,
what did these consist of? Sometimes they met in councils occasionally broken up by the police, as formerly; they presented addresses
to the ministers and the tsar, for which they were reproached as in
the case of the Chernigov address; they compiled earnest plans for
the reconstruction of Russia, which found oblivion in the ministerial
council; and finally, they made lofty speeches at crowded banquets.
In a word, in contrast with the former enforced silence, they won
the right to express opinions until they were told "enough!" Naturally, under these circumstances the liberals began to seek agreement
with the revolutionary parties that had at their disposal more powerful and frightful means than they, even though these were incompatible
with a legal order. Thus liberal society was compelled to join with
revolution and but for this, there probably would not have been any
Liberation Movement.

Now everything was changed. The forbidden constitution became a reality; it was possible to be dissatisfied with it and insist
on changes, but the former autocracy no longer existed. Liberalism
did not need to hide in strangers' clothes now. It became a free, all-
Russian organization that no longer needed to conceal either its opinions or its activities. But above all, representatives of liberal
society did not need to search for roundabout ways to influence the
course of state activity; they became a part of state authority, and
ruled in its highest legislative institution, the Duma. These were
unheard-of opportunities for liberal activity in Russia.

12

However, tremendous as the new liberal opportunities were, compared with the past, the task was as difficult as it had been before.   Transforming vast autocratic Russia into a constitutional monarchy was easy on paper; a manifesto was sufficient for that. But putting it into practice was infinitely more difficult.   A twofold danger threatened.

The state apparatus had long since been solidly built and developed on the basis of autocracy, the submission of all not to law but to the discretion and will of the government.   There were, and of necessity there still remained in this apparatus, people who could not understand a different order of things.   Much painstaking effort was required to change them without simultaneously destroying the whole apparatus.   But an even greater difficulty lay in the fact that the whole nation,   including the intellectual element, had been brought up by the same autocracy, and though it fought against it, had acquired its chief faults.   The nation also had no respect for law and justice and interpreted its victory over the old order as placing the people above the law, in autocracy's former position.   Having submitted to the will of the monarch without question, the nation now thought that nothing should oppose the spontaneous will of the people.

The problem of the moment was not to substitute one autocratic will for another but to introduce a reign of justice, and in the vivid words of S. E. Kryzhanovski, "to erect a bridge between the old Russia and the new, between the government and the people. "   This historic task fell to the lot of the liberal, intellectual society, which was practically the only group in Russia that understood the underlying principles of justice demanded by the constitution and the prejudices and instincts, opposing it from above and below, which would have to be combatted.   The Cadets, as the most intellectual party, deeply steeped in the theory of justice, might have become such a bridge and might have united in this task all sound elements of the government and society.   This, indeed, was their responsibility, an undertaking worthy of the hopes that rested on them.

The Cadets, however, did not understand the difficulty of this problem.   They considered themselves not as the bridge between the nation and the traditional authority, but as the nation itself.   Their election successes, the adulation of the crowds, the flattery of their own press--all these they regarded as the expression of the will of the people, as our tsar saw trust and submission of the people in the welcoming shouts of "hurrah!"   The task, as they understood it, therefore, seemed very simple.   In their opinion, the whole nation stood behind them and the only obstacle to their progress was the government, which already admitted its impotence.

It is strange to recall now the thoughtlessness with which they tried to reach their goal, exactly as did the military parties when they pushed their countries to a European massacre in 1914.   Vinaver tells us[1] how, on the evening of April 27, several deputies, "transported with ecstasy", gathered at his home to settle some urgent questions. Vinaver also, in his biography of Kulisher,[2] recalls "the tempestuous days of rapture in the first period of the February Revolution." Transported with ecstasy, rapture! I can understand going into raptures about the Manifesto that proclaimed the constitution, when theoretical principle triumphed for the first time. But when the deputies met for the great and arduous task, when the very fate of Russia was at stake, when danger threatened on all sides and one careless move might cause everything to crash--then being transported with ecstasy was not an appropriate mood. The Cadets, determined not to yield, set lightheartedly to work. As a result, two months later the superior position of our first-chosen ones changed into a complete and deserved rout.

It is curious to note that the liberal press and society did not blame the Duma for this defeat. No Duma after its failure had so many enthusiastic recollections dedicated to it. What names were given to it! "The Duma of popular hopes, the Duma of popular wrath." One brazen author even proposed naming it "the Duma of great achievements." At the Viborg trial, O. Ia. Pergament ended his defense speech with this tirade: "The garland of their fame is so splendid that even undeserved suffering cannot add to it." Subsequent Dumas were regarded by the representatives of the First Duma with arrogant scorn. Vinaver jokingly compared his Duma, "filled with the inspired flight of a great epoch and glowing with courage and talent," with the "grey and leaderless" Second Duma. The day of the opening of the First Duma became a day of celebration for Russian society and anyone criticizing the First Duma was considered a renegade.

Now, one can be fairer. The undeserved canonization of the First Duma was natural; that is how society defends the vanquished and has its revenge on the victors. Only the victors were accused of the failure of the Duma; to them was ascribed the preconceived intention of undermining the constitution and hindering the Duma in its work.

For their part, the accusers considered such an intention only natural. Of course the autocracy would not be reconciled to a limitation of its authority. At the first opportunity it would certainly begin to prepare for a restoration. Many even contended that the introduction of a constitution must necessarily be accompanied by a change, if not of the dynasty, then at least of the monarch. The constitution, supposedly, perished because that was not done at the time.

In the downfall of Russia it is useless to justify the government; its fault was indubitable. But we must not close our eyes to the sins of our society. During the eleven years of the existence of the constitution (1906-17), there were periods when the government was to blame, just as, more than all others, it was to blame for the distant past. But this does not prevent my admitting that society's conduct in its victorious moments was to blame for its final failure. I recall one of the most vivid of these moments.

Is the legend true that from the very outset the tsar wished to destroy the constitution which he promulgated and that he merely "toyed" with the First Duma? In 1905, at a gathering attended by Sted, Rodichev spoke of the attitude of society to the Bulygin Duma,* saying, "they regard it as an ambush prepared by an enemy." Were such words justified in connection with the constitutional legislative Duma?

A priori it was possible to presuppose that. Every autocrat certainly finds it difficult to reconcile himself to a diminution of his authority. The tsar's personal past; his veneration of the memory and policy of Alexander III; his first political step (hopeless dreams); his stubborn struggle with the Liberation Movement; his hostility to the word "constitution"; his mysterious expressions such as "my autocracy remained as in the past," which he used in speaking to a delegation of the right after the Manifesto; his sympathy for the Black Hundreds, the supporters of restoration; and, finally, his scheme to set aside the constitution in 1917 on the eve of the revolutionary explosion--all these supported this opinion. But that is only one side of the matter. There is another.

The tsar did not wish to grant a constitution; he fought against it and granted it unwillingly. By nature he was not a reformer. All this was true. But on the other hand, he could yield even more than was necessary. Thus in 1917 he abdicated his throne without exhausting all means of opposition, and having abdicated, he reconciled himself to the situation and made no efforts to restore his former position. He did not become the center and inspiration of restoration intrigues even though the surveillance he was under was not sufficiently strict to prevent his doing so. Some people feared his conspiratorial activities without cause, just as others counted on them in vain. The tsar's complete loyalty to the new authority that replaced him was proven by his diaries. The same thing was evident in 1905. Autocracy was an overwhelming burden for him, but he

----

* The Bulygin Duma was created by an Imperial Manifesto in August, 1905, in the face of popular demand for a constitution. This consultative duma was to have the power to discuss all laws and forward its considerations to the tsar. The electoral basis was a strictly limited franchise based on class delegates--landed proprietors, burgesses, and peasants. The publication of the draft law met with general indignation and the Duma was never convoked. [M. B.]

considered its defense his duty. However, when circumstances
revealed that defense of autocracy was harmful for Russia, when
those whom he trusted advised him to yield, he yielded and reconciled himself to the new conditions sooner than did many others.
The tsar was not the first to attack the constitution: the newly
elected Duma did that and, distrusting him, it immediately began
to threaten him with revolution. If war between the tsar and liberalism was renewed, he was not the aggressor--he only began to
defend himself. Then those who started this war began to say "we
were right" and took pride in their foresight. It is not at all difficult to be such a prophet.

Liberal canon, contrary to evidence, denied all this. It was
contended that the tsar did not recognize the constitution, but the
evidence was not convincing. To begin with, the liberals took issue
with words. Why did the tsar continue to call himself the autocrat
after the Manifesto? Why did he never once mention the word "constitution" and not permit his government to do so? In November,
1905, when Miliukov advised Witte in the form of an ultimatum to
say the word "constitution," Witte replied: "I cannot speak of the
constitution because the tsar does not wish it."[3] Yet, in spite of
his undoubted hatred of the word, the constitution was, nevertheless,
first promised by the tsar and after six months actually realized.
Why then did the Cadets insist on the mention of the word when they
obtained the reality of the constitution, and it was not disputed? Was
such insistence worthy of realistic politicians?[4]

Justification for the tsar's preconceived repugnance to the word
could be found in the analogous and much less comprehensible attitude
of liberal society to another word that it hated, the word "autocracy."
It demanded that this word no longer be used. But why? The Fundamental Laws retained the term as a traditional title stripped of its
offensive implications; moreover, the Cadets themselves declared in
print that the title did not contradict the meaning of the constitution
and therefore agreed to sign without reservations the deputies' promise
of allegiance to the Autocrat. Yet they did not permit use of this title which they countersigned and which was rendered harmless by the
Fundamental Laws*. When the Third Duma proposed to put the title

----

* A codification of the principal laws dealing with the constitutional
structure of the empire. The new Fundamental Laws were promulgated April 23, 1906, shortly before the opening of the First State
Duma. Unlike other statutes, the Fundamental Laws could be amended
only on the initiative of the crown. Certain functions such as foreign
affairs and control of the army and navy were prerogatives of the
crown and beyond the duma's competence. Article 87 empowered the
tsar to promulgate emergency decrees without the Duma. [M. B.]

in the heading of the address to the tsar the Cadets rebelled, and on
this issue they carried the Octobrists with them. What could this
word change? Yet failure to recognize the lawful title of a monarch
is always considered insulting. How much blood was spilled on account of the Emperor of Abyssinia! The address of the Third Duma
set the tsar against it because of the arrogant denial of his title.

It must be admitted that the term "constitution" was not understood in the tsar's circles. In february, 1917, when the revolution
had already begun, Grand Duke Paul Alexandrovich went to persuade
the tsar to grant a constitution at last. During the abdication days,
the empress feared that the tsar in his weakness might be forced to
sign a constitution. What, indeed, did "constitution" mean at this
time?

Let us suppose that the court was too ignorant to understand
the true meaning of foreign legal terms. Were conditions any better
among our intellectual élite? The term "constitution" in the strict
sense of the word is a completely formal one; it denotes the combination of laws determining the state order, regardless of their contents.
That is why Stalin, too, now has a constitution. But we will not limit
ourselves to the formal definition and admit, what would be historically correct, that a constitution is the opposite of absolutism, and
that a constitution exists wherever the monarch's rights are limited
by popular representation. I cannot help remembering that Baron A.
F. Meiendorf used this definition in the Duma to defend the existence
of a separate Finnish constitution, in the face of P. A. Stolypin's refusal to recognize it. From this point of view, the Fundamental Laws
of 1906 were undoubtedly a constitution. Their significance did not
change because they might sometimes be violated on the sufferance
of the organs of authority, as unfortunately happens even in highly
advanced countries. Violation was abuse of authority because the
Fundamental Laws were the constitution and no longer permitted unlimited authority of the monarch. Nevertheless, our liberal society
considered it possible to insist that these laws were not a constituion, did not attempt their practical realization, and scornfully nick-
named them the "pseudo-constitution." Miliukov systematically and
intentionally confused "constitution" with "parliamentarianism,"
even though he knew of the existence of nonparliamentary constitutions whose scope was very broad because the monarch's rights were
limited. Was there any wonder, then, that the tsar did not wish to
use a foreign and ill-defined word which the people did not understand at all, and with which it was easy to toy?

That was why the arguments over terminology were insufficient
to determine whether or not the tsar recognized the constitution and
the Fundamental Laws. This question could be answered only by the
analysis of the Laws themselves. But to my surprise, in an article

dedicated to Pares' book and published in Latest News (July 16, 1939),
Miliukov introduced as proof of the tsar's nonrecognition of the constitution, the Act of June 3, 1906. The misprint is unimportant, though
it is symbolic. I shall not deny that later, when liberalism lost out
and the sworn enemies of the constitution again appeared on the political stage, the tsar gradually came over to their side. There are
many proofs of that, not excluding the planned coup d'état before the
revolution itself. However, in 1906 the tsar retorted with displeasure
when Shipov hinted at the possibility of rejecting the constitutional
order or even changing the election law. I shall deal with that further in chapter twelve. Nevertheless, the main point is that the Act
of June 3, 1907, however it may be condemned, did not prove that
the tsar did not recognize the constitution. The tsar himself in the
Manifesto, and Stolypin in his reply to the declaration, justified it
not only by the lawful rights of an autocrat but from the standpoint of
the necessity of this act. "What can prevent the tsar from rescuing
the power entrusted to him by God," exclaimed Stolypin, and this
statement is reminiscent of Mirabeau's famous quotation, "Je jure
que vous avez sauvé la chose publique (I declare that you have saved
the state)," when he justified on April 19, 1790, the National Assembly in exceeding its authority. Then, who would be so hypocritical as to deny that government upheaval, and the violation of formal
law, is sometimes essential, because, as Bismarck said, "the life
of the state cannot halt"? Such upheavals may take place from above
and from below, in the liberal or reactionary sense, depending on
their relative strength. Sometimes they take the form of a coup
d'état, sometimes of revolution, and a jurist may demand only one
thing: that the upheaval is not passed off as a law and the normal
way of things. Miliukov's allusion to June 3 as proof of nonrecognition of the constitution is all the more surprising since in the Third
Duma, in the debate on the address, he himself justly and wisely
pointed out that the 3rd of June was not a "legal precedent but was a
virtual victory of force over justice." Consequently, the 3rd of June
could not be used as proof of nonrecognition of the constitution. Other
reasons must be found to prove this.

But even if these conclusions prove nothing, it is still fruitless
to deny that on the question of the new order there remained one serious ideological difference between liberal society on the one hand,
and the tsar, the ruling classes, and the uncultured mass of the people on the other. At the time this was not taken into consideration
and this difference of opinion was not reflected in our literature and
journalism. Liberal society considered that a revolution occurred
in 1905, and that the new order was a complete denial of the old because it rested on different foundations. From its own point of view
it might have been correct. But the tsar, his court circles, and the

vast mass of the people understood it differently. They did not see
any break with the past; the customary authority remained at the
head of the state, the same tsar whose titles were sanctified by tradition and the Church. The tsar cherished this popular attitude and
did not wish to disturb it. It was beneficial to the tranquillity of
Russia, even if, in reality, a far-reaching change did take place in
the structure of the state. Besides, as far as the tsar was concerned,
it was not a pious deception, for he actually understood the change
in this sense. In his opinion there was no break with the traditional
past. He was convinced that the embryo of what was commonly called
a constitution existed in former autocracy: therefore, simple evolution was sufficient to bring about the change. That is why the tsar
could reconcile himself to it with such unexpected ease. This ideology is of considerable interest.

Since the time of Speranski, the ideologists of autocracy contrasted it with despotism as an example of a legal order. This conception of autocracy was reflected in the old edition of the Fundamental Laws. Alongside of Article 1, which established the "unlimited"
authority of the autocratic tsar "to which God commands obedience,"
there was Article 47, asserting that Russia's government rested on a
"firm basis of laws." This article contained the embryo of a lawful order, as distinct from despotism.

My generation laughed at this fine distinction, considering that
the one article excluded the other. If the monarch was "unlimited,"
then the laws had no "firm foundation," and vice versa. But not
everyone agreed with this point of view. Professor Korkunov, Professor A. S. Aleksieev, replacing M. M. Kovalevski, and others supported the former viewpoint. An unlimited monarch was, of course,
above the laws, not only because if he violated them he was responsible to no one, but also because he could change any law handicapping
him. But the monarch could establish definite forms and limitations
for the expression of his will; so long as they existed, he, too, had
to obey them. In this self-limitation of the autocrat existed the embryo of a legal order. The idealists of autocracy attempted to prove
that unlimited autocracy was an even better safeguard of law because
the autocrat did not need to break the law. He was free to change it.
Breaking laws is the resort of impotence.

This idyll was not confirmed by experience. Our autocracy
became the source of lawlessness. It provided too many opportunities and temptations to violate laws with impunity. But the basic
idea that a law proclaimed by the tsar was compulsory for him also,
so long as he did not repeal it, was a sound one. In theory, it made
out of an unlimited monarch not a despot but a person within the law.
It is true that he was not accountable for violating the law, that the
law he was violating was his own creation. But once he acknowledged

it as compulsory for himself, if he did not fulfill it he broke his
given word. It is significant that the confirmed autocrats like Nicholas I would not admit that an omnipotent monarch would stoop to the
violation of his given word. Faithfulness to his word was a matter
of honor, and compensated for his omnipotence. Here was the embryo of a legal order, which facilitated the painless transition to a
constitution.

    From this point of view, what was accomplished in 1905? The
tsar established a new self-limitation. He decreed that henceforth
"he would not proclaim a single law without the Duma's consent."
This was a very significant self-limitation, but in itself it did not
violate the ideology of autocracy. A lesser self-limitation, but of
the same type, was introduced in Article 49 in the Bulygin Duma.[5]
In its defense, none other than D. F. Trepov made a curious statement: "This article undoubtedly means a limitation of autocracy,
but a limitation coming from Your Majesty and beneficial for legislative work." An analogous self-limitation, but one that went further, was now introduced. Thus the Manifesto of October 17 could
be expressed not as a break with the traditional past but simply as
its development; and the pompous phraseology of the acts of February
18 and August 6 could be justified. No constitutional ideology was
necessary for the explanation of this self-limitation. Furthermore,
the tsar could still say that his "autocracy remained as before,"
even though practically all that remained of it was the traditional title
and a very limited right of pardon (Article 23, Fundamental Laws).
But the former ideology remained firm, and he could not retreat from
it.

    This interpretation naturally helped Nicholas II to accept the
constitution in all sincerity, but in it lurked danger. Enemies of the
constitution could resort to it when it suited their purpose. When the
April Conference discussed the new Fundamental Laws and Article
4 concerning the monarch's authority, which retained the title Autocrat but excluded the word "unlimited," Goremykin considered that
they need not concern themselves with this Article 4 since nothing
had been changed. The monarch remained as he had been; he merely
decreed a "new order of examining legislative activity." This order
had to be introduced into the appropriate places in the Code of Laws,
but everything else was to be left unchanged. What would have happened had Goremykin's advice been followed? The new constitutional
order would have existed only until the day the tsar wished to change
it. That is what happened in the past with all self-limitations which
the tsar imposed. Not only the ideology of autocracy but also its previous practice would have been retained. Under such circumstances
it would have been impossible to speak of any kind of constitution.

But Goremykin was opposed by supporters of the constitution, who pointed out that the Manifesto was also a law. Once the tsar proclaimed that not one law may be changed without the Duma's approval, then this regulation was also a law, and it could not be changed henceforth without the approval of the Duma. Consequently, the monarch, though of his own free will, limited his authority forever and therefore ceased being unlimited. Thus it was necessary to change Article 4 and limit the tsar's authority by law. This was the constitutional interpretation of the Manifesto. An imperceptible distinction separated the autocracy from constitution; it all hinged on the one word "unlimited." Heated arguments went on over it in the conference, in which Witte took an equivocal stand unworthy of him. In particular, he proposed that the tsar in promulgating the Fundamental Laws stipulate that he retained for himself alone their modification. Then the old autocracy would have remained.

The tsar participated in this dispute personally and defended Goremykin's point of view. "I am troubled by the feeling," he said, "of whether or not I have the right to change the scope of authority that I received from my ancestors." His doubts lay not in a personal lust for power, for he did not care for it, but in this feeling of betraying a bequest. However, he raised the question clearly and correctly. The issue was not "the method of passing new laws" but rather the "limitation of the scope of the monarch's authority." After lengthy consideration he postponed his decision till the end of the conference. "Article 4 is the most important in the whole project," he concluded. "But the question of my prerogatives is a matter for my own conscience and I shall decide if it is necessary to leave the article as it is or change it."

These words show that he realized the full significance of this article. It determined whether we would retain unlimited autocracy even if accompanied by "a new order of examining legislative work," or whether a constitution would be introduced. The tsar considered the matter for a few days and then yielded, eliminating the word "unlimited." It is characteristic that he was persuaded by only one thing: the tsar's word had been given by the Manifesto and it would be unworthy of the tsar to break his word. This was the old ideology of autocracy. Thus the Fundamental Laws approved by the tsar introduced our constitution; now we can understand the effect of the tactics of the Cadets, who rejected the Laws with indignation and claimed, to the delight of their enemies, that they were not a constitution.

But society sincerely believed this because its political ideology was quite different. In the proclamation of the constitution it consciously wished to see a break, not evolution; a change in the founda-

tions of our social order. The monarch assumed that the reform
emanated from his absolute authority, which he himself limited for
the good of Russia. Society regarded it as arising out of the sovereignty of the people, which was above the law. The tsar continued
to consider himself a monarch "by the Grace of God," who conferred rights upon the people, while society acknowledged only the will
of the people as the source of even the tsar's power. These two ideologies, of course, excluded one another as logical antitheses, but
the ideologically irreconcilable difference of opinion had no significance in practice. What if the tsar was of the opinion that he alone
conferred the constitution? He still considered himself bound by his
word to observe it and change it only with the consent of the elected
representatives. What if society thought that the will of the people
was above all laws? It nevertheless understood the real strength of
the monarchy and the respect due to the monarch's constitutional
rights. Thus both sides, for different reasons, could equally accept
the constitution. Their ways met at this point.

Certainly--and society was quite right in this--the word of the
tsar might seem an insufficient guarantee for the permanence of the
constitution. But under existing circumstances, what else could
society demand of him? An oath, which later, in 1917, was included
in the text of the tsar's abdication? But an oath is itself merely a
promise. A treaty concluded between the tsar and the elected representatives? But the force of the treaty is also based only on faith in
the given word. It is not necessary to be a Marxist to recognize that
the real guarantee of the constitution rested on the correlation of
forces. In 1905 this correlation was not to the advantage of society;
on that score it would be convinced that same year. The whole government apparatus was in the hands of the traditional authority, whose
prestige among the masses of the people was still very great. To
make the tsar impotent to change the constitution, it was first necessary to take away his authority, i.e. to bring about a revolution.
This was indeed the secret desire of many, but it was not necessary.
The existing relationship of forces was not unchangeable; the very
existence of the constitution would have helped to strengthen it; the
laws passed by it, their tangible results, would have created for it
new defenders. Time was on the side of the constitution, not against
it. That was why it was necessary first of all to make the constitution
work, and until then the solemn word of the monarch was the maximum
that could be demanded of him. All the rest, such as tiresome demands
insisting that he employ the word "constitution," could add nothing to
the strength of the constitution. Worse than that, this word introduced
the delicate ideological conflict under the most unfavorable circumstances, when it should have been avoided, since both sides could agree on
practical conclusions. Each could retain its own ideology and use its

own terminology without forcing that ideology on the other. The tsar
spoke of autocracy, society of a constitution. As long as both sides
remained within the framework of law, they could work together
toward the common goal, as in practical life ideological opposites
such as churchmen and atheists can work together to achieve much.

This interpretation of the new order, as the tsar understood
it, helped him to accept it without reservations. Apparently he did
not do so at once. On October 17 he realized only vaguely where the
Manifesto would lead him; in April it became clear. This was not
all. The events of this half-year showed how serious his decision
was. For life gave optimists a lesson before the problem of the constitution was finally determined in April, 1906. Different results
had been expected of the Manifesto of October 17. On all sides the
tsar was assured of the immediate restoration of order; this persuaded him to yield. But instead of tranquillity, anarchy reigned
supreme, and liberal society together with revolutionary forces continued to strike blows at the government. The revolutionary onslaught
of 1905 was crushed by the forces of the old régime alone, without the
help of liberal society. Many liberal people then turned to the right,
revolutionary leaders went into hiding, and reaction set in. Under
such circumstances it would not have been difficult to recall the Manifesto, limit it, or postpone its fulfillment.

Yet the government did not go back on its word. On the contrary,
those who in July, 1905, still defended the consultative Bulygin Duma
against a constitution supported the constitution at the April Conference.
A number of persons loyal to the tsar declared that though they did not
approve of the Manifesto it must not be tampered with now. The tsar
himself, defending the title "unlimited," declared regarding the Manifesto of October 17: "Whatever happened and whatever may be said,
I will not be moved from my stand on last year's act and I will not
retreat from it." He mentioned telegrams that he received from
"every nook and corner of the Russian land," in which, along with
prayers not to limit his authority, he was thanked for rights that he
granted in the Manifesto. The constitution never had so many supporters as appeared after a half-year of anarchy.

This was no accident; events opened people's eyes. It became
impossible to maintain the earlier conviction that except for a handful of intellectual rebels everyone supported the old order. Military force could annihilate revolutionary "volunteers," but they were
not the issue now. Former autocracy found no defenders, either at
court or among middle-class circles. The election law of December
11 tried to discover supporters of the old order among the simple
peasants, but this attempt was defeated in the elections. Even those
who showered the tsar with requests to safeguard the autocracy at
the same time thanked him for the Manifesto, which limited it. Such

telegrams were no basis for a restoration. Thinking people, who
foresaw long before that such a moment must come, came to the conclusion that the new order must be accepted. In 1903 even Pleve
considered this possibility in his conversation with Shipov,[6] and we
learn from S. E. Kryzhanovski's memoirs, that the latter not only
became a supporter of the new order but tried to persuade the empress to do likewise.[7] Everyone in our bureaucracy who would not
sacrifice Russia to save the régime, except dyed-in-the-wool conservatives and yes men, reconciled himself to the new order much
more sincerely than liberal society thought possible. It was no
longer necessary to defend the constitution against its former enemies;
the enemies of the constitution now came from another direction.

Thus sound tactics demanded of liberal society the postponement of all ideological conflicts with the government, which could
serve no useful purpose, until political circumstances were more
favorable. Instead, liberal society had to support firmly the constitution, which practically gave the country all it needed, and which
was a pledge that later the ideology, too, would change. A useful
agreement with the government to implement urgent reforms could
have been reached on the existing constitutional basis. We shall see
later what course the Duma followed instead.

But our liberal society accused the Supreme Authority of more
than the nonrecognition of the constitution. It suspected those who
did accept the constitution of merely covering up their intention of
leaving everything as in the past. According to liberal public opinion, the constitution was only a police move since the government
would not permit organic reform. That is why the legislative program of the Duma, the scope of the projects it introduced and particularly the land program, supposedly frightened the ruling class and
led to the dissolution of the Duma.

This accusation is even more unreasonable than the charge of
unfriendliness to the constitution. Even before the promulgation of
of the constitution the government recognized the necessity of a moral
reform for Russia. The first ukase of the tsar, on December 12,
1904, announcing the government's liberal program, was issued at
a time when the autocracy did not consider the possibility of a constitutional order or even of a consultative Duma. Granted that this
liberal government program was not original, but it did incorporate
the resolutions of the first zemstvo congress, which represented
mature liberal thinking. Inclusion of the zemstvo ideas was not a
shortcoming at all, making this program the meeting point of the
government and liberal society. Though the political leaders of this
period sought to reach an accord between liberalism and the revolutionary parties, as it happened liberal society and traditional authority

came to a realistic agreement on the practical reform program
beneficial for Russia even sooner. In order to follow the path of
reform together they found a common tongue.

The most typical example of this may be seen in the peasant
question. For a long time not only the autocracy but also the cor-
porate class structure were considered the foundation of Russia's
might. Old semifeudal Russia rested on these, above all on the
reticence and isolation of the peasant world. Our conservatives supported equally both these foundations. Just as before 1861 the state
order was founded on serfdom, until the liberation of the peasants of
necessity resulted in other reforms, so in the 1890s the social and
administrative order of Russia was supported by peasant inequality,
with the peasants serving a large number of state needs. Conserva-
tism stubbornly defended peasant isolation, and naturally, the liberal
program immediately made peasant equality a matter of primary
concern. Witte's historic but unappreciated service to the autocracy
lay in the fact that, as far back as 1897, he put this question point-
blank and broke the harmful tie between the autocracy and the social
hierarchy. Whether he understood, confirmed supporter of autocracy
that he was, that the settlement of the peasant question would undoubtedly lead to a constitution, I do not undertake to judge. But Pleve
understood this perfectly; he used this issue to undermine Witte's influence and buried the work of the agricultural committees. But he
could not stop the march of history, and when the "spring" of Sviatopolk-
Mirski began, the buried "peasant equality" appeared in the ukase of
December 12 in first place, and after that it never disappeared from
the government program. When the Bulygin project was discussed at
Peterhof the conservatives still hoped to preserve the autocracy, but
only the remnant of the most hardened conservatives defended social
hierarchy. The government itself disavowed them. Peasant equality
became the primary issue, and in line with it the whole country was
affected. As was the case after the liberation of 1861, when the
aristocracy lost the foundation of its authority in the country, so after
the destruction of social inequality, the ruling center had to look for
new sources of its strength.

Having become premier, Witte could concern himself with this
vast problem. The Council of Ministers, meeting on March 5, decided to come before the Duma with a purposeful program. Symbol-
ically, in first place was "the ending of preparatory work on the
peasant problem." But that would have been only the first step;
others would have followed it logically. The main reforms of the
1860s, the zemstvo and judiciary, held up in the period of reaction
because of their nonconformity with the autocracy, would have been
completed, since both now conformed to the constitution and the idea

of a legal order. "Freedoms" which contradicted the spirit of the old régime, but without which the constitution could not exist, would have become essential. Once more the trend would have turned to beneficial social reforms: to the defense of the weak, assistance to peasants in their need of land, and the defense of workers against capitalists. Autocracy had long been concerned about this in order to win support among the lower ranks of the population; now this became more urgent, and thanks to the introduction of popular representation, it could be done much better and more completely. Lastly it might be remembered that Russia was not a unitary state, and the national question could be raised in all its profundity. As time proved, its importance for Russia was not understood either by the old régime or society. Such was the incomplete scheme of reforms prepared for the urgent consideration of the State Duma. The government did not deny reforms, for they became part of its program even before the Duma presented its own.

Thus in this program the paths of society and traditional authority actually crossed. The ideological difference, which existed in the understanding of the political order in Russia, did not appear here. The direction of the reforms was the same; there might be some difference as to details or, to be more exact, in their tempo. In this regard not only is agreement always possible, but the very difference of opinion may be natural and useful. As delay and excessive speed are equally harmful, so mutual concessions were logical and would have resulted in cooperation between the government and society.

The government considered this reorganization work of great political significance, for it could prevent unnecessary ideological conflicts with the Duma. In the period of Witte's disgrace, I heard this from him more than once. The most grandiose reform projects of the Duma did not frighten him. At the Council of Ministers on March 5, Witte pointed out that "it is essential to direct at once the activity of the State Duma to definite and broad but sober and businesslike work and thus secure the productiveness of its activity." This is confirmed by the memoirs of Count V. N. Kokovtsev. A few days before the opening of the Duma, the tsar did not share the Count's pessimism. He expressed the same hopes as Witte, that "the Duma occupied with work may prove to be less revolutionary than Kokovtsev expected; zemstvo circles would not wish to undertake the thankless task of snipers in a new flare-up of struggle between the government and the popular representatives."[8] These words of the tsar deny the preconceived accusation that the government did not wish to permit reforms and decided to hinder the Duma's work.

Is this contradicted by the fact that the government actually appeared before the Duma with empty hands, and what is worse,

with projects about "orange groves" and "laundries, "* which society regarded as a joke at its expense? This was an effective argument for meetings but it was not the truth. The liberal program was
publicly proclaimed (May 13) and corresponding legislation introduced soon after (June 1--local courts and breach of official duty,
June 12--extension of peasant landownership). The delay in their
presentation had a different explanation which was   simply that nothing except minor legislation happened to be ready at the time the
Duma was summoned. Did this fact require particular explanation?
It was self-evident. Following the dismissal of Witte's ministry, on
April 22, Goremykin, the new premier, had to select the new cabinet
under abnormal conditions since the tsar insisted that no one of the
former ministers could enter the new cabinet. It was necessary to
find quickly new people, who would be unfamiliar with the plans made
for this period. Everything was done hurriedly. Kokovtsev learned
of his appointment as Finance Minister on the eve of the opening of
the Duma. The new cabinet, with the best of intentions, could not
appear before the Duma with a prepared program. Besides, the
proper time for the declaration had not yet come. The Duma was
not organized; it did not verify the certification of its deputies, and
the first few days it was busy considering the address. Preparation
for legislation takes time if real legislation, not "general phrases, "
is to be introduced. We shall see in the end that it was not the Duma
that should have accused the government of legislative delay.

    Was there reason to suspect that the very dismissal of Witte
was an unfriendly act toward liberal society? Such a conclusion would
be an error because society did not consider the dismissal in this
light. The Cadet party greeted the fall of the ministry and saw in it
a Cadet triumph. Apparent cause for such thinking was Witte's letter
of resignation. When he sent his request for resignation on April 14,
among the reasons for it he referred to attacks to which he would be
subjected in the Duma, which might hinder the joint work. In that he
was right. Liberalism regarded him with enmity, unwilling to admit
that it was itself responsible for what happened to Witte after the
----

    * Goremykin's ministry assumed office on the eve of the opening
of the new legislature and so could not appear before the Duma with
elaborate legislative projects for the reforms which the progressive
public was demanding. Consequently, when the Duma was opened,
there were only two rather trivial legislative projects ready for debate. These were introduced by the Minister of Education. One
dealt with the organization of a laundry at some university (Dorpat)
and the other proposed a winter garden at some other school. Hence
the Duma's indignation. [M. B.]

Manifesto. On the other hand, no matter how righteous was Witte's anger against liberalism, it reached such extremes that he limited his effectiveness in bringing about a reconciliation with the Duma. The stenographic reports of the Special Sessions show this; Witte did not act on a high plane and was beneath his usual stature. The Cadets could triumph; their tactics made impotent and removed from the scene a great and useful man.

Even if the departure of Witte could appear to Cadet conceit as a concession to the Duma, his replacement by Goremykin was a genuine "public calamity. " Society did not understand that at the time.[9] As Minister for Internal Affairs, Goremykin did not mar his record with anything reactionary. In his clash with Witte regarding the North West Zemstvo, society was on his side. He was considered an authority on the peasant question, as he had published two thick volumes on peasant legislation, but society did not realize what dangerous opinions Goremykin himself held on this question. Goremykin's name was not odious at the time, but unfortunately, he was one of the few people who did not understand what had already become clear to others: the necessity for the constitution, the settlement of the peasant problem, and the need for liberal reforms in general. He was not aggressive in the Duma but was quite unconcerned about the problem of agreement with it. He was so little suited to his post that it could be argued that his appointment was intended to provoke the Duma. But even that was not the case.

The memoirs of Count Kokovtsev are revealing in this respect. Rejecting the appointment of Minister of Finance on April 25, he frankly told the tsar that "the choice of the new chairman of the Council of Ministers scarcely serves the needs of the moment. Goremykin's greatest indifference to everything, his lack of flexibility and downright unwillingness to come closer to the representatives of new elements in our national life. . . . " The tsar replied to Kokovtsev that that might be true, but he was certain that Goremykin would leave the post of his own accord if he saw that his resignation would help improve relations with the Duma. Why then was he appointed? "Most important to me [said the tsar] is that he will not make any agreements behind my back, or grant concessions to harm my authority. I can be quite sure that there will be no surprises and I will not be faced with accomplished facts as was the case with the electoral law, and others. "

Such calculations ensured his appointment. It is clear that they were not directed against the Duma or against reforms, but against Witte and the former cabinet, whose independence the tsar could not forgive. This was the tsar's reckoning with them and not with the Duma; it certainly reflected little credit on the tsar's perspicacity, but there was no hint that the tsar wished to use this appointment to hinder liberal reforms.

Thus Goremykin's appointment did not signify desire to undermine the constitution or to prevent the passage of necessary reforms, as, in its time, the appointment of Count Panin in place of the deceased Ia. Rostovtsev did not signify rejection of peasant reform. Supporters of the constitution and liberal reforms entered the new cabinet: they were Kokovtsev, Izvolski, Stolypin, and Shcheglovitov. The last name may cause a smile, but in 1906 he was not what he became later. He was noted for his dedication to the judicial code, was a contributor to the newspaper Pravo (Law), and he openly greeted the issuing of the Manifesto. The Minister of Justice, Akimov, sometimes sent him to interdepartmental conferences, where he took such a liberal stand that Witte asked Akimov not to send him any more. He tried to follow the same course in the Duma, at first, but later turned sharply to the right.[10] However, he was not the only one, for liberalism estranged many of its former supporters.

Thus the composition of the new ministry was not hostile to the constitution or to reforms. Its chief defect lay in the chairman's ineptitude for collaboration with society. This was an obstacle that might have been surmounted if desired; the course of events showed how this was done.

If the struggle between the Duma and the government began from the opening day, its cause was not the constitution, nor the program of liberal reform. The real cause was the Duma's attitude to revolution.

This word is vague, even less definite than constitution. Both were misused. We read about revolutions in books but we did not witness any in Russia after the "Time of Troubles." There were court and military uprisings including the unsuccessful revolt of the Decembrists, peasant disturbances, the destruction of factories, and terrorist activity extending to assassination of the tsar. But not one of these was revolution and none could have deposed the state authority. In 1905 the government saw for the first time, with its own eyes, the ghost of revolution. Organized forces came to the forefront, attempting by joint action to depose the ruling authority and put in its place a different one. The Manifesto of October 17 broke up these forces and, in so doing, halted the revolution, but the government learned the aims and minimum program of the revolutionary parties: a democratic republic, a purely popular government, and the destruction of the army and its replacement by a general levy. Such a program was beyond the realm of possibility and could not serve as a basis of agreement between the government and the revolutionaries. The question of strength was now the only issue between traditional authority and revolution.

The government, still much stronger than the forces of revolution, did not intend to yield and was prepared to oppose them. But the government could not forget the role played by liberal society at the time of the revolutionary attack, its friendly neutrality to revolu-

tion. The anarchy that liberalism hoped to appease with concessions,
even to the extent of disarming the state authority, was suppressed
by the old régime without the support of liberal forces. The government now recognized that there was no safety in autocracy and was
reconciled to the constitution, but it did not wish to yield to revolution and was not disposed to confuse a legal order with the ''dictatorship of the street.'' The victory over the raging Acheront* showed
the autocracy the strength of the government apparatus, but it also
taught the danger of temporary weakness or inactivity. It was now
realized that the government's duty lay in holding on to the rudder,
and retaining enough power to resist the Acheront in the interests of
the whole state, rather than relying entirely on the maturity of Russian society. This necessity was clearly recognized when the Fundamental Laws were debated at the April Conference. These Laws
also prepared the ammunition in case of a conflict not with the constitution but with revolution.

The government did not intend to attack the constitution but
decided to defend it from revolution, and at that time the government
was not the blank it became in 1917, when the tsar agreed to abdication and Grand Duke Michael refused to accept the throne. The government was not even wavering, as in did in 1905, when Witte stood alone:
when the right wing hated him as a traitor to the autocracy, the revolutionaries for hindering their triumph, and intellectual society, in
spite of repeated appeals to it, preferred to stand on the sidelines.
The confusion of the government was now ended and it realized its
own strength. It did not want to violate the new constitution and it
conscientiously planned to carry through within its own framework
the reorganization that liberalism demanded and whose necessity it
recognized itself. In this respect the government was prepared to
go very far, but it refused to pander to revolution. The demarcation
line between the government and liberal society did not pass where
Miliukov attempts to draw it, between autocracy and constitution.[11]
It was drawn between constitution and a ''deepening of revolution;''
between the Fundamental Laws and obvious realization of popular
sovereignty. Opposing sides now came to agreement in the state camp:
far-sighted liberals, who had long supported the constitution but now
perceived the reverse side of society; and those who were formerly
devoted to the old régime but who finally understood the significance
of events and saw things in a new light. A middle-of-the-road policy
was evolving and this became the policy of the government. The

----

*Acheront: This was a term used to refer to the destructive rev-
olutionary spirit which prevailed in Russia during this period. The
derivation is from the Greek. [M. B.]

right-wing enemies of the constitution were compelled to go into hiding and adapt themselves to this new course of events.   They took the offensive only later, when liberalism challenged them; and when it lost its game, they played a fateful role in the general catastrophe.

Chapter Two

THE ATTITUDE OF THE DUMA

TO THE TASK AHEAD OF IT

It is always difficult to understand the popular masses, but what was the aim of their chosen body, the Duma? Elections are one of various imperfect methods of determining the national will which generally cannot be expressed by a candidate, to mention only one difficulty. The nation as a whole has no will and no voice of its own. It resembles a child who cannot speak and utters only indistinguishable sounds that help one guess where he has pain and what he wants; but others must decide what he needs. This should have been the real purpose of the Duma.

Election results are said to resemble a broken mirror, but much can be seen even in a broken mirror. So did the elected Duma reflect Russia in its heterogeneity. Like every representative institution it was generally above the country's cultural level and had no illiterates, but mainly it was a dull mass, unprepared for legislative work. Yet the First Duma contained a particularly outstanding, brilliant minority, who were far above the average level. Later, participation in the Duma made one's reputation, but the members of the First Duma made their reputations before their election. They were a credit to the nation that recognized their worth.

The composition of the Duma also reflected, at a glance, the main characteristic of this time--the moral collapse of the old order. It had no open supporters in the Duma at all, since at that time a conservative reputation ruined people. Even such exceptionally popular, almost legendary figures as F. N. Plevako did not get to Moscow for this reason. On the right-wing benches on which we later saw Purishkevich, Markov, and Zamyslovski, sat such worthy leaders of the Liberation Movement as Count Heiden and Stakhovich. They themselves did not change in any way, but they found themselves heading the opposition from the right. This right-wing opposition in the First Duma represented the authentic liberal principles, and it could indeed have painlessly strengthened the constitutional order in Russia.

The existence of an opposition usually adds interest to parliamentary debates, and in the First Duma, we were indebted in this respect almost exclusively to Heiden and Stakhovich, who bore the whole

brunt of the struggle against the majority. Among their supporters
were people who later, under different circumstances, played a prominent role (for example, Count Olsufev), but in the First Duma they
were silent. The two right-wing leaders were different types, but
they complemented one another. Both were descendants of the privileged class, zealots in its struggle for liberalism, and they occupied
prominent positions until the democratic wave engulfed them.

As a zemstvo leader and chairman of the Free-Economic Society,
Count Heiden long ago had become a constitutionalist. The possessor
of a clear, sober mind, he saw the disintegration of autocracy under
the glistening covering, and understood that without the support of
liberal society the monarchy would perish. Hence his equal devotion
to the constitution and to the monarchy. However, he had no illusions
about the maturity of either the lower or upper brackets of our society.
When the demagogues of the First Duma began to claim that Russia's
salvation could be secured only by full "popular sovereignty," he began to expose this lie with the same insistence with which he fought
against the lies of the old order. Unceasingly, he reminded the Duma
of the fundamental truths of a legal order: that demanding respect for
your own rights necessitated respect for the rights of others. He punc-
tured with irony the soap bubbles of pompous phrases, which at the
time replaced earnest arguments. He did not oppose reform and did
not take upon himself defense of the government, which he considered
the chief offender; but in the First Duma he was the propagator of
common sense and a conscientious attitude to the task ahead. Resembling in appearance America's Uncle Sam, he was neither fluent
nor eloquent, and never tried for oral effects because he stuttered
and at times bellowed. But he was always sensible, approachable,
and his speeches were not only impressive but also commanded the
respect of his opponents.

M. A. Stakhovich was quite a different type. I happened to know
him well, having met him at Iasnaia Poliana in 1898, on the seven-
tieth birthday of Leo Nikolaevich. Later we became close friends.
He was the youngest and most gifted member of a large, exceptionally
interesting, and unique family. Though a brilliant future lay ahead
of him he was not attracted by a career. He could hardly have stayed
on a beaten path since everything appealed to him. His versatility,
eagerness for life ("Life is joy," he used to say), his self-indulgence
(he was spoilt by fate and nature), his everlasting passionate enthu-
siams for people and problems, made him seem thoughtless in the
eyes of superficial observers.

In politics, he was for a long time a supporter of the autocracy.
I happened to read in the minutes of Besiedi (Conversation), [1] the
report of a debate on this theme. Stakhovich was almost alone in his
defense of the autocracy, and his main arguments were characteristic.

In the first place, he insisted that the autocracy was created and supported by the will of the people, who did not understand any other
order; furthermore--and this is most important--that no other régime
could introduce so quickly and completely the social reforms so necessary for Russia. Stakhovich represented the rare variety of the idealists of autocracy, who considered that it could be the basis of political freedom and social justice. He sincerely believed that the autocracy
would justify his expectations, but experience showed how mistaken he
was in this evaluation.

     As chamberlain and government leader, he delivered a speech
at a missionary conference at Orel on the necessity of complete religious freedom of conscience. To him, a sincerely devout man, this
seemed quite obvious, but the speech created such a sensation that he
required all his influential connections to escape serious consequences.
Stakhovich also participated without any ulterior motives in the Zemstvo Conference at Shipov's home in 1903, for which he was severely
reprimanded by Pleve on orders from the tsar. On one occasion,
while taking part in a trial in the capacity of a class representative,
he had the opportunity of seeing with his own eyes the effects of arbitrary local administration, and he wrote an article about it in the
periodical Law, signing his full name. The article was censored but
it was printed without his knowledge in Osvobozhdenie (Freedom).
This brought on Stakhovich the ire of Prince Meshcherski and led to
a curious and highly sensational trial in which Stakhovich accused
Meshcherski of slander.

     Stakhovich never refused to intercede for those who turned to
him--how many people did Leo Tolstoy send him--and so learned
about the life of the lower strata and realized how far his ideal of
autocracy was from reality. But--and this is curious and characteristic of him--he did not become a constitutionalist, which surprised
many of his friends. "I swore allegiance to the autocratic tsar and
cannot go back on my word, " he told me more than once. To many
this attitude seemed insincere: what's in an oath? Who takes this into
consideration in our day? But in this respect he was old-fashioned.
However, when the tsar himself rejected the autocracy, Stakhovich
greeted the action with joy and forgave the monarch for everything.
He became a constitutionalist by "Royal Command"--so quipped
Khomiakov about Stakhovich and himself.

     Stakhovich believed that the constitutional order would cleanse
and save the monarchy and implement the reforms of whose urgency
he had long been aware at first hand. The temper of the First Duma,
its impatience, intolerance, unfairness to opponents, rudeness stemming from consciousness of immunity, in a word, all that captivated
many people as a "revolutionary atmosphere, " outraged not only his
political understanding but also his esthetic sense. He did not yield

to this atmosphere and fought against it. He was not a painstaking, persistent man like Heiden, but rather impulsive, inspired by great parliamentary days but not the day-to-day work; yet in defense of liberal ideas and against their distortion by the left wing, he could rise to great heights. His features and beard resembled Michelangelo's Moses, his speech was hesitant and he often groped for words, but he captivated his listeners by his throbbing passion. His speeches on behalf of amnesty and on the appeal to the people [2] rose to heights that few could attain.

Count Heiden and Stakhovich were, of course, not the only loyal constitutionalists in the First Duma. The majority of them were in the Cadet party, but its discipline and false tactics deprived them of individuality. There were also prominent people outside the Duma and the Cadet party, who were free from discipline and could have defended the constitution, but they were hampered by the unhealthy atmosphere of the Duma and did not dare to resist it.

Take for instance M. M. Kovalevski, a man of exceptional talents, scholarly, with a world-wide reputation. He resided abroad for many years and established a university in Paris where professors expelled from old Russia lectured to students similarly ousted from their homeland. He was familiar with the intellectual as well as the political situation in Europe and knew all its aspects. He had a completely negative attitude toward autocracy, not only as an advocate of principles of justice in national life, but also as a man who himself suffered from the autocracy. From far off he followed with interest the progress of the Liberation Movement in Russia, and during those years I had to report to him every time I visited Paris.

He returned to Russia at the height of the Liberation Movement and participated in the Zemstvo Conferences. Disillusioned by the lack of maturity and earnestness of Russian society, he told me sadly, "I saw only one national figure, Guchkov." Kovalevski did not join the Cadet party, as he was critical of its irreconcilable tactics, whose advantages he failed to see. The revolutionary outbreak after October 17, did not surprise him but caused him great anxiety, and he returned abroad, filled with dark foreboding. His knowledge of history led him to believe that all would yet be well, but the recovery would not be easy. When the revolution was halted by force, Kovalevski returned to Russia once more and was elected to the Duma.

Much was expected of him because of his talents and independence, and he had a good opinion of himself, too, as his surprisingly arrogant first words in the First Duma indicated. Speaking as a man of authority he declared at the session of May 3: "I am a friend of the party called the Party of Popular Freedom, but at the same time I reserve for myself the freedom of independent action, and only with this reservation in mind, can you count on my support." What was the

result of Kovalevski's numerous speeches? One would think he had
lost all his individuality and had forgotten all he had seen. In his
failure to realize that lawfulness was threatened, then, not from the
right but from the left, that we were being pushed toward revolution,
which he did not want at all, he personified liberal society that could
not or would not fight on its left front. Almost all his speeches regarding the address, the declaration, and individual bills only added
fuel to the flame that was raging as it was. His presence in the State
Duma proved fruitless, if not harmful. After the dissolution of the
Duma, when he became a member of the Imperial Council, he found
himself in his element. There the struggle could be carried on against
the right wing, defending human rights and the constitution from administrative arbitrariness. He could command a hearing in the Council and make it profitable to his audience. In short, he was himself,
but while he was in the Duma he was infected by its atmosphere.

Kuzmin-Karavaev was another example of the Duma's deadly
effect. He belonged to the Party of "Democratic Reform," consisting
of four persons, and was not restrained by party discipline. Though
he did not possess Kovalevski's talents, being a rather mediocre man,
he still had much experience and well-merited prestige. He was a
professor in the Military Academy, a town councillor, and held the
rank of general; when participating in zemstvo conferences, he followed an intelligent constitutional policy, often fighting the Cadets.
After 1917 he courageously opposed both army reform and the treatment of officers; on the question of emigration he was in the right
camp. But in the First Duma he swam with the stream. On the questions of capital punishment and the appeal to the people, times when
the voice of experience and wisdom was sorely needed, his speeches
were pathetic. He placed his prestige on the scales of demagogy and
he, too, was ruined by the deadly atmosphere of the First Duma.

Whence blew this harmful political wind that blinded our experienced constitutionalists? In its purest form it was to be found on the
left benches, in the so-called Labor group (Trudoviki)*, which was
the real hero of this Duma.

The Cadets regarded this group with condescending arrogance.
In June, when Miliukov was working on the formation of a Duma Cabi-
net, he wrote in Riech (Speech), June 18, that there would be no
Trudoviki in the new cabinet, "because they have not sufficiently ex-
perienced persons for such work." This was, of course, correct,
but he was mistaken when he saw sufficiently experienced persons
----
* Trudoviki: A parliamentary group representing peasant interests.
Among other agrarian reforms, they demanded nationalization of land.
They advocated bold political tactics in the Duma, were more radical
than the Cadets, and were not subject to party discipline. [M. B.]

among the Cadets and liberal society generally. Another reason for
the disdainful attitude towards the Trudoviki was their lack of a definite program. This made their group a conglomeration of ten different subgroups, one of the largest (eighteen) bearing the picturesque
title "left of Cadets. "[3] The doctrinaire Cadets could not understand
such a party, but in reality, the Trudoviki had more unity than the
Cadets with all their discipline--not unity of program but of political
mood--and there lay their indubitable strength.
    One of the most cultured of the Trudoviki, Professor Lokot,
gives us the key to understanding them in a very interesting book re-
cording vivid impressions of his experiences, Pervaia Duma (The
First Duma), published in 1906. He stated frankly that:

    The Trudoviki came into being as a result of the convic-
    tion that a spontaneous revolutionary spirit had swept the
    whole country, making it even more revolutionary than
    the intellectual élite. Representing such a country, the
    Duma could not be a government institution; it had to be-
    come the organ of revolutionary upheaval. The popular
    wave was destructive and revolutionary, and therefore,
    the Duma could not be other than destructive and revo-
    lutionary.[4]

    The tactics of the Duma had to conform to this attitude, shifting
the center of gravity to revolution, to the "revolutionary mood of the
popular masses, " and not to the proper functioning of the constitutional machine. What was to be done in the Duma? Lokot stated:

    We must strengthen the revolutionary mood and organize,
    rally, and discipline the revolutionary forces of the surg-
    ing upheaval. This is the pressing need of the moment
    and the task of the First State Duma, the political organ
    brought to the forefront by history to realize this aim.[5]

    This was the tactic formerly adopted by the Liberation Movement
against the autocracy, but unruly revolutionary upheaval, because it
was an upheaval, followed its former course even after the promulgation of the constitution. As far as it was concerned nothing had changed.
From the outset its aim was the liquidation of the existing government
order. This according to the Trudoviki was the task of the State Duma.
    Since the Trudoviki were the foremost exponents of this point of
view, Lokot felt that they should lead the Duma. It was impossible to
think of constructive work within the framework of the tottering old
order. First the revolution had to be brought to its logical conclusion
and existing authority overthrown. Then new forces would appear and

create the new order, which would perhaps be quite different from
the one the naive destroyers dreamed of. But this creative effort
was not the task of the Trudoviki, nor of the First Duma generally.
In the opinion of the Trudoviki, the root of Cadet blunders lay in their
failure to understand this. The Cadets could only be the party of the
future. Lokot declared: "Later their time will come, but it has not
come as yet. It will come when the revolutionary wave will overflow
into several calmer streams, in which even the Cadets will be able
to swim; streams that would suit their nature and their class and
group interests."[6]
    Thus the task of the Trudoviki was only destructive: to continue
the revolution using the Duma as the organ of revolutionary upheaval;
and to assist this upheaval by struggling against everything hindering
its triumph. The Trudoviki were consistent if one acdepted their basic premise that the whole country was swept by a revolutionary spirit.
If this feeling was sufficiently strong, the established authority could
be overthrown, and if this perspective was considered beneficial for
Russia, it was necessary to advance it and not play at constitution
making.
    This was the way the Trudoviki's case was presented in the
Duma by their leaders: Zhilkin, a moderate, candid journalist; Anikin,
a teacher, who participated personally in agrarian pogroms; and finally, Aladin, a curious figure of this period.
    I made Aladin's acquaintance in 1904, when I went to London
for the first time. My friends, Shklovskii and Goldenberg, who lived
there, recommended him to me in the capacity of a guide in London,
since he knew the city well and was free at the time. I spent a few
days with him and was intrigued by his eccentric personality. He was
an ardent admirer of England, representing a particular variety of
Russian Anglomaniacs, the democratic Anglomaniac. He ridiculed
Russian revolutionary parties; favored gradual reforms, prefering
practical achievement to pure idealism, and cooperation instead of
war with the government. That is how familiarity with English life
changed a Russian revolutionary. Later, when I learned from the
press that he returned to Russia and was elected to the Duma, I expected much of him. I hoped that he would become the spokesman of
a practical left wing that would finally descend from the clouds. Whether he was infected by the harmful atmosphere of Russia, or he simply
was not sincere in his former conversations with me, I do not know,
but in his demagogic, arrogant speeches in the Duma, I failed to recognize my interesting London guide.
    The Labor group's frame of mind was, of course, incompatible
with the establishment of a legal order. But the strength of the Trudoviki lay in the fact that this mood found a response everywhere. It
was familiar, intelligible, and natural--a primitive, alluring world

outlook. As far as the Duma was concerned, it was quite evident
that neither the subtle criticism of Heiden nor the liberal pathos of
Stakhovich could overcome this mood. Both were too far removed
from it to understand and counteract it successfully. Stakhovich and
Heiden were regarded as traitors by their former associates and
severely criticized by them, but the Liberation Movement passed
them by and disavowed them; they were unable to turn the tide.

Here began the historic responsibility of the Cadet party, since
it was the only one able to combat this mood. Did this mean saddling
the party with a task it did not want? On the contrary, the Cadets
understood this to be their task, and herein lay their real strength.

Even when the Liberation Movement employed the negative slogan, ''down with autocracy,'' the Cadets were not content with this
and tried to write a constitution. It did not suit Russia at all, but in
the midst of the destructive, raging storm, it was a worthwhile effort.
The Cadets also prepared business-like legislation for the Duma, and
even if their agrarian project showed how naive they were, still it was
constructive work. The Cadets understood that the destruction of authority was not the only task ahead of them, for they did not exclude
the possibility of their own participation in a government under the
tsar. Later on, Miliukov carried on secret conversations on this very
subject, and the attitude of the Cadets became even clearer during the
war, when they created a progressive bloc that was an expression of
this same idea. It was no wonder that after 1917 they became the
chief object of revolutionary anger, and the word ''Cadet'' became a
curse. Consequently, though their ideology was not at fault, the ill-
fated tactics of their leaders concealed their nature, prompting them
to act when it was too late and to reject favorable opportunities when
they presented themselves. They let their chance slip in October,
1905, when Witte sent his invitation to the zemstvo; they also missed
their opportunity in the First State Duma.

The chief task of the Cadets was to strengthen the new constitution; they could have done it had they wished. The First Duma assem-
bled all that was best in the country: veterans of the Liberation Movement; deserving community workers; and youthful, rising forces of
science, jurisprudence, and journalism. Their names are well known
and they are too numerous to mention. The Cadet constellation was
far superior to all others; it was eager for action and wished to bol-
ster--not destroy--the constitution. ''We and you are born parliamentarians,'' Kokoshkin told Vinaver sadly, ''but we are following a
different course.'' It is useless to try to calculate the number of supporters that could have been mustered for a loyal constitutional policy
in the First Duma. In June Miliukov declared (Speech, June 18) that
the Cadet ministry could count on a safe majority (305 votes) without
the Trudoviki. But this was not significant. The Cadets could have

challenged the opposing current and won the support of the wavering
and nonparty people, who were everywhere in the majority, if only
they had remained true to themselves and fought the revolutionary
upheaval in support of the constitutional order. Such a battle in the
Duma was more worthy of their talents and their historic role than
the belated exposure of the sins of our past. But the struggle for the
constitution had to be carried on wholeheartedly, without looking to
the left, as was done in the agrarian appeal when the prospect for a
Cadet ministry appeared. The Cadets did not follow the loyal road
when such a policy might have saved the situation because they were
burdened by their recent past.

To carry on a successful struggle in support of the constitution
and against the revolutionary upheaval, they themselves had to accept
the constitution. It was quite in order to be dissatisfied with its original form and attempt to improve it, but a loyal party could not deny
the constitution since it was proclaimed by the lawful authority in a
lawful manner. And yet, after the April Conference, on the eve of
the first sessions of the Duma, the Cadet party published this decision in connection with the Fundamental Laws:

> The Party of Popular Freedom and its representatives in
> the State Duma declare that they see in this step of the
> government an open and flagrant violation of the rights of
> the people, solemnly acknowledged by the government in
> the Manifesto of October 17, and they declare that no obsta-
> cles created by the government will prevent the popular
> representatives from the fulfillment of the tasks imposed
> on them by the people.

This false and insincere phraseology was either a lot of nonsense or it meant that the Cadets did not recognize the constitution.
If so, how could they defend it or the very principle of legality? In
his Contemporary Memoirs, book sixty-five, Vishniak reproached me
for considering observance of formal law obligatory for both those who
created it and those against whom it was directed. In his opinion it
was a misunderstanding on my part, which was consistent, because
he has remained a revolutionary to this day and thinks that 1906 must
be treated as a revolution. But the Cadets had to fight such a viewpoint, for if there were no constitution at that time, there could be no
talk of a legal order; force alone would have been triumphant. Then
the same thing would have taken place as in 1917, when the government surrendered to the Soviets and the notorious Constituent Assembly was dispersed by a sailors' threat. Here lay the chief peril of
this period, and the Cadets should have defended the country from it.
But after passing their resolution this would have meant loss of face

and so was out of question, though they later claimed that the government was the enemy of the constitution.

This was not all. The constitution was not an end in itself for
anyone except professional politicians, but it was essential as a means
of introducing reforms that the nation needed. The chief problem of
the moment was the reorganization of Russia, which the masses expected. Yet, at the January and April Conferences, the Cadet party
forbade "organic" work, so long as the constitution remained unchanged. It is true that this prohibition was only a wily phrase to
conceal the discord and avoid a split. The Cadets still intended to
work under its cover, but by doing so, they surrendered their ideological position. Intrigue was placed above the interests of the nation, and having postponed the satisfaction of these interests until a
complete constitutional victory over the crown was won, the Cadets
still accused the government of rejecting reforms.

Such was the position of the Cadets when the duty of defending
a legal order against revolutionary attacks fell to their lot. Since the
autocracy made a concession, they were faced with a dilemma: either
continue the old policy and finish off the retreating authority as an
enemy that showed its weakness; or accept the surrender, come to
an agreement with that authority, and realize certain concrete tasks,
while opposing side by side with the government further revolutionary encroachments. A choice had to be made since the policy of the
Duma depended on the conduct of the Cadets. This was an historic
moment, when the immediate future depended on the party leaders.
We know how the Cadets solved their dilemma, but it is interesting to
note the way they solved it.

The decision on which everything depended was not even brought
before the party. It was predetermined by the past. Vinaver, the
faithful chronicler of the Duma, tells us that

> on the eve of its opening, the Cadets and the Trudoviki
> held the first joint session of the "opposition." The Ca-
> dets organized it and Miliukov, though not a member of
> the Duma, presided. The subject of discussion was strict-
> ly determined in advance to avoid confusion and speakers
> of the Cadet party were selected in advance to give reports
> and explanations.[7]

On the eve of the official opening of the Duma it was certainly
natural to assemble the deputies for a private deliberation, but this
was not a private session of the Duma. It was a meeting of its left-
wing majority, including the Trudoviki. Right-wing groups, on which
Miliukov counted finally in the selection of his cabinet, were not invited to the session.

Was the program of this left bloc determined earlier, and were
the conditions on the basis of which it was concluded laid down formally, as was the case in France at the formation of the Popular Front?
Nothing of the kind. Everything was simply left as before, as though
the Liberation Movement was still continuing and no discord existed
on matters of principle between the Cadets and the Trudoviki.

This is the way the past influences people. In the liberation
period, liberalism together with the revolutionary parties opposed
autocracy. On the 26th of April they continued to march side by side,
without stopping to consider whether,now that the constitution had been
introduced, they were not on opposite sides of the barricades. They
acted as though nothing had changed since the victory of the Liberation
Movement.

Such a policy was perhaps clear to the masses, whose inertia
equally determines their quiescence and their movement, but it was
the task of the Cadet leaders to reorient themselves instead of blindly following their predecessors. Why, then, did the Cadet leaders
act as they did?

Mainly because we had no leadership. The work of the leaders
consisted of explaining, in a roundabout way, the supposed necessity
of what had happened. Gambetta said in his last parliamentary
speech: "cela ne s'appelle pas gouverner, cela s'appelle raconter
(This is not governing, it is telling stories)." What our leaders
later said about this I have already noted in the introduction and
will not repeat now.

There was one curious detail regarding this session of April
26, and the Duma "bloc." Its significance lay in the fact that this
majority called itself the "joint opposition." Why "opposition"?
This terminology was not a slip of the tongue by Vinaver, as it is
frequently repeated in his book. It was also used by the entire Cadet
press of that period. The Duma's majority was transformed into the
"opposition." When a small Cadet group in the Third Duma called
itself the opposition, it was understandable, since minority and opposition are related meanings. But why did the majority that was in
complete control of the First Duma call itself the "opposition"? The
Cadets lived in the psychology of the past, and this was reflected in the
term "opposition." During the period of autocracy all who were against
it united under the common name"opposition." Struve wrote at the
time, "Since all oposition in Russia is treated as revolution, revolution became simply opposition"--an appealing idea, justifiable, perhaps, in a certain period, but dangerous in a new order. What sense
was there in this name for such admirers and experts of parliamentarianism as were the Cadets? Only that, as N. N. Bazhenov said,
the Cadets continued to live "according to the old textbooks." Thus

instead of using and defending the constitution, the Cadets followed
the tactics of the Trudoviki and their destructive revolutionary upheaval. The Cadets began to apply their own talents, knowledge, and
skill to petty problems of concern to no one and to clothe the revolutionary tendencies of the Duma in a semblance of constitution.

Having accepted this subordinate role, the Cadets still pretended
to be the leadership of the Duma. Their personal qualities gave them
a right to do so, and the Duma would certainly have followed them had
they led it on the constitutional course, for there the Cadets could
have no rivals. However, Cadet attempts to provide leadership on a
revolutionary road foreign to them were a paradox. The Trudoviki
were more consistent in their revolutionary tactics and therefore began to inspire more confidence, until the Duma proved to everyone
the falsehood of their original premise. The Cadets were ruined by
their tactics and the great cause to which history called them proved
to be beyond their strength.

Such was the mood of the Duma at the time of its opening. It
was clear that immediate conflict between it and the government was
unavoidable, but is it possible to maintain that only the "malicious
government" was guilty?

Chapter Three

THE OPENING OF THE DUMA

The opening day of the Duma, April 27, indicated clearly which of the two foes was the aggressor. That day traditional authority faced a representative assembly for the first time.

The meeting was accompanied by pomp and ceremony. As recently as the middle of April, the tsar refused to issue a manifesto announcing the granting of the constitution, considering that an ukase to the Senate would be sufficient. This was a petty manifestation of his displeasure at having to strike out the title "Unlimited." But by the end of April he overcame this feeling and decided to introduce the opening of the new order with the greatest pomp.

This in itself is unimportant, but in determing intentions, exterior form is not insignificant. Everything in the power of the government was done to make the opening a great occasion. There was a grand welcome ceremony at the Winter Palace, and a speech from the throne to mark the dawn of a "new era." There was no need for such ceremonies if the Duma's work was to be hindered.

The speech from the throne held the spotlight. P. A. Stolypin, speaking at the Winter Palace welcoming ceremony, implied that the speech was unexpected by the government and was personally written by the tsar. Whether or not this was true is unimportant, but the speech was significant and I shall quote it in full:

Almighty God entrusted to my care the welfare of the Fatherland and impelled me to summon representatives of the people to assist in legislative activity.

With abiding faith in the great future of Russia, I greet in you the élite, whom I ordered My beloved subjects to choose from their midst.

Difficult and complex work lies before you. I trust that love of your native land, and a burning desire to serve her, will inspire you.

I will safeguard the unshakable tenets I granted, in the firm conviction that your unselfish service to the Fatherland will help determine the needs of the peasants so

near to My heart, and contribute to the enlightenment
of the people and the advancement of their welfare. Remember that spiritual greatness and the welfare of the
nation depend not only on freedom, but also on order
based on justice.

May My earnest desire be fulfilled: may I see My
people happy and pass on to My Son, as his inheritance,
a strong, well-ordered, and enlightened state.

May God bless the work confronting Me and the State
council and the State Duma, and may this day be henceforth remembered as the day of the rebirth of the morality of the Russian land, the day of the rebirth of her best
forces.

Approach with faith the work for which I summoned
you, and justify in a worthy manner the confidence of the
Tsar and the nation.

May God help You and Me.

Of course this speech contained many platitudes, but apart from
them, its political content was very gratifying. I shall stress its
three main points.

The tsar promised to "safeguard the unshakable tenets he
granted." Later, when the existence of the constitution was questioned, one of the reasons for questioning it was the fact that the tsar
did not swear to it. This proof was not only weak, but also incorrect.
There was no oath, but the tsar, under exceptionally ceremonious
circumstances, promised to "safeguard" the new tenets. His promise took the place of an oath. Furthermore, while the deputies entering the Duma took no oath, they made a ceremonious promise to fulfill the duties imposed on them. No more could be demanded of the
tsar, but his promise was particularly noteworthy. At the April session a number of officials, among them unfortunately Witte, tried to
persuade the tsar to declare that he retained the right to alter the
Fundamental Laws. The promise to guard them unswervingly was
his reply to this foolish advice.

No less important was another fact. It was suspected that, having granted a constitution, the tsar would leave everything "as in the
past." The speech from the throne denounced this suspicion also.
It announced an era of fundamental changes: the rebirth of the morality of the Russian land; the settlement of the peasant question; extension of enlightenment; general welfare; an order based on justice--
these were the paths to follow. The political program the speech
outlined coincided with the age-old goals of liberalism.

It is curious to note that, in order to carry out these reforms,
the tsar summoned the Duma to action. He did not speak, according

to the old formula, of his proposals or of legislation that the government would introduce for the Duma's confirmation, but rather he expressed the hope that the Duma would determine the needs of the
peasants, facilitate enlightenment, and contribute to the public welfare. Consequently he expected of the Duma not only approval of
government proposals, but a clarification of the country's needs.
Surely this supported the conception of the Duma's legislative initiative.
        And finally there was a third noteworthy point in this speech.
The very people who were elected to the Duma were, until recently,
considered "enemies of the state and traitors." The composition of
the Duma aroused the indignation of the right-wing press, which could
not find enough insulting epithets to hurl at it. Yet the tsar greeted
them as the élite. Probably he did not think them so, but he followed
the constitutional fiction that they were. Elections do not necessarily
bring into parliament the best people, just as the vote is not always
an accurate gauge of the will of the people, and truth is not always on
the side of the majority. But these are fictions without which a constitutional order is impossible. The tsar overcame his objections
and sacrificed his personal feelings to the constitutional idea.
        It is curious that he understood the sense of this fiction better
than the constitutionalists concerned. Some deputies accepted the
epithet "élite" at its face value. On May 8 Aladin said: "The nation
through its élite, and this is not only my opinion but also the opinion
of the Highest Authority, wishes to rebuild the life of the Russian
people." On May 13, A. R. Lednitskii began his speech with these
words: "Gentlemen representatives, the élite of the land." And at
the Viborg trial, E. I. Kedrin, protesting against the unsatisfactory
condition of the courtroom, the packed crowd and poor accoustics,
declared, "such is the treatment meted out to those, who, from the
pinnacle of the throne, were called the élite." What a queer conception of a polite phrase!
        Society might have been pleased with this nonprovocative speech,
yet it was disappointed. I well remember this mood, and the press of
the period confirms it. No one wanted to evaluate the possibilities
this speech revealed, and influential leaders gave society a pessimis-
tic point of view. Miliukov wrote in Speech on April 28:

> Not a step forward did the government make to meet so-
> cial opinion, at a time when the slightest move would
> have been greeted by the nation with ten-fold attention
> and responsiveness.... Our government is noted for its
> ability to miss opportune moments, and the speech from
> the throne skillfully avoided all controversial topics.

In an interesting and more objective book, Ezerski wrote in 1907:

> The government did all it could to dispel the illustions of
> the most incorrigible optimists. . . . Intellectuals awaited
> the speech from the throne with impatience; but in gen-
> eral, the historic document created the impression of
> something cold, officially gracious. . . . The old ideal of
> Slavophilism was completely destroyed at the very mo-
> ment when it was realized outwardly.

Vinaver appeared more condescending than Ezerski, but even he admitted that "the content of the speech from the throne, even if it did
not irritate, failed to inspire joyous hopes. "

However, what could society have expected from the speech?
What else should have been said to make people evaluate truly the
content and the tone of this document? There was widespread belief
that amnesty to political prisoners should have been mentioned in the
speech, but it is difficult to understand this reproach. Amnesty was
the prerogative of the monarch; he could grant it, but just mentioning
it would have been dangerous.

The Russian people, not only the lower ranks but also the top
strata, could not "differentiate. " When the October Manifesto promised to grant in the future the foundations of freedom, even educated
lawyers understood this to mean that all limitations of freedom were
thereby immediately removed. In fact, the first clashes between society and the government occurred over this very matter. So, too,
mention of amnesty would have been accepted as having the force of
law, to be applied immediately. Our ambassador to England, Count
Benkendorf, observing Russian events through the eyes of an English-
man accustomed to respect the law, in a letter to A. P. Izvolsky[1]
expressed regret that no mention of amnesty was made in the speech
from the throne. "Why fear amnesty?" Sacred simplicity! English-
ment, having heard "mention of amnesty, " would await the new law,
but Russians would rush to smash prison doors. Mention would become provocation, which would benefit revolution and nothing else.

But would our society's mood have been different had the tsar
promised amnesty in the speech from the throne? Would the Duma
have been grateful and pleased?

Doubts of this arise when one reads the stenographic reports
of the meetings where amnesty was discussed. I shall describe an
instructive episode.

On May 3 amnesty discussions were taking place in the Duma.
Many speakers begged the Duma not to prolong the dispute, and

Rodichev made this strange remark: "We are on the eve of being late w'th our Address. If we do not complete it soon, we may find ourselves in the position in which the presentation of the Address including amnesty will prove belated. . . . I think you understand me gentlemen [loud applause]."

The Duma understood him, otherwise there would have been no loud applause. This speech may be impossible to understand now, however, and some clarification is needed. The Duma feared that amnesty for political prisoners might be declared by the tsar, on the occasion of the Tsar's Day, May 6, and the Duma did not want this. It wanted to be the victor in the amnesty issue and did not hesitate to show this openly. What gratitude could the tsar expect of the Duma had he forestalled it on April 27?

The Duma's attitude is exemplified in another instance. The speech from the throne did not mention the tsar's title, "Autocrat," as a concession to the Duma. What was the reaction of the Cadet press to this gesture? P. N. Miliukov wrote the following on April 28: "The warning against further use of the word 'Autocrat,' sounded by the majority of deputies in the report of the joint session of several parliamentary groups, was not sounded in vain." To assess these proud words correctly, we must recall what the "warning" was. The parliamentary groups agreed to sign, without debate, the promise of the deputies, in which the title "Autocrat" was retained. However, they declared that, in their opinion, retention of the title did not endanger the constitution. This decision to obey the government was wise, but what Miliukov calls a "warning" was, in reality, the capitulation of the Duma and the sanction of the title "Autocrat." Nevertheless, the Cadets immediately transformed it into an achievement to be credited to them and their skill--a victory. This is how historians sometimes write history.

But how did society act towards the government on the day of the Duma's opening? Let us examine the second part of the activity that was unfolded in the building where the Duma met.

The opening of the Duma followed the rules laid down in the ukase of September 18, 1905, which the newly-elected chairman of the Duma oversimplified and called a law. According to these rules, the Duma was not supposed to deal with anything on the first day. There was to be only the formal opening by a personage appointed for the purpose by the tsar, signing by the members of the Duma of the "sacred promise to fulfill the duties imposed on them," and election of the chairman. It was difficult to perform an act of political significance within this framework, as the only active person would be the chairman. Nevertheless, several gestures of political significance were made at the opening of the Duma.

As expected, S. A. Muromtsev was chosen chairman. So many votes were handed in for him that a ballot was unanimously declared

unnecessary. This was the crowning point in his career. Extensive
memoir literature about him hardly does him justice. For a long
time he lived in Moscow among us, first as a young professor and
then as a lawyer. He was the Chairman of the Legal Society, a spokesman for city and country, independent as to income and respected by
all from afar, but impenetrable to outsiders. No one foresaw his fate.
He had no political influence and looked for none. He told me himself
that he did not like the practice of law, considered the professorship,
of which the authorities deprived him, his calling, and in general felt
himself out of place. Following the period of the Duma, he became a
legendary figure; but legend, in its turn, began to hinder the understanding of the real man. Muromtsev possessed many qualities of a
chairman, and both in Roman Law, which he taught, and in jurisprudence, formality appealed to him. He liked to change chaos into
order. With absorbing interest, he busied himself putting together
the Instructions for the State Duma, even before the promulgation of
the constitution. I shall not detract from the respect due him if I say
that his skill as chairman was greatly overestimated. It was suited
to a peaceful period, not the confusion of this particular time. The
chairman of the Duma could not be merely a technician; he had to be
a political factor as well. How did Muromtsev measure up as a politician? He had long been a liberal of the European type, a constitutionalist, a parliamentarian: there was nothing of the revolutionary
and demagogue about him. But because of his convictions, Muromtsev
did not reveal his true political colors even in the chairman's high
post. He formulated the principle of democracy in this way: ''Until
a decision is reached, every member of the party must defend his
opinion to the limit; once a decision is reached, unquestioning obedience is his duty.'' However, he did not defend anything ''to the
limit,'' leaving that to others while he listened carefully, but he obeyed
unquestioningly. If it were not for this, he might not have become
chairman of the Duma. Be that as it may, he became a strong technical force in the Duma, but others directed it politically. He never
revealed his individuality in politics, nor did he use the influence he
could have had.

Three symbolic episodes occurred on the first day of the Duma's
activity.

First, there was Petrunkevich's speech on amnesty for political
prisoners. This speech was unexpected; it was not foreseen in the
April 26 meeting of ''united opposition,'' and of course was quite unnecessary. But the deputies were so aroused by the clamor of the
''street,'' which screamed for ''amnesty,'' and by the waving of ker-
chiefs from Krestovskii when their ship sailed by on its way to the
palace, that they decided to respond immediately. To calm the tumult
and provide an outlet for passions, they chose the harmless speech
of Petrunkevich. The mise en scène succeeded admirably. The speech

was brief and stirring. Everyone was uplifted and aroused, though
it was only a symbolic gesture of no practical importance. Miliukov
saw its symbolic significance in the fact that "the first word from the
Duma tribune was dedicated to the heroes of freedom." [2] This speech,
by the way, had another side too, no less instructive. It showed the
overwhelming importance the Duma attached to gestures, preferring
them to results, as well as its disregard for law. The regulations of
September 18, which Muromtsev himself called laws, did not permit
such a speech. But, of course, it was not worthwhile making an issue of this formal defection. And in so far as this gesture could hinder other more risky proposals on amnesty, it was even successful.

The second episode could be ignored altogether, if it had not
been noted and stressed more than it was worth. It remains incomprehensible to this day. In stenographic reports it is recorded as
follows:

> Chairman: I ask outsiders to leave the seats reserved
> for the members of the State Duma; otherwise, balloting
> will be impossible. Let us go on to the voting, etc.

That was all: the incident seems of no significance. And yet it
attracted the attention of chroniclers. Miliukov spoke of it in these
triumphant tones (Speech, April 28): "The chairman rose and ut-
tered his first words, words of firmness, of calm, self-confident
power. It was the master of the meeting speaking, and by ordering
outsiders to leave the hall, he showed their real position as guests,
to those who forgot that they were no longer masters."
What was all this about? Who was ordered to leave the hall?
This distortion of the report, and Miliukov was not the only one to do
so, stemmed from an insignificant incident. A few days later, in
Moscow, I heard the story from eyewitnesses. This is what really
happened. On this great day, office clerks came to see the opening
of the Duma. Unable to find room on the tribune assigned to them,
they spread out into the passageways. This created confusion and
their presence hindered the voting, so Muromtsev, in a loud voice,
asked them to leave the seats assigned to the deputies. Confused,
they quickly went over to other seats. This easy victory over office
clerks was extolled by Miliukov, who claimed that the chairman "ordered the guests to leave the hall."
If there was anything symbolic about this, it was only the satisfaction of Miliukov, the press, and the public--a sorry commentary
on our past. Russian society had so few rights in the past that it
revealed a pathetic delight when it could at last show its authority
about something. In reality, this was so natural that it was ridiculous to pay any attention to it. This delight at the "firmness," the

"calm, " and the "self-confident power in the words of the chairman"
in his "order to withdraw from the hall" makes one think of the
young officer, recently promoted, who is drunk with power because
the soldiers salute him. Such a mood gave little promise of successful collaboration between the Duma and the government.

The day's spotlight was held by the chairman's speech of thanks.
It received excellent publicity and was acclaimed to the point of distortion. I note this humorous detail.

Muromtsev had a well-known weakness for flamboyant style.
He alone employed this mode of address: "Gentlemen of the Senate, "
"Gentlemen, Special Presence, " etc. In his maiden speech to the
Duma, as it was recorded in the press, this non-Russian phrase occurred: Velikoe sovershaetsia (great things are being accomplished).
Journalists fell over one another in their delight at the beauty and
force of the two Russian words, which he actually did not say. The
stenographic report showed that Muromtsev expressed himself more
simply, saying: "Great work is being accomplished. " But his admirers regarded this as ineffective, and they changed this simple
phrase into a more dramatic one, even if it was less grammatical.

However, even without this correction, Muromtsev's speech
was a model--brief, effective, and impressive--but fundamentally it
contained a dangerous idea. It was not apparent at first, but the future revealed its real meaning. This is what he said: "May our
work be accomplished with due regard for the prerogatives of a constitutional monarch [thunderous applause] and on the basis of complete
realization of the rights of the State Duma, stemming from the very
nature of popular representation [thunderous applause]. "

This statement, and the thunderous applause it received, created
a good impression. But only a naive person could suppose that its
first half showed evidence of the Duma's loyalty to the monarch, to
his prerogatives and to his position in the new constitution. Unfortunately, our past did not cultivate such feelings. They would be
branded "as trying to please. " The thunderous applause that greeted
the chairman's words can be explained in a different way. Muromtsev
said later that he was given to understand "from above" that it would
be desirable to avoid the foreign word "constitution. " This would be
as much of a concession to the tsar's dislike of this word as the one
the tsar made to satisfy the Duma when he did not utter the word
"autocracy, " though the earlier veto was removed from it by the
deputies' agreement to sign the "promise" with the word "autocracy"
included. But in the face of such a hint from "above, " Muromtsev,
to show his independence, decided to use the word "constitution" whatever the consequences. It was this particular utterance that called
forth the thunderous applause. The press made the most of it. Miliukov wrote on April 28:

> The gathering, which was silent in the Winter Palace,
> broke into applause during the address to the constitu-
> tional monarch. History will note this first expression
> of parliamentary loyalty: the delicate, fragile feeling,
> which can only be preserved and developed by thought-
> ful care. A promise was given but the condition for its
> fulfillment was also laid down.

These thought-provoking words are clear. There was silence in the
Winter Palace; the applause was for the epithet, constitutional. Miliukov said that the tsar's constitutionalism was the condition for the
loyalty of the Duma. There can be a difference of opinion as to the
suitability of a demonstration accompanying this condition, but history will not be so naive as to see loyalty to the constitutional monarch in this revelation of feelings. Doubt about this was soon dis-
pelled.

The real meaning of the chairman's words was revealed in the
second half of his statement, when he spoke not of the monarch but
of the Duma. It would have been natural, if having declared the
Duma's respect for the constitutional prerogatives of the monarch,
the chairman had pointed to the necessity of the complete realization
of the rights that the constitution granted the Duma. This would have
been a declaration that the Duma promised the same loyalty to the
constitution that it demanded of the monarch. Had such a declaration
been made by the chairman, and had it aroused the applause of the
meeting, it would have revealed the existence of a politically healthy
atmosphere. But this was not done, and had it been done, it would
not have aroused applause.

It is improper to draw conclusions from "silence." But can
there be any doubt that the Cadets did not respect the constitution
and did not intend to observe it? That is why the chairman of the
Duma, the lawyer Muromtsev, did not speak of the constitutional
rights of the State Duma but of rights issuing, supposedly, from the
very nature of popular representation. He countered the constitutional laws defining the monarch's prerogatives by the "natural
rights of popular representation." Such, too, was the point of view
of the April Cadet conference, which declared that until there should
be complete realization of popular authority, there could be no
peace and no organic work done in the Duma. This served as the
basis of compromise between liberal and revolutionary ideology.
Muromtsev could not by nature sympathize with this point of view,
but this is where politics began, and in that respect he followed rather than led. The very first day Muromtsev symbolized the future
role of the Cadets in this Duma; in his speech, he succeeded in
cloaking the revolutionary tendencies of the Duma as natural rights.

But this formula had no concrete meaning. The rights of
popular representatives are determined not by nature but by many
conditions, and above all by the relationship of forces at the given
moment. To speak of the nature of popular representation is as useless as to speak of the nature of the authority of the monarch. But
when Muromtsev countered the constitutional prerogatives of the
monarch by the natural rights of popular representation, he pushed
the Duma on a road from which he, as chairman, should have held
it back. His error was, of course, highly praised by the party
press. Miliukov wrote[3]

> The chairman expressed completely and precisely the
> real feelings of the meeting and pointed out the basic
> problem of the existing political situation. Consequent-
> ly, the amphitheatre, the loges, and today the whole
> country, will feel that, henceforth, the key to the solu-
> tion of the problem is to be found in this very hall. The
> guests and masters have changed places.

Thus Muromtsev himself blessed the transformation of the
Duma from the constitutional setting into the organ of revolutionary
storm. However, at the time, this was not apparent. The higher
authorities remained pleased with his speech. He received a warm
welcome at Court, and at the first official celebration he was given
a place of honor. But the illusion of peace did not last long.

Chapter Four

THE DUMA'S ADDRESS IN REPLY TO

THE SPEECH FROM THE THRONE

The triumphal opening of the Duma was a gala show, but politics went on behind the scenes. The first open political gesture of the Duma consisted of the adoption of the address that determined all future action and showed the Duma in its true colors for the first time.

The address, both in initiative and in execution, was the work of the Cadets. An indication of Cadet leadership and prestige in the Duma was the exit of the eleven members of the right wing, who, though opposed to the adoption of the address, decided not to vote against it. The chairman announced amid thunderous applause that the address was adopted unanimously. The Cadets were so delighted with their triumph that they ignored the wishes of the Right to Maintain unanimity. In Speech, May 6, Miliukov attacked them in these words:

> The strange secession of five members of the Chamber
> (there were actually eleven), who participated in all pre-
> vious stages of the discussion and introduced into the
> text a number of corrections and changes, and at the last
> moment refused to bear joint responsibility for the ad-
> dress, only stressed the isolation of this little group.
> Certainly the ''ministry enjoying the confidence of the
> majority'' will not come from among these people; yes-
> terday's action caused an unalterable rift between them
> and the rest of the Chamber.

This was the way the Cadets reacted to the voice of genuine opposition.

The address was not an improvisation; it was conceived and composed by the Cadets even before the speech from the throne was delivered. At the joint session of the ''opposition,'' April 26, Vinaver
reported on its contents, and before its discussion in the Official
Duma Committee of thirty-three members, its text was prepared by
a committee outside the Duma, consisting of six persons including
Miliukov. Two of its members, both Cadets, were entrusted with

drawing up, independently, two separate projects, one of which was approved as the basis for discussion. Later a Trudovik project was also presented to the Committee of the Duma but was rejected as lengthy and ineffective.[1] Thus only the Cadet project was offered by the Committee, and Nabokov presented it to the Duma.   The Cadets composed it, defended it in the Duma, and succeeded in obtaining unanimity in the final vote.   But in reality they were the only ones who remained satisfied with it.

Lokot, chagrined, wrote: ''The address contained respectful, high-flown rhetoric but did not give a clear understanding and precise interpretation of the words and intentions of the higher authorities, and was in no way different from the addresses recently presented by Zemstvo meetings. Was this address necessary?''[2] The Social-Democrats went even further in their repentance.   Their press asserted that (according to B. and Dan, Labor deputies in the Second State Duma) when the vote on the address was taken the labor deputies supposedly shunned it, which was not true, and Vinaver firmly denied this version in <u>Conflicts</u>.   Nevertheless this shows that the Social-Democrats repented and did not share the Cadets' satisfaction with the address.

However, the Cadets themselves were delighted. Miliukov wrote in <u>Speech</u>, May 6:

> The Duma's adoption of the address in reply to the speech
> from the throne is an act of the greatest political signifi-
> cance, and the night session of May 5-6 is destined to be-
> come an historic event. No party criticism can diminish
> the great significance of this fact for the country, the
> Duma itself, and the Head of the State.

Cadet Novgorodtsev echoed on May 8, ''The deed which we accomplished is already entered in indelible lines on the pages of history, a great historic action that nothing can weaken or disparage.''

The Cadets maintained this view of the address for a long time. In the Third Duma, in which the Octobrists were the dominant group, Miliukov announced during the discussion of the address that the Cadets were in complete solidarity with the historic address of the First Duma, which had remained their ''symbol of faith.''

Since the address was the work of the Cadets one may ask: What did they hope to achieve by it? The results, as is well known, were negligible, but how did the initiatiors regard their project? Being a monarchic party, the Cadets could not fail to understand that it would be impolite to leave unanswered the address of the Head of the State. The greeting had to be answered without the servility with which Soviet society regards Stalin, but with the calm dignity with which the

people reply to their sovereign. In fact, the address was regarded
as a reply to the speech from the throne. It began with the words:
"It pleased Your Majesty in the speech directed to the representatives of the people to announce your determination to safeguard the
unshakable laws, etc...."

Even if the reply was inspired by loyalty and the desire to be
courteous, however, the Duma's wishes might have been added to
the reply, but where was the actual response to the words of the
sovereign?

The enemies of the Duma attacked the address severely and
often unfairly. Professor V. I. Gerie wrote as follows in his book
on the First Duma: "Even persons hostile to the old order were
amazed and considered it a serious political mistake that the address-
in-reply contained not one word of gratitude to the monarch who fulfilled the ancient hopes of Russian liberalism."

While on the subject of these accusing words, I cannot help
recalling a later episode when the Third Duma presented its address
to the tsar. A. I. Guchkov stressed during the debate that the popular representatives to this day had not paid their debt of gratitude
to the tsar for granting the constitution and the Third Duma must
do so. According to the European tradition, the extreme Left departed from the hall during the voting period but the Cadets voted
for the address. They did not realize that in doing so they condemned
themselves; if this expression of gratitude was necessary it should
have been expressed earlier and by themselves.

If reforms are justified only by the benefit they bring to the
state, there should be no need for personal thanks, which might explain the Duma's omission. But gratitude for a constitution is one
thing and gratitude for "greetings and good wishes" is another. To
leave the latter unanswered was equivalent to ignoring a greeting.
The Cadet party was sufficiently refined and cultured to understand
this. Yet it did not answer the greeting nor the "appeal for God's
blessing" on the future work of the State Duma. The tsar's greeting
remained unanswered. The people were silent; but was this lack of
good breeding, or was it intentional?

A minor episode provided the answer to this question. On
May 4 an ignorant peasant, Bocharov, proposed adding this phrase
at the end of the address: "The popular representatives affirm
their allegiance and loyal devotion to Your Majesty."

It was an awkward expression, in Russian, as far as style
was concerned, and as such it did not fit in with the address. But
Bocharov's proposal showed the right feeling about the omission.
The Cadet stylists could have revised it had they wished, but they
did not. The speaker, Nabokov, rose to object. He pointed out
that in turning to the monarch the Duma appeared before him as
"the highest legislative institution," and the tsar himself in his

speech from the throne did not address the deputies as "loyal subjects"; therefore, the Duma ought not to stress this point. Nabokov
added that "the address was not composed with this in view and the
expression of loyalty was not the reason for addressing the monarch." This characteristic declaration was received with stormy
applause. Bocharov was confused and withdrew his proposal. He
was unequal to the task of disputing with Nabokov, and furthermore,
a dispute on such a subject was embarrassing. But the whole address was regarded in a new light; Bocharov's correction dotted the
"i's." The omission of gratitude for the greeting was transformed
into intentional neglect. Why did such an unnecessary blunder arise
and why did the Cadets, the initiators of the address, allow this to
happen?

This is an interesting question, one that should facilitate
understanding of Cadet tactics in general. It showed, of course,
that the Cadets were not true monarchists, in the sense that Heiden
and Stakhovich were, when they refused to approve the address, or
they would not have permitted such a demonstration. But the Cadets
were not republicans, either, and they did not want to make an antimonarchist demonstration; in fact it was they who introduced the
idea of the necessity of the address and persuaded the revolutionary
parties to accept it, though this contradicted their traditions. But
once the Cadets were willing to side with the left bloc on the question
of the address, they were compelled to make concessions. The
Trudoviki already criticized the address both for the respectfulness
of its tone and the presence of "titles and conventions" in it.

M. M. Kovalevski found himself compelled to give an equivocal
approval: "I praise your address," he said on May 3, "because it
is expressed in polite, moderate words." One had to be very un-
assuming to rejoice in the fact that there were no impolite words in
the address to the tsar. But more could not be demanded of the
revolutionaries in their existing mood, and the Cadets paid dearly--
in the form of an antimonarchist demonstration--for the revolutionaries' support of the address. This occurrence became the symbol
of long-term results of Cadet tactics of trying to combine constitutional and revolutionary principles. It also explains the fruitlessness of their tactics.

Involuntarily I contrast this masked demonstration with another
one that took place at the opening of the Second Duma. When I.
Golubev opened that Duma he announced that "the Sovereign Emperor
commanded that the Duma be told," and he paused; all the ministers
rose and the right wing of the Duma did likewise, but the left wing
and the Cadet center remained seated. Since no one wished to make
a demonstration then, the situation became awkward. The chairman's transmission of the tsar's words caught the Cadets unprepared
and they were not too familiar with etiquette. Some of them, following

the example of the ministers, at first arose, but seeing that others
remained seated, they, too, sat down. The Cadet press defended
their improvised demonstration by saying that etiquette did not require their rising and the action of the ministers was excessive
zeal, like uncovering one's head before an empty court carriage.[3]
Later, however, in the Third and Fourth Dumas, under analogous
conditions, the Cadets acted differently; the left wing departed in
advance while the Cadets rose at the mention of the tsar's words.
Consequently the episode in the Second Duma was an accident. But
in the First Duma the address was discussed for several days; debates about it went on in the committee among people to whom amen-
ities were not foreign; there could have been no element of surprise.
Yet having agreed on rudeness in their relations with the tsar the
Cadets betrayed their true selves. They considered loyalty to the
monarch a minor detail that could be sacrificed to the historic significance of the address; but actually, loyalty to the constitutional monarch would have had historic significance. Without it, what was the
significance of the address?

This disloyalty was an ill omen for strengthening the constitution. Even more ominous was the disloyalty of the Duma to the
constitution itself. The monarch's authority was at the time beyond
question, and whoever did not recognize this was ridiculous. But
the constitution was the subject of contention and attack from the
right and the left: from the "Union of the Russian People" and from
the "revolution." It was up to the Duma, at least, to defend it.
Some indication of determination to do so might have been expected
in the address of the Duma, particularly since the tsar declared his
loyalty to the constitution in the speech from the throne, promising
to safeguard it and greeting deputies as the "élite."

As the Duma did not approve the content of the constitution it
had the right to say so and point out desirable changes; it could even
try to improve it through its own efforts. But as long as the constitution was not changed by lawful means, the Duma should have considered it its duty to submit. Having been created by the constitution the Duma could not be above it. Since the sovereign promised
to safeguard it, the Duma might have declared its intention to work
for the improvement of the constitution, employing means provided
by it. The Duma and the tsar would then speak a common language
and have grounds for agreement. But the Duma did not say this.
Its reference to the tsar's promise to safeguard it served only as
a reminder of his obligation to continue the evolution of strictly
constitutional principles. Yet the Duma gave no indication that it
would act in a constitutional manner. This was not a case of forgetfulness or omission, but of revolutionary ideology, according to
which the constitution limited only the monarch but not the Duma,
which expressed the will of the people. Like its chairman, it

claimed its rights emanated not from the law but from the "nature of popular representation." Such ideology was more dangerous than personal rudeness to the tsar.

What, then, did the Duma say in its "historic address?" It dealt mainly with its program of work, which the Duma considered necessary to communicate to the tsar. In the opinion of the Cadets this was the chief significance of the address. Miliukov wrote on May 6: "It is important that that which constitutes the pith and marrow of the liberation movement is repeated and unanimously adopted by the Russian popular assembly as the practical program, subject to its immediate realization in the institution that has the right to accomplish this."

These words implied a serious misunderstanding, for this part of the address could not and did not have such significance. One might ask first of all: why was it necessary to inform the tsar of the Duma's program of legislative work? Lokot was right when he wrote on May 5, "The will of the people could have been expressed more completely and correctly in a series of bills passed by the Duma." No one questioned the legislative initiative of the Duma; the tsar himself summoned the Duma for this work. The revision of the Fundamental Laws excepted, its initiative was unlimited and its agenda was exclusively its own concern. It could examine and adopt whatever it wished, without asking permission or approval of the tsar. Indeed, it was neither loyalty nor the particular respect of the Duma for the monarch that compelled it to set forth its program of work beforehand.

On the other hand, the Duma was not the only legislative authority; its legislative initiative might even fail to reach the tsar if it was not approved by the Imperial Council. That is why, when Miliukov wrote that the Duma set forth a program "subject to the immediate relization in the institution that had the right to accomplish it," he misinterpreted the constitution. The Duma undoubtedly had the unconditional right to reject undesirable legislation, but not the sole right to bring to fruition the legislation that it desired. Journalists may write what they will and consciously mislead readers. For example, Miliukov wrote that if the work of curing the ills of Russia should be prolonged, it was important to create the conviction that, in any event, the work would be accomplished.[4] Such exaggeration was the privilege of the press, but the address was the responsible and serious work of a government institution; here eyewash was inadmissible.

Traces of this pretended or real ignorance of its powers were revealed even in the terminology of this part of the Duma's address. Thus it stated that "the Duma will bring for your Majesty's approval a law concerning popular representation, based, by the unanimously expressed will of the people, on the principle of universal franchise."

Nowhere in this statement is there any mention of the rights of the
Upper Chamber, yet a bill could be presented for the tsar's approval
only if it had been approved by the Second Chamber, and only its
chairman could present it (p. 113, Fundamental Laws). What would
the Duma have said had the Imperial Council used such a procedure
for projects it initiated? Yet according to the constitution their
rights were equal.

Here is another instance. "The Duma will become the spokesman of the aspirations of the whole population the day it enacts the
law repealing the death penalty forever." The Duma had no right
to enact a law.

Then came the announcement disregarding both the Imperial
Council and the tsar himself as supreme leader of the army: "The
Duma will concern itself with strengthening the principles of justice
and human rights in the army and fleet." In the face of Article 96
of the Fundamental Laws, how could the Duma do this, without
going beyond the limits of its competence?

Had such statements been made at meetings, or had this been
said by ignorant people, it could have been explained by their constitutional ignorance. But the address was written by first class jurists who understood what they were doing. Such use of words was
the conscious manifestation of a grasping policy. The Duma did not
recognize the constitution, considered that the Imperial Council should
be abolished, and regarded itself both as the sole legislative authority and spokesman of the sovereign will of the people. This anti-
constitutional conception permeated its address to the tsar. Certainly such tactics would not benefit the constitution.

But if that was the case, why was the program of work set
forth? This was the Cadets' explanation: they had to do so, supposedly against their will, because the speech from the throne was
incorrect and did not say what it should have said. Miliukov wrote
on May 3 as follows:

> The program outlining the order of the activity of the
> Duma should have been given by the speech from the
> throne, but in that case it had to be supported by a min-
> istry enjoying the confidence of the country (?). In
> reality, the ministry has no firm basis, and that is why
> it had to come to the Duma with empty hands. The Du-
> ma itself is now providing the program; the popular
> representatives are fulfilling the obligation shirked by
> the ministry. This is only natural and of course, desir-
> able.

This was absurd; but was it a case of misunderstanding or of tactics?

From a constitutional point of view this was quibbling; Miliukov's reference was to a parliamentary, not a constitutional, order.
The speech from the throne did not have to outline the program of
work. This is done in parliamentary countries where relations between the government and the popular representatives are quite different. Where the monarch does not rule but only reigns he may
himself read the speech from the throne; but it is the ministry's
declaration of policy to parliament. The monarch's personal opinion
is not expressed. If the composition of parliament or the cabinet
changes, he reads an entirely different speech. The changed content
does not compromise him, since he is not the ruler. Parliamentarianism, however, was rejected by our constitution. The monarch
was not a figurehead, and according to the Fundamental Laws, all
government remained in his hands. But even in such a constitutional
system the monarch is not accountable for his actions; the ministry
is responsible for him and speaks for him, and the monarch does
not make personal political appearances, as this would be unconstitutional. The ministers, therefore, make such appearances on
their own, even if in reality they are carrying out the instructions
or even orders of the tsar. In this way the fiction of the monarch's
irresponsibility is preserved. Such an interpretation is not very
consistent and is somewhat difficult to understand, but without it
there could be no dualistic constitution. That is why the speech
from the throne, in so far as it occurs, and the declaration of the
ministry in such constitutions are two entirely different things. The
speech from the throne was delivered in our Duma only once, not at
the opening of a regular Duma but at the introduction of the whole
new order. Our tsar revealed more constitutional understanding
than the deputies when he did not set forth a legislative program,
in his speech from the throne, but limited himself to greetings and
general good wishes. The real government declaration came later,
on May 13, and then the ministry quite properly read it as its own
statement. In subsequent Dumas--the Second, Third and Fourth--
these two acts were always differentiated. The personal greetings
of the tsar were conveyed by the person opening the Duma, and later
when the certification of half the deputies was verified and the Duma
properly constituted, the government declaration was read by the
premier. This same constitutional logic was observed in the First
Duma. The leaders of the Duma revealed grave inexperience or
else lack of etiquette when they hastened to reproach the government
for not presenting a program, and particularly when they decided to
take upon themselves the government's responsibilities. By doing
so the Duma placed itself in a false position, for which, as was its
custom, it blamed the government.

It is even more difficult to understand why Miliukov considered
desirable this obvious confusion of functions, for the Duma chose

not only an unsuitable role, but one that was beyond its strength. Though de jure, the Duma was unrestricted in its legislative initiative (with the exception of the Fundamental Laws); de facto, it could not cope with it. Only the government with its apparatus is in a position to draft laws. No wonder parliamentary initiative does not play an important part in any constitution. So, too, with our Duma, its chief concern should have been the examination of government bills. Miliukov's assertion that the Duma's work could be accomplished best if the Duma replaced the government was only a way of saying that the Duma could do the job better than the government, and perhaps even take over the functions of the ministry.

But whatever its aims, the address was not successful. The Duma failed in this task not only when it finally undertook to draft the laws it announced, but in the very program that it set forth in the address. It was not difficult to draw up the program. Miliukov correctly noted that the Duma's program of reforms was not new. All this has been discussed and approved from every kind of social tribune for several years. The essence of necessary reforms was already the official program in 1904. Now was the opportune time to clarify it, bring it into sharper focus, and integrate it more closely; but this was not done. The Duma's program of reforms was a logically disconnected list of platitudes, interrupted by excursions into other problems. From a purely literary standpoint it was unintelligible and suffered by comparison with the November Zemstvo Conference of 1904. Nor could it be immediately realized as claimed by Speech. What for instance, did the words "the Duma will turn its attention to the purposeful use of national resources" signify? Or: "the Duma will concern itself with strengthening, in the army and fleet, the principles of justice and rights?" What was the meaning of "thorough reorganizations of local government?" On what basis was it proposed? What are the "just needs of nationalities?" The address said nothing concrete about all this. However paradoxical it may seem, the ministerial declaration read to the Duma later, on May 13, proved much clearer and most important, more profound than the business part of the Duma's address.

Let us take the most characteristic example, the peasant problem. All programs of recent years assigned it a special place as the most important, integral, and independent problem. Everyone understood that it was basic to the welfare of all Russia, and its solution should not be postponed. What did the Duma say about it? "The clarification of the needs of the rural population and the adoption of suitable legislative measures will become the foremost task of the State Duma." That was all. Was this a practical program that could be immediately realized, or rather a testimony to the bankruptcy of the State Duma in this most important part of the work? It is a curious coincidence, but these were the very words used in the speech from the throne summoning the Duma to activity. It stated: "You will devote all your strength to the clarification of the needs of the peasants so near to my heart." But the speech from the throne did not put forth these general words as a program. Yet the Duma, which demanded immediate passage of definite constitutional reforms, was merely intending "to clarify the needs of the peasantry." It would have been better had the Duma remained silent on this question. The government in its declaration proved to be superior to it.

Why did the results of the work of "the social élite," people of exceptional talents and devoted to their task, prove to be so meagre and incomplete? The explanation of this must be sought not only in the debasing influence of a collective body. There were two other special reasons for this.

The first reason was the early Cadet decision that the Duma must not occupy itself with vital work until it changed the constitution. This decision in all its implications was, of course, not implemented, but it was occasionally recalled. Vinaver mentions a characteristic instance.[5] Deputy Bondarev proposed that the committee dealing with the address include the statement that the State Duma "will concern itself with popular enlightenment." What could have been less controversial and more desirable? For a long time this matter had been the favorite concern of liberalism, and achievements in this field a source of pride to the Russian zemstvo. Now this program could be unfolded on a nationwide scale. Objections were not to be expected. The speech from the throne itself twice mentioned enlightenment. Yet the Cadets immediately raised objections. Vinaver tells us:

> We argued that Bondarev's proposal was a glaring violation of the slogan of the opposition professed by people who were to the left of us. We pointed out that this subject would be accepted with delight by the government, which would add similar, politically inoffensive objectives for harmonious work with the popular representatives.

This is a significant admission. The Cadets were afraid that the government might find itself in agreement with them and therefore did not want to undertake this project (!), which did not prevent them afterwards from blaming the government for lack of agreement. It is interesting, too, that this tactic of the Cadet leaders was neither understood nor supported by the common sense of the man in the street. As Bondarev's proposal was approved by the Trudoviki and the Right, in spite of Cadet protests, their intrigues failed.

There was another reason that contributed to the fruitlessness of the business part of the address. Cadet leaders insisted on the

unanimous adoption of the address. Lokot correctly noted that
unanimity was not essential and could not be sincere. The Duma
was in accord in its negative attitude to the old order, but there was
a divergence of opinion regarding positive plans. Thus unanimity
could be secured only at the price of ambiguity, half-truths, and
superficiality. To the Cadets, achievement of unanimity at such a
price was the customary party tactic that determined the party
line. Now this purely Cadet tactic was adopted for the whole Duma,
and it was bound to have repercussions. I shall note two typical
instances.

The Cadet party included the "four-tail"* in its program, extending it even to women. The address started its list of reforms
with franchise reform. It became evident during the debate, however,
that the "four-tail" was not such a widely accepted slogan as the
Cadets claimed, and finally they were compelled to admit that themselves. There was opposition against direct elections and particularly against participation by women. Thus D. I. Shakhovski, himself a supporter of the "four-tail," testified as follows: "If the
question of direct elections were put to the vote of our peasantry,
the answer, because of misunderstanding, of course, would probably be negative." To avoid a split, the Duma decided on the expression "universal franchise," which appeared in the Manifesto of
October 17, with the result that the parties of the Left concluded
that the Cadets rejected the "four-tail" and betrayed the national
cause. Such was the consequence of Cadet insistence on a unanimous
decision.

However, this was not a tragic misunderstanding; the agrarian
question fared worse. The opinions of the members of the Duma and
the party varied greatly on the agrarian question. This was demonstrated by the introduction of three different agrarian projects and
confirmed by the divergence of opinion in the agrarian committee.
Unanimity or even a secure majority would be possible only as a
result of patient efforts and mutual concessions. But as the authors
of the address demanded immediate and unanimous decisions, in
their attempt to secure deceptive achievements, the words of the
address acquired this enigmatic aspect:

> The working peasantry awaits with impatience the satis-
> faction of its urgent need for land, and the First Russian
> State Duma would fail in its duty if it did not introduce a
> law for the satisfaction of this urgent need, by means of
> diverting to this task crown, appanage, ministerial,
> monastic, and church lands, and the obligatory expropri-
> ation of private lands.

----

*"Four-tail": The equality of suffrage rights of peasants, wom-
en, Jews, and nationalities, and direct elections. [M. B.]

No matter how carefully one reads these words, taken by themselves they can mean only one thing: the Duma decided to confiscate, by compulsion and without any reservations, all privately-owned land. Would it have been worthwhile to include in the address these words: "and under certain conditions also compulsory alienation of privately-owned land," to avoid this misunderstanding? Everyone would have agreed with such a formula and it would have been only a question of these conditions. But all corrections of the original interpretation were rejected by the Duma and the ambiguous edition of the address was retained. As it was stated, no differentiation was made between large-scale ownership and small, nor was there any definition of the maximum land ownership permitted, but the question of the very principle of private ownership of land was raised. Expropriation of privately-owned land was promised without any reservations.

Actually the Duma did not want confiscation, but implied it for the sake of the Left; and here the Duma played with fire. Its address to the tsar appeared to the people as a more important act than the published programs of political parties and decisions reached at meetings. For uninformed persons and even for many members of the Duma itself, its expressed desire was already accepted as law. Thus with the Duma's blessings celebrations would follow, and these in turn would be used by orators to prove the necessity of speedy confiscation. Did the Duma understand that by this unanimously adopted provocative formula it pushed the government toward the violent objection in its declaration, which later aroused the Duma's anger? Who was the real aggressor in this case?

These misunderstandings were unavoidable if the Cadets insisted on unanimity. But like Lokot we may ask ourselves: why was it necessary if it was bought at the price of half-truths and deceit? Who was being deceived? Unanimity would vanish into thin air anyway when they advanced from declarations to work. It was a bad omen for the success of the Duma's work that while the Cadets knew this would happen, they still preferred fine gestures to realistic results. The fictitious unanimity made it possible to refer to the acceptance of the address as "the symbol of the unity of the Russian opposition movement indicating the trememdous strength of the Duma's majority (Speech, May 6)." This confusion of realistic politics with literary effects and party journalistic practices was disastrous to the fortunes of liberalism.

Chapter Five

THE DUMA'S WISHES AS EXPRESSED

IN THE ADDRESS TO THE TSAR

It would have been better if the Duma had not unfolded its agenda in the address to the tsar. Its inclusion was an unfortunate idea and the manner of its presentation reflected no credit on the Duma's skill. More comprehensible was the intention of expressing to the tsar the Duma's wishes, whose fulfillment did not depend on the Duma. As Miliukov stated in <u>Speech</u> on May 3, "the reply to the speech from the throne presented the only convenient opportunity for bringing the Duma's wishes to the attention of the government."

The desire to change the constitution had a special place among them and there was nothing unlawful about it. With the exception of the clauses included in the Fundamental Laws, the amendment of the constitution was not barred from the Duma's initiative and its revision was possible in a variety of ways. It is interesting to note that the Duma rarely resorted to this normal method. On May 23 the Cadets introduced a bill regarding "the changed procedure of examining legislative business," which, as we shall see, was quite unsuccessful. This bill proved to be the only attempt at revision of the constitution, and though much was said about the unfortunate procedure of "interpellation,"* no legislation was introduced to change the system though it was not difficult to do so.

This attitude was characteristic of the Duma, which regarded all such work as too trivial. Instead, the Duma at once undertook major changes in the very foundations of the constitution. The Cadets found three major basic defects in it, which Miliukov later called the three "locks." Without first removing these locks, supposedly, nothing could be done. First it was necessary to introduce the "four-tail," then to abolish the Second Chamber and establish the responsibility of the ministry to the Duma. Only then would we have a constitution. It was decided to declare this in the address without delay.

----

* The Duma had the right to expose publicly the irregular activities of the authorities and demand the government's explanation for them. As a check on wayward officials, the Duma could question ministers concerning charges of illegal activity involving them or their subordinates. [M. B.]

Having in mind Russia's condition in this period, one might
question the necessity of immediate passage of these constitutional
reforms. But I shall not enter into that now. Instead I shall pause
to consider a less important question: even if such an aim were considered desirable, what would have been the best course to follow to
get results?

No one could conceive that the autocracy, by agreeing to a constitution, simultaneously acknowledged the benefit of these radical
reforms as well. In that case the Fundamental Laws would have been
different; they would have implemented complete popular sovereignty
instead of providing for an order based on cooperation and compromise between the autocracy and mature Russian society. On this
point, therefore, a struggle with the autocracy was imminent.

But how was the struggle to be carried on? If the revolutionary
course was to be followed then everything was, of course, very simple: overthrow the autocracy without fear of revolution; work towards
the establishment of revolutionary authority; and summon a Constituent Assembly that would decide all these problems. That was one
way.

However, such a course might be considered undesirable. The
constituted authority, supported by the country, was still very strong
and could cope with open revolution. Besides, the harmful effects
of revolution were self-evident and it was desirable to avoid them.
In this case, if the Duma wanted to win constitutional reforms, it
should have approached the matter in a constitutional manner.

This course was not entirely barred to the Duma even in the
realm of the three locks of which Miliukov spoke. It is not worthwhile to pause at the first lock, the "four-tail," since the revision
of the franchise was not prohibited by the Fundamental Laws. The
Duma had complete authority to introduce a new electoral bill, which
it did, as announced in the first lines of its address. But even in the
case of the other two locks the Duma was not by any means impotent.

It is true that complete abolition of the Second Chamber was
out of question for the Duma. The existence of the Second Chamber
and the scope of its rights were guaranteed by the Fundamental
Laws. Moreover, there were many supporters of the two-chamber
system in the Duma itself. The Duma was unanimous only in criticizing the composition of the Upper Chamber, which could be changed.
Its composition was not determined by the Fundamental Laws but by
Clause 12 of the Establishment of the Imperial Council, according
to which not less than half the members of the Imperial Council
were to be chosen from the privileged class. The Duma could take
the initiative in changing this and remove any partiality for the upper classes. In fact the Duma should have tried this before approaching the tsar. If this were done simultaneously with raising
the question of the composition of the Upper Chamber, which was
quite within the competence of the Duma, the more general question

of the significance and necessity of this Chamber could be raised for
lawful discussion, if not for final decision. It is interesting to note
that in regard to appointed members, the Fundamental Laws prescribed only one thing: the number of appointed members could not
exceed the number elected (Clause 100, Fundamental Laws). Thus
there were no obstacles to having the number of appointed members
much smaller than the number elected, by changing Articles 12-17
dealing with the Establishment of the Imperial Council. This would
result in a radical alteration of the Chamber's composition, making
it, from the Duma's point of view, harmless.

If the Duma undertook such legislation, of course, it would not
have been easy to get it approved by the Second Chamber--difficult
but not impossible. I spoke of this in my first book and will not repeat my conclusions, but I shall add one thing. If to please the Duma
the tsar took upon himself the initiative to pass this reform, even
then the consent of the Upper Chamber would have been necessary.
Surely the Duma did not intend to push the tsar to a government upheaval at the outset of its constitutional existence. What kind of a
constitution would it have been?

There remains the third lock: parliamentarianism. But this,
i. e. political responsibility of the ministry to parliament, is established not by law but by practice. Formally, the ministry always
remains responsible to the head of the state who appoints it; this
does not prevent him from asking for its resignation if it loses the
confidence of parliament. This principle cannot be expressed in the
form of law, and this was not necessary either. Parliamentarianism
could easily have become established here without changing the text
of the Fundamental Laws. To facilitate this, it might perhaps have
been necessary to alter a few clauses of the regulations concerning
the Duma, and to extend the right of interpellation by changing Clause
60, which sanctioned it. But these clauses were not outside the
competence of the Duma, and a slight change here and there could
have aided the introduction of parliamentary procedures. Nevertheless, in the final analysis, parliamentarianism would be introduced
to the degree that the Duma's prestige grew in the eyes of both the
country and the tsar. In 1915 when the Duma's prestige was great
and there was no doubt of its patriotic mood, the tsar, to pacify the
Duma, had to sacrifice four of his ministers, though he did not
change his attitude towards them. Parliamentarianism is achieved
by winning esteem for earnestness and loyalty, not by demanding it
from the supreme authority.

This was the course that might have been followed instead of hinting
in the address that the tsar should take upon himself the initiative for
these reforms. The course chosen by the Duma had other disadvantages, too

The new order had powerful enemies and few defenders. The
popular masses did not yet realize what the constitution meant. It

was unwise to begin the Duma's activity by criticizing the constitution and insisting on its revision. This meant playing into the hands
of those who contended that society could not be pacified by anything.
Every day of the existence of the new order would have strengthened
it. Prescription is a factor not only in the case of private property
but in contributing to the permanence of the state. The gesture that
the Duma was making by pointing out in the address the necessity
of immediate revision of the constitution was not only unnecessary
but even undesirable.

Above all, in order to achieve success while making this gesture, it was imperative not to reject the constitution in general.
Only by acknowledging the essential need for a constitution, and having shown loyalty to it, could the Duma attempt changes with some
success. The more radical the improvements desired, the more
evident should have been the loyalty of the Duma to the constitution
that established it.   If the whole constitution was unlawful and not
binding on society, then what talk could there be of constitutional
methods for its revision? The whole question would then revert to
the revolutionary plane: the clash of the will of the tsar with the
will of the people, the contest of material forces that each side could
muster. Raising the question this way meant not only provoking the
autocracy to opposition, but preventing it from making concessions.
Had the Duma intentionally decided to initiate the constitutional reforms it desired in such a way that the tsar could not agree to them,
it would not have acted differently.

Let us consider the question of the Second Chamber. No principle is involved in its existence in a constitution; it is simply a matter of practical convenience. Furthermore, the single chamber
theory has not withstood the test of experience, while the advantage
of a second chamber is recognized even by democracies. The Duma
might have tried to establish the desirability of a single chamber by
practical means. For example, the speech from the throne annnounced
the restoration of the Russian land, yet the Imperial Council was specifically composed of representatives of the old order in the persons
of appointed members and representatives of privileged upper classes through elections. This contradiction could be pointed out without offending or frightening anyone.

As I noted earlier, there was an ideological difference between
the autocracy and the Duma. The tsar considered himself the source
of authority; he believed that he, voluntarily, limited his powers for
the benefit of the people. Society, on the other hand, considered
that the source of authority was the will of the people that was expressed through its representatives; therefore the monarch had to
submit to it. It was impossible to reconcile this conflict, but the
issue should not even have been raised. This was an academic dispute since the rights of both were defined by the constitution, re-

gardless of theoretical conceptions. The introduction of a clash of
different ideologies was detrimental to the task to be accomplished.

Yet this was the approach adopted by the address in requesting
the abolition of the Upper Chamber. It stated:

> To achieve fruitful activity in the State Duma it is neces-
> sary to implement the basic principle of truly popular
> representation, i. e. only the unity of the monarch and
> the people constitutes the source of all legislative power.
> Therefore all obstacles between the supreme authority
> and the people must be removed... the State Duma con-
> siders it its duty to inform Your Imperial Majesty in the
> name of the people that the whole nation will fulfill the
> creative task of restoration with true strength and inspir-
> ation, with faith in the coming prosperity of the mother-
> land, only when the Imperial Council, composed of ap-
> pointed officials and elected members from the upper
> classes of the population, will no longer stand between
> the people and the throne.

Thus the question was raised entirely on the basis of pure ideology, without consideration for circumstances or the scope of the
problem. The "basic principles of true popular representation"
apparently required the abolition of the Imperial Council. Was such
an argument convincing? Admitting the existence of such a basic
principle would mean that the British House of Lords is an inadmissible obstacle to the proper function of parliament. The competence
of the Duma might be trusted when it reported on the needs of Russia,
but it was not its business to instruct others in scientific theories of
government, since the Duma was itself in the infant stage of development. Besides, even science recognizes only the relative value of
government forms and not their absolute usefulness for all.

How scientific is the assertion that the source of legislative
authority is the "unity of the monarch and the people"? The relations between the government and the representatives of the people
may be determined by a constitution that clearly defines the specific
position of each. But if we recognize some basic principles of popular representation, and speak of its nature, as did the chairman of
the Duma, how, in the light of such a theory, are we to understand
unity? What is to be done if the monarch and the representatives of
the people disagree? Unity was simply a Cadet subterfuge for making
the monarch submit to popular representatives as to the will of the
people. If, according to the Cadets, the monarch did not even have
the right to grant the constitution, because this supposedly violated

the rights of the people, then how could he contradict the expressed will of the people? Whom were they trying to deceive by this plausible term "unity"?

Let us now examine the motives for introducing parliamentarianism. The address pointed out the following:

> Only the transfer of responsibility of the ministry to the people can strengthen in the minds of the people the conception that the monarch is not responsible; only a ministry enjoying the confidence of the majority in the Duma can strengthen confidence in the government and only when such confidence and tranquillity exist will the State Duma be able to carry on its work properly.

We have a repetition of the irrelevant conclusion reached in connection with the Second Chamber: unless its ideology is implemented the Duma cannot work calmly and properly. But there is an ulterior motive in this tirade. Only the responsibility of the ministry to the Duma, it was said in the address, can implant the conception that the tsar himself is not responsible. What responsibility is referred to here? Responsibility of the tsar to state institutions were unknown in either the old order or the new, and the tsars could not shake off responsibility to conscience, history, and God. They also remained responsible for the use of former autocratic power, for its limitation, and for abdication from the throne. Such responsibility was the destiny of those who became monarch "by the Grace of God." The tsar could only be convinced that he must surrender his authority if it were established beyond a doubt that such a concession would benefit Russia. Tempting him with relief from responsibility was an affront; he did not try to escape his burdens, and even by limiting his authority he did not shirk his duty.

It might be asked: why did the Duma continue to formulate its wishes in such a way that even if the supreme authority were inclined to fulfill them, this could not have been done without rejecting all traditional autocratic ideology? It must be concluded that the address did not pursue practical aims. Its task seemed to be the imposition of its ideology on the tsar, and so it was rebuffed.

The Duma's wishes regarding constitutional changes occupied a special place in the address. They did relate to the Duma's competence as a legislative institution, since the Duma was barred only from initiating such changes. Therefore, in spite of the unfortunate form, the Duma remained within its legal rights when it explained its attitude toward these questions. In particular the Duma also expressed judgment of matters exclusively within the monarch's pre-

rogative. This was in the realm of administration: the removal of
the Exceptional Regulations, modification of the administration, suspension of capital punishment, and finally, most important, the question of amnesty. The Duma could speak of this, too, and express its
desires, but it should have done so without magnifying its rights and
diminishing the rights of the monarch. The chairman himself, in
his opening remarks, promised appropriate respect for the "prerogatives of the monarch."

In order to see how the Duma observed this respect let us take
the main question of amnesty. The Cadets had long ago prepared
and even published a bill on amnesty, but after the proclamation of
the Fundamental Laws amnesty was excluded from the competence
of legislative institutions, and the Cadets submitted. No one insisted on it in the First Duma, in contrast to the Second Duma where,
disregarding the law, similar legislation was introduced by the parties of the left. Amnesty was not forgotten, however, but it was
decided to approach it in a different way.

The whole Duma wanted an amnesty, though it was an exaggeration to say that amnesty was a general popular desire. The parties
of the Left knew this perfectly well. When a recommendation concerning amnesty, threatening a clash with the government, was introduced at the session of April 30, the Cadet orators pointed out that
amnesty was not a fruitful ground for conflict because the people
would not understand it. The Trudoviki also adhered to this view
and the recommendation was rejected. Nevertheless, this did not
prevent inclusion of a statement in the address that "amnesty is
agitating the soul of the whole nation and is the demand of national
conscience."

On April 26 at the session of "the opposition," it was decided
that reference to amnesty would be made in the address. But the
press and "the street" were more impatient; they did not want to
await the address. So Petrunkevich's symbolic speech at the opening of the Duma was devised to give vent to these feelings. It had
the desired results, but the unrest was renewed next day. Others
wanted to speak. Another safety valve was provided by permitting
"exchange of opinion" in regard to Rodichev's recommendation "to
choose a committee to compose the address and instruct it to include, without fail, the item about amnesty." This ingenious proposal provided an opportunity to talk over amnesty lawfully.[1] Speeches
were unnecessary since all were in agreement, but even pointless
oratory was a minor evil since it provided relief for pent-up emo-
tions. After several oratorical effusions the recommendation was
adopted. Knowing what was behind it, it is amusing to read Rodichev's words in proposing adjournment of the session after the vote:
"Let us disperse, gentlemen, inspired by what we have done."
What had really been done?

The next day new proposals appeared. Labor deputy Churikov proposed that the Duma approach the tsar with a petition for an amnesty, without waiting for the address. Kovalevski supported this recommendation, expressing himself in these words: "...to bring to the attention of the Tsar Emperor the unanimous intercession of the Duma in favor of granting amnesty to political prisoners." Petrunkevich was indignant at such a proposal; according to him it transformed the Duma from "a legislative institution into a petitions agency... we do not wish to be intercessors, we wish to be legislators." Vinaver recalls in Conflicts that "the party of Popular Freedom with a proud cry from the lips of Petrunkevich rejected the idea of Kovalevski."

The proud cry of Petrunkevich was only an empty phrase. As a legislative institution, the Duma had no competence to deal with an amnesty. As legislators, the deputies should have been silent, for appeal for amnesty was not a legislative act. Here an interesting constitutional question arose: what did this appeal of the Duma mean legally? The granting of an amnesty was exclusively the prerogative of the monarch, but if the Duma wanted to obtain it while remaining within the bounds of existing legislation, it could only petition for it. One might ask why this would be humiliating for the Duma since a decision did not depend on it. The Duma could have petitioned with marked dignity and it might have been very difficult for the tsar to refuse the Duma's request.

But what could the Duma do if it considered petitioning humiliating, and preferred the maintenance of its self-esteem to saving lives of the condemned? Individual orators were not at a loss for a solution. Amnesty, they said, must be demanded.[2] Here is a scene from the session of April 30:

> Reverend Trasun: I adhere to the opinion of the Duma member who spoke before me [Shershenevich]; I am of the same opinion; we can demand an amnesty and we must demand it, but it must be done firmly....
> Chairman: Can not the word "demand" be avoided. I find it inappropriate in this case.
> Voices: Why? "Demand"...particularly "demand" [applause].

The chairman's desire not to exaggerate the incident was understandable, particularly in view of the sympathetic reaction to the orator by a section of the State Duma. That was why he did not stress that the word "demand" was not only inappropriate but unlawful. Muromtsev wanted the incident to pass unnoticed as much as possible. When Count Heiden objected to the expression "demand," insisting on the necessity of "respecting the rights of others,"

Muromtsev, without complete regard for reality, explained specifically that "the matter of demanding was already rejected by the announcement of the chairman." Actually, though the word "demand"
was repeated many times in speeches, it did not appear in the address
and was not voted on.

What could the Duma do if it could not demand and would not
petition?[3] Not in vain were the Cadets masters at inventing compromise formulas, and Miliukov invented one to suit the occasion. "The
address," he said in Speech on May 3, "expresses those expectations
which the Duma rests on the crown." For an experienced writer like
Miliukov such a turn of speech--"rest expectations on the crown"--
is evidence of confusion, which is understandable. If the Duma observed the constitution it could only petition for an amnesty. If it
were a sovereign body, expressing the supreme will of the people,
it could decree an amnesty. But it was the lot of the Cadets to sit
on both sides of the fence, so the Duma emerged with something in-
termediate and even illiterate: "resting expectations on the crown."

Suppose the word "demand" had been avoided in the address.
I knew a family where the children did not want to call the stepmother
"mother," and they were forbidden to call her by name; as a result
they did not call her anything. It was not the word itself that was
important in the address but the way the question was raised that
made an amnesty impossible.

Normally an amnesty is an act of state authority concerning
those whom this authority has previously judged i. e. an act of victors toward the vanquished. It is an indication of subsiding conflict,
the release of prisoners upon the conclusion of peace. There may
be different grounds for it: remoteness, which presupposes forgetfulness; restoration of order or change of policy, as was the case in
the amnesty of October 21, 1905. The same motives could be found
for an amnesty in 1906. A new life was beginning, signifying the
end of the former war. Grounds for an amnesty were given in these
words of the speech from the throne: "Let this day be remembered
henceforth as the day of restoration of the morality of the Russian
land."

But there are different kinds of amnesties, some being like
the amnesty of 1917. A new authority is created which does not forgive its former enemies, but the rules are reversed, the condemned
of the preceding régime being now the victors. Even if they are supposedly granted "amnesty," as was done by the Provisional Government, it is only for want of a better term. The general mass of
obscure people come under the flag of amnesty, but the well-known
ones return in triumph, as conquerors. This is not all; they immediately begin to condemn former opponents. In 1917 the Provisional Government issued the ukase establishing "a supreme Committee of Inquiry to investigate former ministers, executives, and
other high officials who committed a criminal breach of trust."

On what grounds could an amnesty be discussed in April, 1906, when it was still the prerogative of the same monarch, bearer of traditional authority, in whose name these people were condemned? For an amnesty to be successful, it had to be shown clearly that the former war had ended with the promulgation of the constitution, and that the restoration of the Russian land had indeed started. Only thus could the question of amnesty be presented to the tsar. Its inclusion in a provocative address was, of itself, harmful to the cause of amnesty. But, unfortunately, during the acceptance of the address it was clearly revealed that the Duma regarded amnesty as it was regarded in 1917. The Duma did not petition for the release of the guilty who had been condemned by the government; rather it wished to free its supporters because it was victorious.

This pointed presentation of the question did not arise at once. When the debate concerning amnesty began on April 29, Rodichev at first struck a correct tone. He spoke as follows:

> Let there be no doubt as to the meaning of this measure. Whoever thinks that amnesty sanctions crime is mistaken .... If you want to destroy the hatred which is now blazing on both sides, be the first to forgive generously. This would be an act of the highest political wisdom. When the country is swept away by the spirit of restoration, when it craves tranquillity, the past must be wiped clean.

By nature, Rodichev could not be a tactician; he was always, even when he contradicted himself, sincerity itself. He must have felt that, under the existing political circumstances, this was the only way to put the question of amnesty. But he was followed by people who were in a different mood. Trudovik Anikin, having acknowledged Rodichev's speech as brilliant, rejected it completely. "You heard the call for mercy, I shall speak of justice. It was said here that those who had gone astray must be forgiven, and I say--we must liberate the innocent...." The demagogue, Aladin, went even further:

> I do not appeal to you, for I know there is not one among you who would dare to think that we must not grant so-called amnesty. I appeal not to you, but to those who have yet time to realize with whom they have to deal and whom they have met face to face. The nation is on our side--city and country stand behind us. Our brothers in prisons, exile, penal servitude, may be confident that we release them ourselves, and if not...
> Voices: Enough.
> Aladin: So that is why...
> Voices: Enough...continue...
> Aladin: That is why we are affording the last opportunity to

understand and conciliate us by an act which will restore
our brothers to our midst. I appeal to him who can, in
clear, simple words: have mercy on our land, take this
task in hand and do not compel us to take it into ours.

The Duma should not be judged by individual speeches, particularly because this speech aroused some protests. But the inaction
of the chairman created a strange impression. His silence at Aladin's
conduct might have seemed symptomatic, but it was only a manifestation of Muromtsev's basic weakness: his lack of presence of mind,
the inability to react quickly. His eternal solemnity also contributed
to this effect. However, it created a poor impression.
        We will not judge the Duma by the speeches but by its decisions,
which were expressed not only by the adoption but also by the rejection of recommendations. To understand the meaning that the
Duma attached to amnesty it was significant to realize that the demand to liberate the condemned, corresponding to 1917, was accompanied by another demand, namely trial of the authorities. This was
declared in the first speech made by Cadet Mikleshevski regarding
the address. He declared:

> With pain in my heart I was conscious of a significant
> omission in the address... we must stress at this time
> the necessity of judgment of those who perpetrated the
> dreadful deeds we have lived through. It seems to me
> that the Manifesto of October 17 offers us the opportunity
> to implement this idea. Sincerity demands saying that
> immediate trial is essential [applause].

It is true that this demand was not included in the address; but
the address so described the actions of the authorities that they could
not be regarded as other than crimes. Still the Duma was not content with this. On May 23 it decided to establish a special committee,
"to investigate unlawful activities of government officials and institutions and present the results of its deliberations for the consideration of the State Duma." So that no doubt might remain that the
committee must investigate activities carried on by authorities even
before the Duma was summoned, a memorandum signed by thirty-eight
members was handed in during the discussion of the project, recalling
"the crimes of the authorities during the suppression of the armed
uprising in Moscow," with the announcement that "the guilty ones
were not punished and must be subjected to legal responsibility."
This is the behavior of victorious revolutions, and it was this conception of an amnesty that the tsar was invited to share.
        The events that followed the amnesty of October 21, 1905, were
described as follows:

Seized by a unanimous impulse, the country loudly proclaimed that the rebirth of the morality of Russian life would be possible only on the basis of freedom, unrestricted action, and the participation of the people themselves in the realization of legislative authority and control over executive power. It pleased Your Imperial Majesty to declare, from the pinnacle of your throne, your firm determination to make these very principles the foundation of further improvement in the fortunes of the Russian people, and the whole nation greeted this news with a unanimous cry of enthusiasm. However, the very first days of freedom were clouded by grievous ordeals to which the country was driven by those who were still barring the people's path to the Tsar. Trampling all principles of the Sovereign Manifesto of October 17, they plunged the country into the infamy of illegal executions, pogroms, firing squads, and imprisonment.

Thus it was the Duma's conviction, and not only the opinion of its individual orators, that after October 21 criminals were to be found among the authorities rather than among the condemned. With such an opinion prevalent in the Duma it was impossible to speak of reconciliation, tranquillity, and forgetfulness, the only things that could become the basis for an amnesty. The judges and the condemned simply had to change places. Under the flag of amnesty the tsar was invited to take the side of revolution. Such a conception of amnesty permeated the whole address of the Duma.

Then, as if to remove all doubt, the episode in connection with the speech of Stakhovich occurred. The liberal press tried to suppress it or present it in a ridiculous and unattractive light. Yet anyone taking the trouble of reading the stenographic notes of May 4 will see how unjust, but unfortunately typical of society, these criticisms were.

Although many excellent speeches were made in the First Duma, I know of no other that could have compared with this one in profundity and enthusiasm. I heard, from people who did not like Stakhovich, of the impression it made on the meeting. Had the Duma proved capable of rising to his level, it would not only have gained an amnesty but it would also have proved worthy of the role that it failed to play. It is difficult to convey the essence of this speech in my own words, so I shall quote a few excerpts. Stakhovich voted for an amnesty and said:

I am completely confident that my electors will back me up when they learn that I voted for a complete amnesty which we approved as far back as April 27. [This was

a reference to the speech of V. M. Petrunkevich.] The
more I think of it, the more I am convinced that the Duma as a representative of the people should have expressed itself and voted as it did; that only a lofty measure, a vast sweep of faith and love can express the
feelings of a great people. The Duma expressed it in its
opening words.... The start made on April 27 was the
Duma's gesture as a representative of the whole nation.
But a start is not all.... There is also responsibility for
consequences, and this responsibility rests on the emperor. He knows that he is not responsible to us here;
we spoke of this earnestly yesterday in connection with
ministerial responsibility. But he knows that if he is
not responsible here, it does not release his soul from
accounting to God not only for each tormented prisoner
but also for each innocent man shot down in an alley. So
I believe he is pondering, and is not as impetuous as we
who are moved only by generosity in reaching our decision. I also believe that he must be helped to accept
this responsibility. He must be told that past enmity was
so dreadful in its arbitrariness and severity that it made
people forget the law, and conscience forget mercy. We
must say that this fratricidal war, this mutual brutality,
is a basis for future amnesty. But the goal of amnesty
is different; it is the future peace of Russia. It is most
essential to add that in this, the State Duma will give the
emperor its staunch support. Crime must vanish with
past lawlessness as a means of struggle and quarrel.
May, henceforth, everyone live, manage his own affairs,
and attain his own or communal rights, not by force but
by law, the new Russian law in which we are participants
and of which we are guardians, and by the old law of God
which thundered down 4,000 years ago and said to all people forever: Thou shalt not kill.

Stakhovich connected amnesty with the proposal of expressing
simultaneously the hope "that with the establishment of a constitutional order, political executions would end, as well as other acts of
violence which the Duma condemned severely,considering them an
outrage to the moral sense of the nation and the very idea of popular
representation." This was the famous "condemnation of terror" in
our parliamentary history.
    Leaving out of consideration the editing of the proposal, which
could have been improved, this was a basis on which the amnesty
could not only be defended but from which the emperor would have
found it difficult to reject it. Presented this way it corresponded to

the emperor's call for the restoration of the "morality of the Russian land." The Duma's declaration would have been the very first step towards this restoration. It would have been a new approach, never used before. The emperor's vacillation, of which Stakhovich spoke, was not just a supposition. He was telling me later that when the question of amnesty arose in the Duma, the emperor received many telegrams containing protests and reproaches. "Would he permit an amnesty and pardon those who killed his faithful servants and helpers?" What if these telegrams were fabricated in the Union of Russian People? The emperor accepted them at their face value. To win over the emperor to the side of an amnesty, in spite of these protests, it was necessary to find a new approach that would make it possible to forget the past and its bitterness. Such an approach could have been the moral condemnation of terror. But the Duma proved incapable of this and continued the war.

How discouraging were the replies to which Stakhovich had to listen. Cadet Lomshakov was the first to reply to "Mr. Stakhovich." He said, "I declare that the whole responsibility for the crimes discussed here rests entirely and completely on the government which criminally trampled on the rights of men and citizens." Cadet Shrag would not permit censure of those who "gave their lives for their friends," refusing to take note that they were not accused of anything--on the contrary, Stakhovich, along with others, sought amnesty and pardon on their behalf--that the moral condemnation referred only to those who committed crimes after the proclamation of amnesty and the establishment of a constitutional order.

But reading Rodichev's speech is saddest of all. The stand taken by Stakhovich could not have been unfamiliar to him, yet this is what he said: "I listened with enthusiasm to the fine words of deputy Stakhovich and fully understood the sincere passion which inspired him with the noble words of love. But I could not agree with his political conclusions." Rodichev, who on April 29 himself spoke of "love" and "elimination of hatred," now said: "If this were a preacher's pulpit or a church, such an appeal might have been made, but we are lawmakers." Inspired by the applause and the enthusiasm of the Duma, Rodichev attacked only the representatives of the government:

> It is they who have sown murder and crime in Russia. It is they who have drenched the land with blood... we must say in plain words: there is no justice in Russia, the law has become a mockery, there is no truth. This year Russia suffered more than in all the years since Baty. ... This must come to an end.... Much toil and effort will be needed to obliterate from our souls the bitterness which has been accumulating there for years....

[He closed with the following words deadly to amnesty:]
It is too soon to point to the triumph of benevolence. We
trust that the time will come; it has not come yet.

The speech aroused "stormy, prolonged applause" and the proposal of Stakhovich was rejected. Morally this was the death knell of
the amnesty. If the time for benevolence had not yet come and the
war was continuing, if while fighting for amnesty for past crimes the
Duma refused to condemn them from the moral standpoint even in the
future under the new order, if it found words of condemnation only
for the representatives of the government, what sense would such an
amnesty have? Peace had not been concluded, and prisoners are not
released in wartime.

The Duma not only buried amnesty, it buried itself. A meeting
of several hundred persons cannot be expected to rise to the level of
moral enlightenment. Furthermore, politics was involved here and
that is far more moral. But the Duma could and should have risen
at least to the level of its constitutional role, i. e. the guardian of
law and a legal order. This role imposed obligations. No matter
how much the Duma might be inclined (in individual cases) to justify
crime by the noble motives of the criminal, as an institution granted
the right to draft laws and denounce lawlessness it could not, in the
expectation of a time of benevolence, refuse as a matter of principle
to condemn crimes. Refusal to condemn could not be interpreted as
other than approval. Thus the Duma was transforming itself from a
state institution into an instrument of revolutionary upheaval. The
vote on Stakhovich's amendment irreparably undermined the chances
of a constitutional majority, which would have been created had the
Cadets sided with Stakhovich and had Rodichev repeated his speech
of April 29. But on this day the Cadets rejected the constitutional
course. Later Stakhovich was accused of provocation, a petty and
unworthy accusation. If Stakhovich had not forgotten party politics
at this time he could not have made such a splendid speech.

This is what Miliukov insinuated in his newspaper: "The speech
of M. A. Stakhovich was not directed to the Chamber's address. The
Orlov deputy well remembers the instructions of his electors, 'not to
knock but to support the sovereign authority.' " I shall clarify this
for those who fail to understand it. In Stakhovich's speech on amnesty, alluding to the reference of various speakers to the instructions of their electors, he related what the peasants exhorted him to
do:

They instructed me as follows: "try to obtain for us the
other liberties"--it is what we call freedoms.... But they
also told me what apparently was not said in other prov-

inces to other speakers. The peasants quite definitely
instructed me: ''do not knock the tsar, but help him to
pacify the land, support him. ''

This mild protest against the excesses of the Duma's oratory gave
Miliukov ground for insinuating that Stakhovich, that manly, independent deputy, least resembling a ''yes-man'' and a flatterer, did
not direct his speech to the Chamber but was trying to win favor with
the emperor. Such were the ''elegant'' customs of party controversy.
    What did remain for our tacticians to say in favor of an am-
nesty? Here is the famous finale of the address in reply to the speech
from the throne:

> Your Imperial Majesty! One question is facing us on the
> threshold of our activity. It is agitating the soul of the
> whole nation, disturbing us, the representatives of the
> people, and depriving us of a calm approach to the first
> steps of our legislative activity. The first word heard
> within the walls of the State Duma and received with the
> sympathetic response of the entire Duma was the word
> ''amnesty. '' The country craves an amnesty, embracing
> all activities under the jurisdiction of criminal law that
> result from religious or political convictions, as well as
> all agrarian disturbances. These are demands of na-
> tional conscience which cannot be denied, whose fulfill-
> ment must not be delayed. Emperor, the Duma expects
> You to grant complete political amnesty as the first
> pledge of mutual understanding and agreement between
> the Tsar and the people.

This was a literary masterpiece. Even the word ''demand''
was mentioned and in a form impossible to reject. But if we turn
from literary form to political reasons, we are struck by their in-
adequacy and insincerity. It was not enough to declare that without
an amnesty the Duma would be unable to ''approach calmly the first
steps of its legislative activity. '' It was not true to say that ''amnesty agitated the soul of the whole nation, '' that ''the country craved
an amnesty, '' and that it was ''the demand of national conscience. ''
All this was said after the Duma refused to petition for it so as not
to humble the dignity of the ''lawmakers, '' after the Duma admitted
itself that amnesty was not a fruitful basis for conflict. Such words
were rhetorical and were not convincing.
    The address concluded with the words that ''an amnesty would
be the pledge of mutual understanding and agreement between the
Tsar and the people, '' in spite of the fact that besides amnesty, the

address presented other equally ultimatum-like demands regarding a
single chamber and ministerial responsibility. The Duma also applauded on hearing that "the time for benevolence has not arrived
yet," and it refused to condemn political terror--in short, the war
still continued.

The passage on amnesty was the finishing touch to this strange
address, and it was typical. The Duma wanted an amnesty and yet
presented it in such a way that the tsar could not grant it without
capitulating to revolution, and the Duma preferred to reject the amnesty rather than surrender the position it had taken.

In so far as this position was reflected in the address, it was
not easy to understand it. If one were a revolutionary, he might consider the monarch a usurper, a relic of a distant past; he would then
encourage the revolution and when all obstacles were removed, create
a new order. But people with such convictions do not as a rule present addresses, and when they do, they avoid conventions and respectful expressions. The address of revolutionaries would be a menacing,
accusing act, the declaration and actually the beginning of a decisive
war. This, in fact, was the way the revolutionaries regarded the
address.

One could also take the point of view of supporters of the constitution. Since the head of the state granted a constitution and promised to safeguard it, true constitutionalists had to reply to his personal greeting and accept the constitution. They had the right to
desire improvements in it and point out the changes they wished to
make, but all this would be done frankly, without threats and ultima-
tums, without ideological quarrels with the tsar or attempts to in-
flict their ideology on him. The tsar's rights, guaranteed by the
constituion, were not to be denied or contrasted with the sovereign
will of the people, which supposedly only the Duma represented.
Such an address would be a basis for agreement, not the beginning
of hostilities.

But what did the Duma hope to achieve with the address that
it adopted? It did not contain any disrespectful words which so com-
forted Kovalevski; there was even a verbal respectfulness that dis-
tressed the revolutionary Anikin. But in reality the address turned
out to be "nonrecognition of the constitution." What was its goal?
If the tsar were to satisfy all the desires expressed by the Duma--
abolish the Imperial Council, subordinate his ministers to the Duma,
remove all Exceptional Regulations, declare an amnesty, and at the
same time put on trial those who formerly carried out his will; in
short, do all without which the Duma could not work calmly--he
would have proclaimed the victory of revolutionary ideology. He
would have acted as did Grand Duke Michael Romanov in 1917, when
he signed his abdication and surrendered complete authority to
society. For at that time Grand Duke Michael Romanov was also

assured that society could not halt the revolution unless he abdicated.
In reality he prescribed revolution for the country from the pinnacle
of his throne. Perhaps no better way out was apparent then, but in
1906, too, under cover of traditional phrases about the "unity of the
monarch with the people," the same capitulation to the sovereign
authority of the people was proposed to the tsar. At the same time,
the Duma did not want to say this openly and did not reveal itself as
an outspoken enemy but as a hypocritical and false co-worker. By
this very tactic, this sitting on both sides of the fence and combining
constitutional and revolutionary ideas, Cadet liberalism destroyed
the confidence of its supporters and lost their respect. Unabashed,
it had the audacity to request an urgent audience for personal deliverance of such an address to the tsar.

Chapter Six

THE GOVERNMENT'S REPLY TO

THE ADDRESS OF THE DUMA

No wonder such an address aroused a violent reaction. The emperor would not even hear of receiving a delegation to present it. This in itself had no significance. More dangerous was his first impulse to reply to the Duma in person.[1] One can imagine what a reply that would have been, to say nothing about the fact that controversy between the monarch and popular representatives would have violated all conditions of a constitutional order. Whether this would have resulted in a reversal to the autocracy or in a quickened leap to revolution it is difficult to judge, but the constitution would have suffered in any case. Fortunately, there were in the government people who dissuaded the emperor[2] and so saved the constitution from destruction in this first skirmish. The incident shows that the constitution had friends in the government's camp. It was decided that instead of a personal appearance of the emperor, the government would reply to the address when the government declaration was read to the Duma. The emperor insisted that the reply be as curt as possible, but as we shall see, the government did not follow this imperial wish.

The refusal to receive the deputation made a deep impression on the Duma, which was strange. The Duma considered it quite in order to say nothing in reply to the greeting it received, considering that this courtesy was not obligatory, but it was incensed because the government would not receive its deputation. When the chairman was informed by Goremykin of the emperor's wish that the address be sent to him, and was even preparing to comply with it, prominent Cadets, having heard about the matter, maintained that he had no right to do that without the Duma's permission. The dispatch of the address was immediately halted. Vinaver tells us, "Had we not acted in the nick of time, there is no doubt that to the likely conflict between the Duma and the government would have been added the certain conflict between the Duma and its chairman."[3] This was not all. In the course of the day, Muromtsev took steps to try to rescind the refusal to receive the deputation, or at least to have the communication made in a different manner, not through the chairman of the

84

Council of Ministers. So that was the significance the Duma attached
to the question of etiquette that it previously despised. But all these
efforts failed.

The emperor's refusal to receive the deputation thus had to be
reported to the Duma. Why did the Cadets have to magnify a petty
incident and, by their unexpected insistence on etiquette, put the Duma in a foolish predicament? What should the Duma do now? Not
to send the address at all, after it had become famous as an historic
act, would make the Duma ridiculous. Only one way out remained:
to submit and to try to minimize the importance of the incident. To
do that no decision of the Duma was necessary; it merely had to make
the best of a bad situation. Novgorodtsev announced, in the name of
the Cadets, that the idea of sending a deputation was chosen by the
Duma as being most respectful. Kovalevski gave several historic
examples as proof that the deputation would have been the most defer-
ential form of presenting the address. Whom were they trying to
deceive? As a result of these hypocritical speeches, the following
formula of procedure was adopted: ''The significance of the reply to
the speech from the throne lies in its content, not in the method of
its presentation.'' This was a self-evident truth for which a decision
of the Duma was hardly necessary. But the Duma did not forget this
insult for a long time.

Writing in the periodical <u>Conflicts</u>, Vinaver insists that ''the
refusal to receive the deputation was not only a question of court
etiquette, pure and simple. They undoubtedly wanted to nettle us and
halt our sovereign march with this miserable court etiquette pin.''
Miliukov, proud of the new Cadet victory, wrote in <u>Speech</u> on May
10, ''Casting aside with a single stroke the stone that the court party
placed in their path, the representatives of the people snatched some
bright examples from the ocean of government lawlessness and put
them face to face with the ministers in the first encounter.''

The Cadets presupposed that the refusal to accept the deputation was part of some clever maneuver that the Duma could escape
only through its skill and poise. It did not occur to anyone that, without the slightest desire on the part of the government to infringe on
the ''sovereign march of the Duma,'' the reception of the deputation
just to deliver the address would have been too respectful. Evidently
some speeches were to accompany the ceremony, and since by its
contents the address was an ultimatum, long publicized in the press,
accepting it in silence, without controversy, would have been impossible for the emperor. The personal presentation of the address put
the tsar in an untenable position.

The Duma's resentment at the rejection of the deputation itself
explains the reception that our society had to accord the government's
reply. A fair attitude towards it could not be expected. The reply
was branded in advance as impertinence, as an effort by a pathetic

bureaucratic clique to oppose the "sovereign march" and the declaration of the "sovereign will of the people." Even such reasonable
people as Heiden condemned it.[4] The liberal press vented its indignation for the failure of the address on this reply, and prepared to
ridicule it in advance. Now, thirty-three years later, it is difficult
to believe that fair-minded people could have been so prejudiced.
There were also people who were insulted by the fact that the ministers, not the emperor, replied to the address, which shows how far
we were from understanding a constitutional order.

    Under normal conditions, the address of the Duma, which was
itself a reply to the speech from the throne, required no reply. A
reply to a reply leads to controversy in which it is improper for the
monarch to participate. But the Duma itself distorted the normal
order; unable to wait for the government's declaration, the Duma
decided to replace it by a program of its own, which it presented to
the emperor. Such a program was unnecessary, but once it was
received by the emperor, he could not fail to turn it over to the ministry. Otherwise, we would have had a "personal" régime instead
of a constitutional order. On the other hand, the ministry had every
right to reply to the Duma program in its own name, rather than in
the name of the emperor. These elementary rules of a constitutional
order proved too subtle not only for the uneducated Duma but also
for our most learned jurists.

    It would have been easy to make the ministry's reply insulting
to the Duma. The emperor himself insisted that the Duma be taught
a lesson. The government could have accused the Duma of making
use of revolutionary tendencies, and thus strengthened its own position as the defender of the constitution. It could have countered the
Duma's doctrinaire reasoning about the "sovereign foundations of
popular representation" by the obligations imposed upon that body
by the constitution. Furthermore, the government might have reminded the Duma, which was created by the emperor, that all its
rights stemmed from the constitution and not the mystic will of the
people; that the emperor was by popular conception and by law the
head of the nation, and though he intended to share his authority with
the Duma, he would not place it above himself. The Duma's argument that unless some of its desires were fulfilled, it could not work
calmly and fruitfully was simply ridiculous, for the deputies pledged
themselves to work "thinking only of the good and welfare of Russia,"
and not of their own frame of mind. All this and more could have
been said and the government had sufficiently skilled men to say it.
A sample of this may be found in the correspondence between Muromtsev and Goremykin regarding the telegrams from the ultrareaction-
aries.

    But such a reply would have led to unavoidable conflict. It
would have emphasized the irreconcilable differences of ideology

between the Duma and the government. Yet the ideology of the Duma was the concern only of an insignificant cultured minority of the population. The masses did not yet think of a government without an emperor. The nation acknowledged the authority of the emperor and was more accustomed to it than to the authority of the newly-created Duma. By taking such a stand and rebuffing the unlawful pretensions of the Duma, the government would have defended not only the constitution but also the intelligence of the common masses. And if, as liberal opinion later asserted, the government dreamt only of excuses for the dissolution of the Duma, why did it not take advantage of this situation?

It is clear that neither the emperor nor the ministers wanted a break; after the address they still hoped to work with the Duma. They rebuffed the pretensions of the Duma in the mildest possible way; and at the same time, they stressed and hailed all the constitutional actions of the Duma, avoiding hopeless ideological conflict. Concerning the unconstitutional desires of the Duma such as the abolition of the Upper Chamber, the responsibility of the ministry to the Duma, and the extension of its competence to areas from which it was specifically barred (e. g. military affairs), the government declaration confined itself to this announcement: "The Council of Ministers does not consider that it has the right to dwell on these assumptions, as they concern a radical change of the Fundamental Imperial Laws whose revision is outside the scope of the State Duma."

Could anything have been more inoffensive? The ministry went almost too far in its desire not to provoke the punctiliousness of the Duma. The Fundamental Laws prohibited the Duma's initiative in these matters, but the Duma could express to the emperor its thoughts on these subjects. For its part, the government had a right to object to the opinions of the Duma, particularly because their ideology was not in agreement with the constitution, but it refrained from an academic controversy with the Duma. What more could have been expected of the government, if we reject the idea that it should have submitted to the Duma in everything?

Though it avoided a discussion of these questions, the government did not evade the question of administration where the Duma entered the area of royal prerogative, reminding the Duma that in this area its powers consisted only of the right of interpellation. While declaring that

> henceforth it would be the particular concern of the government to introduce in the fatherland strict observance of the principles of law and order, and the activities of various authorities would be watched closely to make sure that they do likewise, in conformity with the expressed wishes of the Duma,

the government did not conceal its objections to some wishes of the
Duma. Characteristically, it did not express absolute disagreement
with them, but rather it introduced reservations whose force could
not properly be denied.

Let us take the question of the Exceptional Regulations. The
Duma in its address claimed that they must be repealed. The government replied that it recognized the unsatisfactory nature of these
laws, and that it would work out new ones to replace them. Here was
a practical way along which the Duma was invited to follow. But the
government maintained that it was necessary to resort to the Exceptional Regulations because of the unceasing, and recently daily, murders, robberies, and violence. This deplorable fact could not be denied, and the government, obliged to "defend the life and property of
peaceful citizens," was duty-bound to struggle against these excesses.
So the government came to this conclusion: "As long as disturbances
continue, and until new laws are drafted, the authorities would have
no alternative; the government would be compelled to protect communal and personal property by all existing lawful means." This
dilemma had to be faced. We shall see later how the Duma attempted to solve it.

Another provocative question was that of an amnesty. The
government did not oppose it, as a matter of principle, in spite of
the provocative ideology with which the problem was invested in the
Duma's address. It merely stated that "pardoning participants in
murders, robberies, and violence was not in the best interests of
the common welfare at the present disturbing time."

Such was the government's attitude to the wishes of the Duma.
It left room for agreement in the area of the Exceptional Regulations,
and pointed the way along which the Duma could pass from wishes
and phraseology to concrete work. The question of an amnesty was
connected (and quite correctly) with the restoration of order in the
country, which the Duma could aid or hinder. What might have happened had the Duma, through its chairman or leaders, found it desirable to take the government at its word and attempted to reach an
agreement with it? But the Duma would not even hear of it. It considered itself the victor.

Turning now to the area that remained within the competence
of the Duma, the government treated the Duma's legislative proposals earnestly and favorably. Here too, it might have ridiculed
the self-confidence of the Duma and pointed out that it would postpone consideration of these matters until the Duma's legislative
projects became sensible and ceased to be meaningless phraseology;
in particular it might have noted the unconstitutionality of the expressions that intentionally avoided the rights of the Upper Chamber.
However, the government did nothing of the kind. Its attitude was
clearly revealed in the opening words of the declaration:

First of all the government expresses readiness to co-
operate fully in the solution of questions which do not
go beyond the limits of the competence of the Duma. The
Council of Ministers regards with particular interest the
questions raised by the State Duma concerning the immediate satisfaction of the urgent needs of the rural population, and the passing of laws confirming the equality of
peasants with persons of other classes; the satisfaction
of the needs of the working class; the drafting of a law
for universal primary education; extending the burdens of
taxation to the more prosperous elements of the population; the reform of municipal government and self-
government, taking into consideration the peculiarities
of the border lands. The Council of Ministers attaches
no less significance to the problem stressed by the Duma of passing a new law safeguarding the inviolability
of personal freedom, the freedom of conscience, of the
press, of assembly and association, in place of presently existing temporary regulations, etc.

I copied these lines from the declaration intentionally, to show
how sympathetic the government was to the exercise of the Duma's
initiative, particularly in regard to laws that aimed at the "restoration of the morality of the Russian land."
    The government promised its cooperation in all these matters,
but it maintained its right of "clarifying to the State Duma the government's opinions regarding these problems and defending its objections in each case." Who could deny the government this right,
which exists in every country with a similar constitution? The government also promised to fulfill its obligations in cooperating on the
question of suffrage, though, "For its part it did not consider that
this question required immediate consideration, since the State Duma was just starting its legislative activity and therefore there had
been no time to determine the need for changing the mode of its
election." Speaking of "freedoms," the government stressed this
fact:

The Council of Ministers stipulates that in accomplishing
this legislative work it is imperative to arm the administrative authority with realistic means, so that laws intended for an orderly course of national life (without
resort to the Exceptional Regulations) would permit the
government to prevent abuse of the freedoms already
granted, and to counteract encroachments threatening
society and the nation.

Who could take issue with this? One can, of course, question the
extent and quality of these realistic means, but the principle involved
cannot be denied. In discussing the law on freedom of assembly, the
Cadets showed that they understood this themselves. This example
later revealed how useful the cooperation of the Duma with the authorities could be. Each would have had its role to play. The Duma
would have insisted on greater freedom, and the government on
methods of lawful struggle against abuse. A desirable compromise
might have been reached as a result.

I wish to pause now to consider a question that proved to be
critical and overshadowed all the rest. This was the only instance
when the government issued an emphatic "veto," which was wrong,
or at any rate, it opened the way for conscientious objections. However, even in this case, the real culprit was the Duma.

In the address, the Duma promised to introduce a bill "to
satisfy the peasants' land-hunger, by turning over for this purpose
all crown, appanage, ministerial, monastic, and church lands, and
allowing the compulsory alienation of privately-owned land." The
government had a perfect right to disagree with the section concerning the compulsory alienation and oppose it. Furthermore, the government could substantiate its objection and, in passing, expose the
demagogy of the address. All this would have been lawful. But the
government should not have forgotten that it did not "legislate,"
that its role was confined to "cooperation" or efforts "to convince"
the law makers. In saying "that the solution of this question on the
basis of the Duma's proposals is absolutely inadmissible," the government employed phraseology that went beyond the limits of its
competence. Acknowledging inadmissibility was the combined task
of the Duma, the Imperial Council, and the emperor--that is, the
organs of legislative authority, not of the government. By its wording, the declaration gave reason to believe that the government
either considered itself, too, a legislative authority, or was speaking in the name of the emperor. Of course, in reality, the emperor
was in agreement with the government in this respect, but the government did not have to reveal his views, since this did not conform
with the constitutional order. However, the Duma had no cause to
be provoked by the government's illegal stand, as the Duma declared
in the address that it "would pass the law" as if it were the only
legislative authority. Still, the government weakened itself by this
inaccuracy.

But if the government was incorrect in this respect, how right
it was in reality! It objected, for the time being, only to the address,
which on this point was demagogy and deceit. Following the address,
on May 8, the Cadets introduced their agrarian bill, which definitely
did not correspond to the text of the address; it proposed the minimum land allotment that would not be affected by alienation and ac-

knowledged compensation rights to owners of alienated land. Under
such circumstances alienation was not a denial of landownership
rights, but rather, for land-rich Russia, an extension of a lawful
practice. But in order to reach unanimity, under pressure from the
parties of the left, the Cadets kept quiet about all this in the address.
They encouraged the peasants to think that the property of the landowners would revert to them, immediately and unconditionally. The
consequences of this deception were quite understandable. A pogrom
atmosphere, for which a basis had long existed, was created and
strengthened by the Duma. The government felt itself obliged to
warn the peasants about this deception. Perhaps the warning was
too decisive and too sharp:

> The Council of Ministers considers that it is its duty to
> declare the solution of this question on the basis proposed
> by the Duma as absolutely inadmissible. The govern-
> ment cannot recognize the rights of private property for
> some people and deny them to others; the government
> cannot, generally, deny rights of private ownership of
> land without at the same time denying ownership of every
> other kind of property.

All this is too "undeniable," too simplified for such a complex
problem, but if we recall the demagogy with which the ministry had
to contend and the social group it was addressing, it could not be
blamed. The sharpness was the result of the Duma's intentional
demagogy in dealing with the peasantry, too dangerous a game to
play.

This is the impression one now has of the ministers' reply,
and it is strange to recall the attitude towards the government's
stand at that time, and all that was said and written on this subject!
Had the question of a suitable government reply, in the light of existing circumstances, been put up for competition, a milder and
more favorable one could not have been discovered.[5]

However, the government not only replied to the address but
also presented its own declaration, and thus established a useful
precedent that was never interfered with later. The address, in
which the Duma hastened to include an absolutely unnecessary program of work, disturbed the harmonious relations between the government and the Duma; the declaration restored them.

At first the emperor rejected such a declaration, for it reminded him of the constitution. But he yielded, and as long as the
monarchy existed, the sessions of each new Duma always started
with the declaration. Of course, in a dual constitution it did not
have the same significance as under parliamentarianism. The ministry did not require the approval of the Duma and could not be

defeated suddenly by the Duma's negative vote. Still, the declaration
helped to elucidate attitudes. The Duma's consent was needed for
legislative activity and the government had to be aware of the Duma's
temper and so know in advance what it could count on. Exchanging
points of view and clearing up misunderstandings was beneficial to
both, but the presentation of the program was, of course, the prerogative of the government. The declaration was a tribute paid by the
executive to the legislative institutions, the admission of their authority and power. Thus the government presented the declaration,
and it was the business of the Duma to consider it.

This time, thanks to the Duma's haste, the roles were changed.
The Duma was first to present a program, and when this was subjected to the ministerial judgment the Duma found the criticism offensive. But the ministry itself had the right to tell what it was planning to do: to quote the words of the declaration, "the government
would point out in general outlines its forthcoming proposals in the
field of legislation." This part of its declaration, of necessity, became only supplementary.

Nevertheless the declaration proved to be more profound than
the "historic address" of the Duma, differing from the address as
the work of specialists differs from improvisations of self-confident
amateurs. It had an advantage over the address because it was
linked to two main ideas: the peasant problem and the reorganization
of Russia to correspond with the principles of a new order.

The peasant problem was raised in Russia even under the autocracy, and was independent of the Manifesto of October 17. But we
must admit that neither society nor the Duma understood its full
significance. Above all they did not understand the problem's ramifi-
cations. There were three separate references to the peasant question in the address. First, there was one in the paragraph about
universal equality, calling for "abolition of all restrictions and privileges stipulating class, nationality, religion, or sex." Created by
the special conditions of Russian history, the complex peasant problem was thus placed on a level with the fashionable feminist problem.
Secondly, there was the main statement which meant nothing: "Clarification of the needs of the agrarian population and the adoption of
appropriate legislative measures will become the immediate task of
the State Duma." Had that been merely the modesty and the realization of the Duma that it was time to study the peasant problem
which was unfamiliar to the deputies, that would have been laudable.
But without studying the problem, the Duma, in a third reference,
decided that "it is necessary to give the peasants crown, appanage,
ministerial, monastic, and privately-owned land." This was the
entire baggage that the Duma possessed at the moment regarding
the peasant problem.

Let us contrast the address with a brief extract from the declaration of the ministry:

The strength of the Russian nation rests primarily on the strength of its agrarian population; the welfare of our fatherland is unattainable so long as the conditions necessary for the success and prosperity of agrarian labor, the basis of our economy, are not secure. Consequently, considering the peasant problem in the light of its universal national significance as the most important of the matters now to be reviewed, special solicitude and discretion are required in investigating ways and means for its solution. Care must be exercised in order to avoid radical upheavals in the historic, singularly fashioned peasant mode of life. However, in the opinion of the Council, the approaching reorganization of our national order with peasant representatives participating in legislative activity predetermines the chief basis of the forthcoming peasant reform. Class isolation of peasants must give way to their merging with other classes with respect to social law and order, administration, and justice; also all restrictions of ownership on allotment lands, which were established to secure the orderly payment of redemption dues, must be abolished. The equalization of peasants' civil and political rights with those of other classes by no means releases the government from the right and obligation of showing special concern for the needs of the agrarian peasants. Measures undertaken in this field must be directed both to the improvement of the conditions of peasant land tenure within existing limits and to the extension of the landownership area of the landless part of the population, at the expense of crown lands and by the acquisition of privately-owned land through the cooperation of the Peasants' Land Bank. In this respect the forthcoming field of government activity is wide in scope and fruitful. Raising the level of the agricultural industry, now on quite a low plane of development, will expand the productivity of the land and thus raise the level of national prosperity. Vast spaces suitable for land cultivation now lie waste in the Asiatic regions of the Empire. Extension of emigration will, therefore, be one of the first concerns of the Council of Ministers.

In this brief excerpt I noted three ideas that were not included

in the address, and so would not appear in the Duma's legislation.
Yet they were very important for a correct solution of this truly basic
Russian problem. The government noted that equalization of rights
was not enough and did not "release the government from the obligation of expressing particular concern for the special needs of the
peasants." While the address was silent in this regard, the ministry's declaration stressed the necessity of improving conditions of
land tenure on allotment lands and, finally, incomprehensible to the
Duma, the declaration expressed the idea that the most desirable reforms "must avoid radical upheavals in the historically singular
peasant mode of life." Neither Cadet nor Labor bills introduced in
the Duma showed such concern.

Another part of the ministerial declaration had in mind the reforms that logically follow the introduction of a "constitution." The
address of the Duma paid more attention to these than to the interests
of the peasants. All that remained for the government was to sub-
scribe to these reforms and promise cooperation in elaborating them,
which it did, adding to these proposals characteristic and useful
riders. Speaking of different kinds of freedom, the declaration added that these freedoms run the risk of remaining a dead letter,

> without the establishment in the country of real principles
> of law and order. Therefore the government gives pri-
> ority to the introduction of the question of local courts
> and their organization to achieve better relations between
> the courts and the people, and the simplification of judicial
> organization to accelerate legal procedure and make it less
> expensive. Simultaneously with the introduction of the bill
> on local administration of justice, the Council will bring
> before the State Duma plans for changing existing regula-
> tions regarding civil and criminal responsibility of of-
> ficials. These projects emanate from the belief that
> consciousness of the sanctity and inviolability of the law
> may become rooted in the population, side by side with
> the assurance that violation of the law, not only by the
> ordinary citizen but also by representatives of authority,
> will be impossible.

The government was correct in taking this stand; it was the
only way to go from words to practical deeds. And the government
did not deceive the Duma. It actually introduced both these laws
pertaining to local judiciary and responsibility of government officials, and characteristically, the Duma left them sitting there, without even turning them over to a committee. This proved the difference between a policy of gestures and words and a policy of practical

achievements. Society did not yet learn to go beyond the first, which we shall see when we come to its legislative work.

It is easy to explain all this. Of course, the government had infinitely more experience and opportunities for legislative activity. The Duma could be blamed only for not wanting to understand this, and imagining that it could do everything itself. But that is getting ahead of myself, as I am not speaking of this now. I merely wished to show that in spite of the provocative address, the government did not break with the Duma, did not set any traps for it, and eliminated from the declaration anything that might lead to a morass of unsolvable ideological conflicts. It stressed points on which agreement was possible, and common effort desirable. Official liberal opinion which claimed that the government was the aggressor, that it intentionally hindered the Duma's work, was contrary to reality. The government's hand was extended to the Duma even after the address, but the reply came in the session of May 13.

Chapter Seven

OPEN CONFLICT BETWEEN THE

DUMA AND THE GOVERNMENT

The session of May 13, 1906, may truly be called historic. It marked the parting of the ways, for the Duma irrevocably chose its course and so decisively rejected the government's extended hand that henceforth all hope of agreement with the government had to be abandoned.[1] Not only does the stenographic report of this session convince one of this, but it is also the impression obtained from various memoirs of the time. Thus the Trudovik Lokot recorded on May 13: "The Duma accepted the challenge which the existing government had flung at it and the nation and, with remarkable unanimity, began a determined and merciless struggle, the like of which had probably never been witnessed in any constitutional country or in any parliament." Of course this savors of exaggeration similar to that of the Soviets when they speak of "the unheard-of achievements of Soviet Russia."

No less enthusiastic was Miliukov when he wrote:

Yesterday we experienced another historic day, one that marked an epoch in history, one of tremendous significance, for it meant the meeting of the representatives of the people with a ministry not responsible to them. Not only was the day unquestionably interesting, but, in the opinion of various deputies, it proved to be a great victory for the Duma. Two worlds met and measured strength with each other [he continued] and no matter on which side physical force ultimately prevailed, the moral victory undoubtedly proved to be on the side of the new order, that of popular freedom. While attempting to teach a lesson to the resprsentatives of the people, the ministry was itself compelled to hearken to the severe admonition of the Duma, which proved to be the sterner and more earnest tutor.

Thus not only did a historic parting of the ways occur, which need not be denied, but at the same time a great victory was, supposedly, won. Was this true?

96

We all know how wartime reports are colored. Each side pro-
claims itself the victor and retreats and havoc are transformed into
victories. Only naive people take such reports seriously, but they
are the majority. So, too, everyone has become accustomed to the
existence of party deception, but the faithful still believe it. Such
systematic deception flourishes best wherever only one official
press exists, but even under conditions of freedom where a varied
press opinion exists, the uncultured masses usually read only their
own newspapers and actually know only their official version. Devia-
ation from this was considered treason even in the period of the First
Duma.

Thus the historic session of May 13 has long been remembered
by our society as the day of great victory. But after thirty years one
may ask oneself: what did this victory consist of? Who was conquered
and what was there to be proud of?

It was considered a victory because events in Russia were regarded in the light of European parliamentary life. There the vote of
nonconfidence in the ministry always appears as some sort of victory,
even if it is some times undesirable for the work at hand, because the
ministry resigns. This means that the majority group on which the
ministry depended in the Chamber until then is now breaking up. It
is a victory in the sense that the enemies of the ministry convinced
the ministry's former supporters of something.

But what constituted the victory of May 13? The ministry was
never supported by a majority, and according to the meaning of our
dual constitution, it did not even require it. Even before the convocation of the Duma, Miliukov contended that the ministry should resign merely because of the election results, and the Duma's address
unanimously demanded resignation before the ministry had an opportunity to say or do anything. If the Duma adopted the very same
resolution after the session of May 13, who was vanquished? Who
was persuaded to change his mind? And what was the practical
achievement of a vote of nonconfidence?

Was there at least what is called a moral victory? Was there
superior eloquence, revelation of national understanding, profound
thinking? Eloquence perhaps, but parliament is not an oratorical
tournament and eloquence is generally of little worth, particularly
when the judge is a large gathering and the measure is its applause.
But if eloquence was to be measured in this way, the deputies were
victorious on May 13; there was "stormy" and "prolonged" and
"loud" and every other kind of applause. But what of it? The First
Duma cannot be denied the gift of eloquence for it had many first
class orators, all of whom made speeches on the first great parliamentary day. Moreover, the Duma had prepared for this day, since
the ministry's declaration was known in advance, though not by all.
I recall my conversation with Stakhovich in the Second Duma regarding the composition of the presidium. The "majority" of that period

did not admit any opposition elements and Stakhovich was indignant
about this. He explained that this was not only a question of justice
but also a practical concern. In the First Duma, he said, the presidium knew in advance the text of the declaration, which it distributed
in printed form to all deputies, but its own members were informed
earlier and given an opportunity to prepare their speeches.

This episode is characteristic. Muromtsev, chosen by the
whole Duma, formally left the party because of the incompatibility
of party affiliation with the position of chairman. However correct
he was personally, he utilized the post of chairman to the detriment
of the minority, whose interests he, in particular, should have guarded.
Thus at the dawn of the constitution, party affiliation was already destroying proper conduct of affairs.

But the advance notice of the declaration had its advantages.
Thanks to this the spectacle had been prepared in advance and there
was no tediousness or repetition. The number of orators was limited.
In short, the stage setting was a model one. But for all that, what
victory was there to be proud of? The chief condition of victory, a
battle, was lacking and the orators were smashing through an open
door, with no one to contradict them. Goremykin read the declaration in a quiet, indifferent voice, and when the indignant speeches of
the Duma began to flow in a stormy torrent, he sat silently, smoothing
his whiskers with indifference.... Opponents of the ministry told me
that they did not rejoice at its misfortune but suffered for Russian
authority. When the intermission was announced all the ministers
left and did not return to the session. Only Shcheglovitov returned
and spoke a few conciliating words, but though he had good intentions
this gesture was not appreciated. This was still the former Shcheglovitov, adherent of Court Law and supporter of the constitutional order,
who wanted to correct the evil that occurred and heal the breach.

He had never been a powerful and skillful orator, but he was a
good lawyer, a very cultured and educated man and a sympathetic
one. I remember him as a representative of the Ministry of Justice
at one of the most interesting cases in which I had an opportunity to
participate, the case of the Pavlov Sect. Even in appearance, their
trial in no way suggested justice. The crime was so monstrous--
they devastated two churches--that they were denied trial in ordinary
courts. Unfortunately for the accused the Ministry of Justice defended
the case. The Senior Chairman of the Chamber, Cherniavski, generally an independent man, called the defense into his office and informed
them that the "court enjoys national confidence and he must justify
this confidence." The Chamber justified it by refusing psychiatric
examination even to a person who long before this had been an inmate
of an insane asylum, on the ground of religious madness, to say
nothing of the estimation of the whole incident, which was a clear
example of mass religious insanity. The envoy of the Synod, the

notorious V. M. Skvortsov, was, of course, pleased with this, but
Shcheglovitov was indignant about the whole trial and succeeded in
getting a pardon for the accused. So, too, as the Minister of Justice
he wanted to begin the joint work with the Duma as speedily as possible and he spoke with this aim in mind. He did not pick up the
gauntlet or take the offensive. Rather he apologized to the Duma.
He began by saying:

> The attacks of the State Duma compel me to say a few
> words, of course, not to appraise or discuss these attacks,
> because the ministry does not consider itself authorized
> to do so. [Quite an incomprehensible humiliation for the
> government. He mitigated the offensive words of the
> declaration ''undeniably inadmissible, '' saying:] Why
> should the members of the Duma worry about the exis-
> tence of opinions with which they do not agree? A matter
> is clarified from the clash of different opinions and truth
> is born, so to speak. [He closed with this strange state-
> ment:] The government regards the difference of its
> opinions from those of the State Duma as a guarantee of
> the perfection of the new laws, which consequently will
> be a truer expression of the will of the people whom the
> Duma represents.

This almost ingratiating speech served as a further example of
the extent to which some ministers tried to avoid a break, and how
easy it would have been to come to agreement with them. But to
speak of the Duma's victory over Shcheglovitov for the stand he took
and which aroused against him strong displeasure in right-wing circles is to be too extreme.

Although the ministry had a great deal of material, not only
for defense but also for attack, it did not defend itself. This was
done in spite of the fact that it had in its midst people who were second to none of the Duma's speakers in eloquence. I recall Stolypin's
remarks after the declaration in the Second Duma, powerful, brilliant and profound; its weakest part was its famous closing: ''You
will not frighten us. '' But he was not the chairman of the Council of
Ministers in the First Duma. That was Goremykin. Stolypin could
not bypass him and Goremykin was incapable of making any reply,
so there was no struggle at all. This was, of course, the fault of
the government, but it was improper to take pride in such victories;
this was the same as pride in having hit an adversary who is down.
The Cadets should have been above that.

But, apart from eloquence, the Duma could have won another
victory which could easily be appraised now, after so many event-
ful years. It might have shown its superior political understanding,

revealed the innate defects of left-wing policies, which the right
wing was preparing to do; it might have undertaken the defense of the
constitution from its distortion by supporters of the old order, and
at least in this way strengthened its demand for the resignation of
the ministry.

But, unfortunately, this was not done and could not be done.
After the address the Cadets could not defend the constitution. We
shall see this from Cadet speeches, which were quite enlightening.
This was a field day for the revolutionaries; they had nothing to defend. But the national party, which had pretensions of becoming the
government, had to show that it was capable of it; that it understood
correctly the task of government in this difficult time and knew how
to deal with it. It could not be satisfied with mere rejection, but the
Cadet speeches did not reveal this.

I shall take as an illustration Nabokov's speech, which was the
first and was the highlight of the day. [2]   By nature Nabokov was not
a revolutionary but a liberal, and he understood the obligations which
this entailed. By birth and upbringing he belonged in the revolutionary
camp, but he parted from it consciously and finally. In the new environment he remained what he had been: convinced but not a fanatic,
educated and cultured, possessing a great literary talent, an elegant
figure, and refined, fluent speech. The greatest success of his
speech was due to the fact that it was calm, without any hysterical
excesses.

Yet, this speech did not prove to be a defense of the constitution.

It is to his credit that he alone correctly appraised the most
vulnerable part of the declaration, the agrarian problem. This dis-
tinguished him from the other speakers and it was to his advantage.
He discerned in the declaration of "absolute inadmissibility" of the
principles of the address, "the government's former arbitrary tone,
a habit which it was time to relinquish and renounce." To the ministerial absolute veto he replied, in accordance with the constitution,
that regardless of the opposition of the minstry, "We shall continue
to introduce our legislative proposals and we consider that the country
is behind us." This objective position, compared to what others said,
was a credit to Nabokov, but the sensational success of his speech
was not due to this.

The stormy applause and Nabokov's later renown were the result of two points in his speech. Speaking of amnesty and the ministers' negative attitude toward it (Nabokov added "categorically negative" which was actually not true, for the ministry questioned the
suitability of amnesty only for some kinds of crime--murder, robbery,
and violence), Nabokov said: "We consider amnesty to be among
the prerogatives of the Sovereign Authority to which we appealed, and
we shall not permit any intermediary voice between us and the Supreme Authority on the question of amnesty; we reject it [stormy
applause]."

These famous words of Nabokov undermined the whole constitutional system. Under a constitution the ministers speak for the
monarch; they advise him. How can that be rejected without simultaneously rejecting the constitution and returning to a personal régime?
A well-educated lawyer like Nabokov could not help knowing this. But
the Cadet party intentionally, as a matter of tactics, confused two
completely different conceptions: constitution and parliamentarianism.
It asserted that when there is no parliamentarianism there is no constitution, either, and the war continued. It was not ignorance that
made Miliukov write in Speech, on April 19-20, that strictly constitutional principles demanded that the ministry be composed of the
majority which won the elections. He substituted one term for
another; parliamentarianism, not the constitution, called for ministerial responsibility, and Miliukov was well aware of this also, but
he was playing politics. Nabokov went even further. He described
a government order where nothing stands between the popular representatives and the monarch. "The Duma does not permit the mediation of the government between itself and the monarch." This would
be neither constitution nor parliamentarianism but simply a Slavonic
idyll. Nabokov's statement was a legal monstrosity but for this reason it met with pronounced success in the Duma.

An even more serious anti-constitutionalism was revealed by
Nabokov's second famous statement, which came at the end of his
speech:

> Since we are told that it is not the business of the govern-
> ment to fulfill the demands of popular representatives,
> but rather to criticize and reject them, then from the
> point of view of the principle of popular representation,
> we can only say one thing: "the executive authority shall
> submit to the legislative authority."

This statement aroused prolonged applause and became famous;
it was regarded as the résumé of the whole session. Yet it was constitutional heresy. The Duma was not the "legislative authority"
but only part of it. Legislative authority was shared by the Duma,
the Imperial Council, and the tsar. Only their union constituted
legislative authority. To such authority, of course, the ministers
had to submit, but there was a vast gulf between submission to legislative authority and submission to the Duma alone. By calling the
Duma the legislative authority, Nabokov grossly distorted its competence. He repeated word for word the historic error of Barnave,
which was so cruelly exposed by Mirabeau on May 22, 1790, in his
famous speech "sur le droit de la paix et de la guerre (the rights
of peace and war)." Barnave argued that the declaration of war
depended on the legislative assembly for it is "pouvoir législatif
(legislative power)." Mirabeau accused Barnave of juggling the

facts, for he substituted the words "pouvoir législatif" for "corps
législatif (the legislative body)." "vous avez forfait la constitution
(You have forfeited the constitution)," he then told Barnave.

About a hundred years later Nabokov made the very same error,
confusing the legislative assembly with legislative authority. He
could see the perniciousness of this interchange of ideas in the following speech made by Aladin:

> All ministers are obliged to be the executive authority;
> they must accept what we, the representatives of the coun-
> try, find necessary, indispensable, and urgent; they must
> study the laws which we decree and as our faithful ser-
> vants they must execute these laws. That is their duty
> [applause].

The drunken helot arose before the eyes of the aristocratic Nabokov,
who realized the error of his statement sooner than his admirers.

A few years later, in the Third Duma, Shcheglovitov, then a
changed man, recalled this "historic statement" of Nabokov as
proof of the fact that the First Duma wanted to compel submission
of the ministers to its authority. The circumstances under which
it was then made were already forgotten. I replied that this interpretation of the statement disregarded the existence of the tsar.
Legislative authority is not vested in the Duma alone, but it includes
the Imperial Council and the tsar. Did Shcheglovitov consider that
the ministers should not have submitted to this legislative authority?
This change of front met with success. Having learned of my criticism, Shcheglovitov sent A. H. Verevkin to the Duma to explain his
statement, and Nabokov thanked me for giving his "unfortunate statement" such a plausible and unexpected, as far as he was concerned,
explanation. But, of course, on May 13 it was meant as Shcheglovitov
interpreted it; that was the way everyone understood it then, and for
that very reason praised it, seeing in this legal heresy the moral
victory of the Duma over the government.

Besides Nabokov, other great politicians and lawyers spoke.
But to what extent did their opinions prevail upon the government?

Kokoshkin undertook to prove that the government revealed an
"ignorance of constitutional procedure and an absence of a truly national point of view." No one was in a better position than he to
fulfill such a task, since he was a man of exceptional gifts, well-
armed with scholarship and creative ability, a fanatic whose faith
prompted original interpretations of this rewarding theme. How
stupefying was the Duma's atmosphere when a man like Kokoshkin
made such an ineffectual speech on such a theme!

Kokoshkin showed no appreciation of the government's desire
for peace, on account of which it avoided a conflict over the anti-

constitutional declarations of the Duma. He blamed the government
for this evasion, regarding it as "ignorance of constitutional procedure." He declared that the government erred regarding the Duma's
indication of the desirability of changing the constitution as its "legislative initiative." Kokoshkin's conclusion was too hasty, for the
government did not commit such a gross error. An address generally is not a form of initiative, and there was no initiative either in the
proposals to change the Fundamental Laws or in the reforms that the
Duma announced. Initiative had to come in the future. But the government could not be condemned for refusing to express itself on
questions that were beyond the scope of the Duma's competence.
Kokoshkin failed to show a real understanding of the constitution when
he contended that the government was obliged to consider these wishes
of the Duma as "the possible scope of the government's legislative
activity." The government was not obliged to consider everything
that happened to be said by the Duma, particularly since the Duma
did not request the tsar's initiative but contented itself, according
to Miliukov's words, "to rest expectations on the crown." Why was
the government obliged to give consideration to all possible expectations? It is amusing to note that Kokoshkin affirmed this while Nabokov was declaring that the Duma would not permit mediation between
itself and the monarch. Which of these two Cadet leaders was ignorant of constitutional procedure?

In addition to ignorance of constitutional procedure, Kokoshkin
reproached the government for lacking a national point of view. Such
a theme was also profitable. A new conception of nationhood was
being born, which the supporters of the old order found difficult to
accept, and the revolutionary parties rejected. It was the particular
task of the Cadets to strike the true note that could have helped
strengthen the rule of law. What, then, did a man like Kokoshkin
say in this regard?

He spoke of an amnesty. I noted how unsuccessful the address
was in initiating the demand for an amnesty, but the address was compiled by a group and consequently had its flaws. However, Kokoshkin
himself replied to the ministry. He was unrestricted and could explain what he meant by a new basis for national life. What did this
new basis consist of? Kokoshkin contended that the declaration of
the Council of Ministers

> revealed complete lack of understanding of the essence
> of an amnesty, by comparing it to an individual act of
> pardon. An amnesty, that is mass pardon, has a special
> meaning. The very term is borrowed from international
> law and indicates restoration of peace. When peace
> treaties are concluded a clause on amnesty is included.
> Such moments arise in the internal life of a nation when

it is essential to end internecine war of one form or
another. [The comparison was correct, and Kokoshkin
concluded:] No one can deny that what has been taking
place in Russia the last few years is a condition close to
internecine war. We must restore political peace and
this requires an amnesty.

Was this a national point of view? An amnesty is appropriate when
peace is concluded; but amnesty does not bring about peace; it is
rather the consequence of peace. A political conception of amnesty,
in fact, is that it is concomitant with the conclusion of peace. But
the Cadets did not prove that peace was concluded, or that they even
desired it. Yet, if the war continued; if the Duma did not recognize
the constitution and was not prepared, because the time of benevolence had not yet arrived, to condemn violence against the government, then there was no ground for an amnesty.

To continue Kokoshkin's comparison, an amnesty under such
conditions would be the equivalent of freeing the prisoners of one
side before the conclusion of peace, which would be capitulation and
a proof of weakness. The government pointed out this fact in its
reply: ''An amnesty is untimely in the present troubled period.''
The struggle between the government and revolution was continuing,
and by raising the question of amnesty this way, the Duma, and following it, Kokoshkin, robbed amnesty of its national meaning.

Kokoshkin also touched on a more general problem that later
permeated all the activity of the Duma. Until the present, society
could be preoccupied with composing theoretical constitutions, which
was not a difficult matter. It could propound the latest ideas on
theories and practices of civilized countries without having to worry
about the difficulties that their application in Russia might encounter.
But after 1906 Russia turned from theories to a period of practical
realization; the Duma was no longer an outside observer but a part
of state authority, and the government was in a difficult position at
that time. On the heels of belated reforms, there flowed the revolutionary waves that even tried to do away with the tsar to whom Russia was accustomed, and to substitute in his place a Constituent
Assembly of the intelligentsia. These revolutionary waves, as usual,
struck at the old autocracy as well as at the newly-announced constitutional order. When the monarchy fell in 1917 and the revolutionary
government was created, the revolutionaries still continued to
''heighten the revolution,'' weakening the authority created by revolution. In 1936, when the Front Populaire ministry came into power
in France and compulsory occupation of factories began with the
S. G. T. (trade union) claiming control of the nation, these revolutionary activities were an attack on the new ministry. So, too, after
the promulgation of the constitution and the convocation of the Duma,

what orators called civil war became intensified. Revolutionary
upheaval did not want peace at all, and aimed at complete victory.

What should the government have done under such circumstances? Either acknowledge revolution as the will of the people
and submit to it, or, in defense of law and in the name of the new
order, repulse revolution with force. There was no third alternative.

In its declaration the government took up the second position,
announcing that "it was its duty to safeguard order and the life and
property of peaceful citizens." The government understood that old
methods were outdated and promised to enforce strict observance of
law. While agreeing that the exceptional powers, which it had at its
disposal until now, were no longer of any use and should be changed,
the government raised a question that could not be brushed aside by
quibbling. What was to be done in the meantime when no new laws
have as yet been passed? So the government announced that until
such time as new laws are passed, it would of necessity have to rely on old, unsuitable laws for necessary powers.

This question was a test of the national maturity of the Duma.
It was not difficult to foresee the stand the revolutionaries would
take. They did not want to struggle against revolutionary upheaval,
which they regarded as the will of the people. To them the constitution of 1906 meant coercion, and they consistently awaited, with joy
and hope, the downfall of state authority and the complete triumph of
revolution.

But how was this question answered by the constitutional party,
which in a few weeks was to start secret negotiations for the creation
of a Cadet ministry that would then become not a revolutionary government as in 1917 but the government of a constitutional monarch?
Did the Duma, which was a part of state authority (Muromtsev even
contended that it was a part of the government), have the right to
look on indifferently while the unrestrained Acheront tried to destroy
the constitution?

The Cadet party, by providing the guidance expected of it,
should have shown that it differed from both the representatives of
the old order and the revolution. This required clarity of purpose
and courage, but, because of tactical considerations, the Cadets
proved to possess neither the one nor the other. They had to defend
the legal order against revolutionary forces, and at the same time
introduce principles of law into the defensive activities of the government. These were two aspects of the same policy. The procedure of the government could have been changed: some odious powers could have been totally abolished immediately, while others
could have been placed under the control of the courts by establishing
responsibility for abuse of authority. But the Duma, which was demanding the government's submission to laws and observance of

rights, should have supported the government in the chief struggle
against revolutionary violence. Without doing this, the Duma's
protests and accusations were not acts of state authority but only an
aid to revolution.

Neither at that time nor later would the Duma take such a
stand. What did Kokoshkin say to the ministry in reply to the tragic
alternative of the government? ''If the law is unsatisfactory, it must
not be preserved...It should not exist a single minute....''

This rhetoric showed no statesmanlike comprehension. To
whom was it directed? The ministry itself could neither change nor
set aside any laws. The Duma's consent was necessary for that,
and as we shall see later, the Duma was not in any hurry to change
these laws. Meanwhile new laws had not been passed and the old
ones were not abolished. What was the government supposed to do
in the face of the raging Acheront?

The Duma was faced with this question many times later on.
When Stolypin raised it in his famous example about the firelock, the
Duma laughed, but it is easy to laugh at nothing. One reply was al-
ways given: govern without exceptional regulations. On May 13
Kokoshkin used Switzerland and the United States as an illustration
that exceptional regulations need not exist.

This was almost convincing but, in the first place, even without exceptional regulations, the government is not impotent in these
countries. A month or so later, during the discussion of rights of
assembly, this same Kokoshkin explained to Kovalevski the nature
of the extensive powers with which English administrative authority
is endowed for the maintenance of order. Furthermore, the coun-
tried to which Kokoshkin alluded had no civil war at the time and respect for law and order was deeply ingrained there. Liberal parties
in those countries were not afraid to say that the state apparatus
existed to safeguard order established by law from attacks made on
it, supposedly in the name of the will of the people.

The autocracy did not develop such a conception of order in
Russia. The mark of the enemy it had conquered lay on liberalism.
Our conception of rights was so confused that some of our cleverest
lawyers could not understand the Manifesto. Here is a graphic example. In its declaration, the ministry undertook to review all
existing regulations regarding administrative arrests. In this connection Kokoshkin gave vent to this tirade: ''This completely disre-
gards the fact that, since the issue of the Manifesto and the proclamation of the inviolability of personal freedom, every executive detention
is a violation of the law.'' While preaching this to the government,
Kokoshkin knew that this was not true. First, because no proclamation of the inviolability of personal freedom was made on October
17, the government was instructed to draft a new law based on the

principle of inviolability, but it did not have the time to implement
this instruction; there were extenuating circumstances for this.
Second, no new law could totally prohibit every administrative detention. Only on some examination did Kovalevski get a student's
definition, that habeas corpus means that no one may be arrested
without his consent. This was not all. Our lawyers were so confused about human rights at this time that while demanding from the
government immediate realization of all kinds of freedoms, they
were arguing, at the same time, that after October 17 no new laws
could be passed without the consent of a Duma that had not yet come
into existence. This was not a case of theoretical reasoning in a
vicious circle. On the basis of such thinking, society attempted to
refuse submission to the new laws concerning press and assembly.
How could anyone compare life in Russia, with its ignorance of
human rights created first by the autocracy and later by the ideology
of revolution, with the orderly course of life in civilized, law-abiding
nations in peacetime?

Yet the support of a legal order was the task of this epoch. It
was easy to proclaim idealistic principles of a new order, but it was
difficult to implement them gradually and carefully, in practical life,
so as not to topple the government at the same time. It was evident
that the traditional authority, seeing its salvation in the exceptional
powers to which it was accustomed, and revolutionary society,
dreaming of the complete triumph of revolution, could not agree on
anything between themselves; with them it was only a question of
superior force. Only joint action on the part of liberalism and the
new governmental forces could solve this problem by limiting unavoidable conflict. To accomplish this, liberalism had to defend
the legal order from its enemies from above and below. It could
criticize the lawlessness of the government as a spokesman for
principles of justice, but not as a servant of revolutionary upheaval.
Liberal society could not condemn the government if, in order to
fulfill its duty, it resorted to obsolete laws when it was not given
new ones. Nor could all the lawlessness of the revolution be justified by the fact that we live in a revolutionary period, for then,
under cover of neutrality, society would have taken the side of revolution.

That is why liberalism could do nothing useful at the moment;
if it dared not condemn revolution, the problem of halting it became
the squaring of a circle. Thus liberalism did not pass the test of
nationhood either, and dragged at the heels of revolution.

Let us consider now liberalism's attempts to solve problems
where it could limit itself to criticism. Here its political sense
was not put to the test, and only the fairness of its discussions entered into consideration. Abbé Sieyès was right in his observation:

"Ils veulent être libres et ne savent pas être justes (They wish to
be free but they cannot be just)." How fairly did liberalism criticize
the government's declaration?

The declaration's most vulnerable point was the categorical
manner in which it announced that the settlement of the agrarian
problem on the basis proposed by the Duma was "absolutely inadmissible." Everyone passionately attacked these unfortunate words.
I shall not speak of the revolutionaries but pause for a moment to
consider the Cadet speeches.

I paid tribute to Nabokov for his moderation in dealing with
this question. He pointedly indicated the weakness in the government's approach to the Duma's agrarian proposals, and said all that
could and should have been said in this regard. But what of Kokoshkin? In spite of his personal scrupulousness, he did not hesitate to
accuse the government of "ignorance and illiteracy," as though it
really did not know that legislatures of all countries, including the
Russian, recognized the right of expropriation of private property
only under certain conditions. Kokoshkin himself pointed out one of
these conditions when he said: "The inviolability of property consists merely of fair compensation paid the owner of the expropriated
property." Whom was Kokoshkin ridiculing then? The question of
compensation was not mentioned in the address, not because it was
forgotten but because the Cadets did not want to bring it up at the
time. This was something, according to Kokoshkin, that every lawyer knew, though the people did not know and did not accept it. In
their election campaign the Cadets frequently met with opposition to
compensation for expropriated land, a question that was brought up
and discussed at the First Peasant Congress in 1905. Later thirty-
three deputies in the Duma introduced legislation for the complete
abolition of private land property rights without any compensation.
With the peasants in such a mood, the address suggesting unconditional expropriation of privately-owned land was like an incendiary
torch. Thus Kokoshkin's objection to the government's announcement of the "inadmissibility" of this clause, and his allusion to all
European countries, cannot be considered sincere.

Kovalevski even surpassed Kokoshkin. How could this happen
to a man who was not inclined to fanaticism nor easily swayed by
enthusiasm? This is how he attacked the ministers: "How dare you
contradict the will of the Tsar-Liberator; how dare you deny the
greatest act in Russian history--the liberation of peasants with land
[prolonged applause]?" How can we explain such a distortion coming
from Kovalevski's lips? This statement was as inappropriate for
him as his repetition of Mirabeau's famous words: "allez dire à
votre maître...." Yet he literally said: "We here are the spokesmen of the people and we shall fulfill the mission with which they
entrusted us. Only brute force shall drive us from here." N. N.

Bazhenov, a fellow countryman and friend of Kovalevski who was present at that session, told me how false these bombastic phrases sounded coming from him, and how Kovalevski himself laughed about them later. Such was the unhealthy atmosphere of the Duma.

I want to consider two more interesting Cadet speeches that have baffled me. How could the speakers have failed to understand how unjust their accusations were and how much harm they caused?

To begin with, let us consider Vinaver's speech on the Jewish question, which was a profitable theme. Vinaver, an exceptionally clever man and an excellent orator, could put the Jewish question bluntly better than anyone else, and no one would then have taken a stand against equality of rights for the Jews. He touched on this theme more than once in the First Duma and always with complete success, but that day he failed to realize that the blows he directed against the ministers really struck at the Duma. Vinaver accused the government of silence on the Jewish question:

> The Duma categorically demanded equality and what re-
> ply did it receive? Empty silence [applause]. The min-
> isters rejected a just solution of the agrarian problem;
> they brusquely rejected many other things, too, which
> rejection was courageous though politically senseless.
> Only in regard to social equality did they prefer to re-
> main cowardly silent. We have the right to pillory them
> for this shameful silence [applause].

How did Vinaver reach this conclusion? In its address the Duma itself remained silent as far as the Jewish question was concerned.[3] It was a peculiar and exceptionally important problem, but not a word was said about it in the address except for a hint in this statement: "The Duma will work out a law for complete equalization of the rights of all citizens and for the rescinding of all limitations and privileges resulting from social position, nationality, religion or sex." Thus the Jewish question was merged with the other problems of inequality, including the question of women's rights, though one might not be an anti-Semite and yet not recognize equality of rights for women. Such a formulation of the question of equality might be criticized from various points of view, but this was done by the Duma itself, not by the government. What was the government's reaction? It expressed readiness "to give full cooperation to the solution of questions raised by the Duma which do not go beyong the limits of its legislative competence." This referred to the law of equality and so to the Jewish question also.

If the Jewish question was not dealt with separately and in sharp relief, it was the fault of the Duma alone, whatever may have been its reasons. If this was so obvious, why did Vinaver complain

only about the government's silence? Or did the Duma remain silent
because it feared discord within its ranks, and if so, why did Vinaver
accuse the government of cowardice? That the condemnation of the
government was unjust was revealed in a published letter of Stolypin
to Nicholas II on December 10, 1907, in which Stolypin expressed
the opinion that social equality was already granted by the Manifesto
of October 17. Thus the Jews had a legal basis for demanding full
equality of rights. On this question, however, the government
clashed with the personal prejudice of the tsar and it needed the
cooperation of the Duma to overcome it. Such speeches as Vinaver's
did not make the government's task easier. Soon after this session
I met Prince P. N. Trubetskoi in a railway car. Fate connected him
with the liberal movement though he belonged in the right-wing camp.
During the conversation he told me of the depressing impression
that Vinaver's speech made on his listeners. When I expressed surprise and asked "Why?" he replied: "Because he demanded that
the ministers put the Jewish question in first place; they think only
of that, we have other problems, too." This did not reflect Trubetskoi's personal opinion, but Vinaver's speech accusing only the government of cowardly silence and confusing friends with enemies
encouraged such unfortunate moods.

I cannot help comparing this speech with Lednitski's speech on
the Polish question, which had much in common with it. The Cadet
program on the Polish question--Polish autonomy within Russian
boundaries--was well known, and had been adopted at the April
Zemstvo Congress, 1905. But on April 30, 1906, twenty-seven Polish deputies presented a declaration to the Russian popular representatives, protesting the violation of the rights of the Polish land.
They said: "Our rights are inalienable and holy and the autonomy
of the Polish Kingdom is the sacred demand of the entire population
of our country." Thus, when the address was composed, everyone
knew full well that the Poles wanted autonomy.[4] Yet this was not
mentioned in the address. The paragraph on nationalities limited
itself to this statement:

> Finally, the State Duma considers it necessary to note
> among its urgent problems the long delayed satisfaction
> of the demands of various nationalities. Russia is a
> country inhabited by a great many tribes and races. We
> must meet their need for safeguarding and developing
> the peculiar aspects of their mode of life. The State
> Duma will concern itself with meeting these just demands
> on an extensive scale.

In addition to this reference, I have more than once quoted the
statement about equality of rights without differentiation of classes,
nationalities, religion, or sex.

The Duma did not consider it necessary to say more on the
Polish question than on the special Jewish question. Why? Evidently
for the same reasons: there would have been no unanimity. There
were enemies of Polish autonomy in Russian society in both right-
and left-wing circles. Some members of the Zemstvo Congress opposed Polish autonomy because this would give them more privileges
than others had. On the other hand, I recall a pre-election meeting
at Tula where a blunt and confirmed opponent of Polish autonomy was
a respected and liberal Jewish lawyer, who, apparently with the Jewish problem in mind, pointed out how dangerous Polish autonomy
would be to national minorities. This comparatively minor question
involved the very serious problem of state antinomy in a democracy:
what is to be done if the principle of national rights results in a denial
of the rights of the individual? Which should receive preference?
Should national rights be limited in the name of rights of the individual, or should individual rights be sacrificed in the name of national
rights? In the Third Duma we came face to face with this problem
during the discussion of self-government in the Polish Kingdom. The
same problem is posed now in a tragic form by the totalitarian countries. This alternative has not yet been resolved even theoretically;
everyone evades it. During the discussion of the address it was also
avoided by silence, as was the "four-tail," the Jewish question, and
other matters. The Duma's opinions were expressed in such a way
that they could be construed to mean anything: national autonomy or
only so-called cultural self-determination. So acted the Duma for
tactical reasons, and the government answered just as vaguely, expressing readiness to assist with all reforms that did not go beyond
the competence of the Duma and stipulating particularly "the reform
of local government and self-government, taking into consideration
the particular problems of border areas." These words could allude
to the Polish question also. In any case, if nothing more definite was
said, it is because the Duma said nothing definite, and the question
remained wide open. No objections were made against it by the government; nevertheless, Lednitski considered it just to attack the
government for malicious silence: "We, too, are sons and citizens
of Russia, but the ministers' declaration had no word for us either
about rights of nationalities, or national equality and a just satisfaction of national demands, which the Russian people already declared in the great historic reply to the monarch." If, instead of
striving for apparent unanimity, the Duma should have presented a
clear and concrete program of its majority, it would have had the
right to draw conclusions from the government's silence, but when
in place of such a program a collection of general statements was
introduced, the government did not need to bother reading between
the lines. The Duma's attacks were a typical transfer of guilt
"from a sick head to a healthy one."

I shall not deal any longer with this historic session. It closed with the adoption of a motion to pass on to other business. It was a typical, cheap, stereotyped formula* of the kind now produced in Soviet Russia at the order of the party and calculated to win popular favor. The formula read as follows:

> Discerning in the declaration of the chairman of the Council of Ministers definite proof that the government absolutely refuses to satisfy the popular demands and expectations for land, human rights, and freedom, which were outlined by the State Duma in its address in reply to the speech from the throne, and without whose satis-faction tranquillity in the land and fruitful work of the popular representatives are impossible;
> And finding that by its refusal to satisfy national de-mands, the government reveals an obvious disregard for the real interests of the people and no desire to save from new upheavals the country exhausted by poverty, injustice, and continued domination of unpunished, arbi-trary authority, we express to the entire country complete lack of confidence in the ministry which is not responsible to popular representatives, and recognize as the most essential condition for the pacification of the nation and fruitful work of its representatives the immediate resig-nation of the present ministry and its replacement by a ministry enjoying the confidence of the State Duma,
> The State Duma is proceeding to the next order of business.

Was there any justice in this formula? The declaration con-tradicted the Duma's conclusion that the government had absolutely refused to satisfy the expectation of land, human rights, and free-dom. It was not true to say that the government refused the satis-faction of these demands and that it revealed an obvious disregard for the interests of the people, etc. This type of oratory might be effective for meetings. It was possible to suspect that during con-sideration of concrete laws the government's acquiescence might be greatly diminished, but to declare before the entire country that the government refused everything was an obvious untruth.

Of course this is often done in the contemporary party struggle: slandering enemies, doing the very thing for which opponents were criticized, voting against their own laws when they are proposed by the opposition--all these are stereotyped methods of present-day

----

*Formula of transition: A procedure adopted by the Duma which consisted of summing up the preceding discussion before going on to the next order of business. [M. B.]

democracies. Or rather they are the perversion of democracy, and
the reason why democracy and parliamentarianism are now exper-
iencing the crisis they deserve.

In well-established régimes such practices are accepted as the
unavoidable weaknesses of every government system, but it was not
so with us. We were just approaching this new order, which we
idealized as flawless and contrasted with the organic defects of the
autocracy. However, the aura of idealistic faith vanished the very
first day as rampant falsehood, self-confidence, and boasting were
exposed in the Duma, striking a moral blow at the new order in the
eyes of ordinary people unspoiled by politics. Such behaviour compromised the constitution.

So I return to the question: who was the victor that day? The
formula adopted before going on to the next order of business was
proposed by Trudovik deputy Zhilkin. I recall Rozhkov's article
which claimed that the significance of that day lay in the fact that
the leadership of the Duma was transferred from the Cadets to the
Trudoviki. Vinaver exposed this falsehood, because the formula of
transition was composed at a greatly enlarged meeting of Cadets and
Trudoviki, of which Miliukov was chairman. It was only by accident,
and yet it might have been intentional, that Zhilkin introduced this
accepted formula as his own and thus strengthened the legend of
change of leadership.[5]

But this apparent falsehood had some truth in it. The Trudoviki
actually were the real victors that day. The acceptance of the address
was a victory of the tactical, if misdirected, skill of the Cadets, but
at the session of May 13, Trudovik ideology triumphed all along the
line. Cadets made Trudovik speeches; they were inspired by a revolutionary spirit and transformed the Duma into an organ of revolutionary upheaval. They made the choice that they avoided until
then. Nothing remained of their constitutionalism and political understanding. In this session the Duma was only the weapon of revolution. Such was the Cadet reply to the conciliatory declaration of
the ministry.

Chapter Eight

THE INTENTIONS OF THE GOVERNMENT

IN REPLY TO THE CONFLICT

The session of May 13 revealed the impossibility of collaboration between this Duma and the government. The Duma lasted another two months, but it could not recover from the blow which it dealt itself that day.

The problem, of course, remained the same: the peaceful transition from an autocratic Russia based on a system of legal classes to a constitutional monarchy. If this task were impossible to realize, two alternatives remained: restoration of autocracy or revolution with its consequences. The latter occurred eleven years later. But during these years efforts to solve this problem continued, involving different combinations of the same forces: the old imperial authority that now retreated, now advanced; the revolutionary parties that did not spare their ammunition: and liberal society that continued to vacillate between the government and revolution. However, the opportunity for agreement never again appeared under such favorable circumstances as in the First Duma.

Never again was the tsar so ready to make concessions. His personality was more complex than it appeared to those who were jealous of him and hated his memory, but I am merely undertaking consideration of his actions, not the judgment of his personality. At the opening of the Duma, he met it half-way in every respect. He personally greeted the élite elected to the Duma, did not mention his lawful title, "Autocrat," promised to safeguard the Fundamental Laws, and asked the Duma to work with him for the rebirth of the morality of the Russian land. The tsar's desire to bring about normal relations with the Duma did not vanish after the address, nor even after the Duma's conflict with the government. Even then the tsar made concessions beyond all expectations, and discussions about the formation of a ministry from the Duma show that he still had faith in the maturity of Russian Society. The Duma itself brought about its dissolution. But after the dissolution the tsar's attitude toward liberalism changed. This was not because his fear of revolution--with which our leaders tried to justify their former tactics-- disappeared, but because he became disappointed in the loyalty of

114

liberalism. Could it have been otherwise? When the very people who
were negotiating for Duma participation in the ministry, including
the chairman of the Duma, could sign the Viborg Manifesto, such an
action contradicted all their former declarations, as much as the
seizure of Czechoslovakia and Albania contradicted the declarations
of Hitler and Mussolini at the Munich meeting. The tsar could no
longer believe in the loyalty of liberalism. Stolypin remarked once,
"In politics there is no revenge, but there are consequences"; this
proved to be true when others tried to set right the work ruined by
the Duma.

But there was another consequence of the failure of the first
attempt. The task of bringing together the government and liberal
society fell into less competent hands. No matter how great the
errors of the Cadets were, they undoubtedly were a liberal party and
wanted to introduce necessary reforms. But their tactics pushed to the
Right the government as well as a considerable portion of liberal society. This gave rise to a complex attitude called "Cadethood", as a
result of which the former Octobrist party came to the forefront, and
was ruined. The purely reactionary forces that joined it freely only
in order to fight the Cadets proved more harmful than the revolutionary ties of the Cadets. The position of Guchkov, for on his shoulders lay the mission neglected by the Cadets, was at the same time
made more difficult, because of both the tsar's loss of confidence in
liberal society and the decline of liberalism in his own party. This
was another consequence of the failure of the first attempt.

There was still a third consequence. On the day of the opening
of the Duma, the enemies of the constitution had to go into hiding,
for to attack the Duma was the equivalent of assaulting the tsar. But
when the Duma adopted its provocative address, the really reactionary
elements raised their heads. Their mode of attack was patterned
after recent practice. As in 1904, when a speech and banquet campaign against the autocracy began across the country, so in 1906 a
campaign of telegrams was started against the Duma. It was well
organized, supported in the highest circles, and had promoters
among local and central authorities. Before long these telegrams
addressed to the tsar began to appear in print in the Government
Gazette. A loyal stand by the Duma in the early days would have
made such a campaign impossible, for it would have proved to be
directed against the lawful order. However, when the Duma itself
did not recognize this order, the telegrams took on a different character; they defended law and order against a revolutionary threat.
The constitutionalists in the government found it more difficult to
oppose them and the tsar sympathized with them, at first in secret
and later openly. Politically the tsar's attitude was a mistake, but
psychologically it was quite easy to understand. When there is a
threat from without, supporters are not generally pushed aside.

The resurgence of purely reactionary forces was one of the consequences of the tactics of liberalism.

Of course, this was revealed only later, and the Duma could
not be blamed for failing to foresee it. And yet, why did its leaders
celebrate a victory? This optical illusion was characteristic of our
politicians, who were so isolated from the realities of life that they
judged them in their own fashion. What seemed a success in their
own narrow circle they considered a joyful event for the whole country. Besides, the Cadets were so familiar with the life and customs
of politically advanced countries that they considered the external
aspect of parliamentary régimes as the most important. "The
struggle" between the opposition and the government, the seizure of
ministerial portfolios, the defeat of cabinets, authoritative parliaments that control the administration, party supremacy, the role of
the press--in a word, that distorted atmosphere which is the cause
of the contemporary crisis of democracy--was in their eyes the sign
of healthy political life. They tried to introduce these practices and
their Western terminology in Russia. This was the explanation of
their tactics, but it was not understood by the ordinary citizens. The
country had not yet attained the constitutional stage of development,
nor were the rank and file ready for a legal order. The leaders
were too astute and too learned for Russia. They sought the rebirth
of Russia through parliamentary battles and successes and did not
want to consider the effect of these successes on the country. This
explains their delight at the first steps of their Duma. On May 30
Miliukov described the victories of the first month as follows:

> What has remained of the self-assurance and prestige
> of the government after the first month? The very first
> blow, seemingly so cunningly devised by the experts of
> petty etiquette, only disturbed their own balance and
> struck an empty spot. What became of their skill in na-
> tional administration and their experience? What has
> been the world's reaction to the government's program?
> The shallowness of their wisdom was revealed at the
> first breath of parliamentary and press criticism, and
> finally the nonconfidence vote crushed the ministry with
> the ponderous weight of public condemnation of 130
> million people. Only a month had passed, and the min-
> istry lies vanquished and cannot rise; and take note, this
> ministry has not had a chance to commit any crimes, but
> it is weighed down by its own past crimes and those of
> others....,
>
> Now everyone, without exception, is amazed by the
> contrast between the government's lack of plans and the
> constructiveness of the Duma's plan, and all emphatically

demand, as does the Duma, the resignation of the ministry which is discredited before the country and is absolutely devoid of any governing ability....

If, indeed, the Duma's vote defeated the ministry and it lay
vanquished and unable to rise, a victory celebration was appropriate. But how far was such a picture from reality! Evidently the
party's press and the party's delight blinded no less than the praise
of courtiers and led to a misunderstanding of the situation. For during those very days of brilliant victory over the government, the
vanquished and powerless authority was deciding the question of immediate dissolution of the Duma. The always exact Count Kokovtsev[1]
reveals what was going on in the camp of the vanquished at that time.
There was not a single person who had not reached the conclusion
that further collaboration with such a Duma was impossible. No one
doubted, either, that the dissolution could be carried out without any
trouble, that the authorities had sufficient strength to do this, and
that the Duma's threat of a popular uprising was bluff and delusion.
But the supporters of the constitution did not want to hasten
the dissolution. The tsar himself showed more penetrating insight
than some leading members of society. The memoirs of Kryzhanovski
recall a curious scene. Witte once tried to convince the tsar that the
Duma would become his bulwark, but the latter answered in a tone
filled with regret:

> Do not tell me this, Sergei Iulievich. I understand per-
> fectly that I am creating an enemy, not an ally, but I
> console myself with the thought that I may nurture a
> national force which will prove useful in securing for
> Russia, in the future, a path of peaceful development,
> without marked destruction of those foundations on which
> it has rested for so long.

If this reminiscence is correct, and if the words of the tsar were
sincerely meant, it shows that his understanding of the situation was
superior to our society's, which tried to assure the tsar that popular
representation would immediately pacify Russia. The tsar understood
that this could not be accomplished quickly and not without a lengthy
struggle. The first two weeks showed him that, even if a constitution was a good thing for Russia, the First Duma unfortunately did
not want pacification, and its leaders did not make the attainment of
tranquillity their goal.
But the supporters of the constitution in the camp of the government, disregarding all this, correctly considered that the main
effort had not yet been made. Agreement between the government
and the Duma could take place only on the basis of active constitu-

tional work, and that was not yet started. Not a single law had yet
been introduced by the government. There was the Cadet agrarian
legislative project, but its discussion could not begin for a month.
Of necessity, the first days of the Duma's activity were devoted to
lofty matters: the address, and those ideological disputes in which
there could be no agreement and where agreement was not necessary
for practical purposes. Only active work could sober the Duma and
open its eyes, and supporters of the constitution claimed that this
opportunity should be given the Duma before its dissolution. This
explains why there was no decisive reaction to the Duma's aggressive
formula of transition.

There was another reason for this. If liberalism was mistaken
in its confidence that it won a victory, the government, too, undoubtedly fumbled badly that day. It did not appear at its best and was unable to reply to the unjust attacks leveled against it. It is no wonder
that the ministry found no defenders in the Duma that day. When
Count Heiden, who made it his specialty to debunk the Duma's excesses, stepped to the tribune, he, too, disassociated himself from
this ministry. His unexpected announcement, made at the end of the
session, was met with thunderous applause. It is difficult to shake
off the impression that it was provoked not so much by the declaration as by the conduct of the ministry at the session. The dissolution of the Duma at this moment, while the same government remained in office, might be interpreted incorrectly, and the perspective
distorted. It was better to wait for a more opportune time, and until
then try to work with the Duma.

There was no ulterior motive in the decision to attempt to work
with the Duma. The government permitted the Second Duma "to rot
at the root," as the saying goes, and would have been glad to find an
excuse for its dissolution without having to resort to the unworthy
provocation of a plot. However, there was nothing like this in its
attitude to the First Duma. The government earnestly hoped that
the Duma would stop playing at revolution and maintained throughout
the same stand that it took the first day, April 27.

Thus, in spite of its mistakes, the Duma received another
chance and was given an opportunity to rectify its mistakes, but it
was not in a position to take advantage of this opportunity. It would
have been easy for the Duma to start its work from the very first
days of its existence. Many legislative proposals were ready for its
consideration. Circumventing the monthly deadline with the government's consent posed no difficulty; for, even without the government's
consent, it was circumvented in the agrarian legislative measure,
and the government, by its participation in the discussions, gave its
sanction to such action. But after the declarations that the Duma
made at the session of May 13, collaboration with this government
suggested retreat and was impossible for the Duma. Its position

after the skirmish was worse than the government's. As the government did not start the conflict, it could continue working with the Duma without loss of face and regard the vote of May 13 calmly, as older people regard a prank of playful schoolboys.

But the Duma could not regard the matter in this light, for it had demanded the resignation of the ministry. In the session of May 23, following the speeches of Stishinski and Gurko in connection with the agrarian bill, deputy Onipko protested the chairman's action in permitting them to speak, as follows: "Since the State Duma expressed nonconfidence in the ministry and the desire that it should resign immediately, I consider that the Duma should regard the representatives of the ministry as outsiders." His opinion was not clearly expressed and formally it was even unlawful. But this Duma which did not recognize the constitution without parliamentarianism, which considered it had the right to demand the removal of the ministry, could not work with the same ministry, after May 13, without making its previous vote a matter of ridicule. It was necessary either to insist on it, end relations with the ministry, and compel dissolution, or, of necessity, to suffer humiliation. This was the price the Duma had to pay for the thoughtless tactics of the first few weeks.

But the chief obstacle to the Duma's new attempts at work lay in the very composition of the Duma's majority, the so-called "opposition bloc."

The legislative work in the Duma might have been limited to the activity of the Cadets. Though they rejected organic work as a matter of tactics, they still prepared for it and had a number of bills ready for presentation to the Duma. However, their legislation proved to have as pathetic an ignorance of life as their attitude to the constitution: it was fortunate that the Second Chamber existed to make them face the facts. Collaboration of the Duma with the traditional authority was necessary to carry out these reforms.

Such a policy would inevitably have resulted in a clash between the Cadets and the Trudoviki, and the common front of the opposition would have fallen apart. The Trudoviki did not want to work actively in the Duma and used it only to heighten the revolutionary mood. They maintained the same tactics towards the Cadets as the Cadets did toward the government. Everything was always too little for them. The Cadet legislative projects regarding the press and assembly were declared inadequate, and when the Cadet measure on Assemblies was sent to a commission, the Trudoviki voted against its being sent because it was completely worthless.

They riddled the Cadet legislative projects with corrections which contradicted the constitution, but it was difficult for the Cadets to vote against them. The Trudoviki also made a series of proposals, such as the adoption of a legislative measure regarding the death

penalty without waiting for the constitutional one-month deadline;
the establishment of a committee that would take executive authority
into its own hands; and the creation of local committees, elected according to "the four-tail," for the preparation and implementation
of future land reform.

From their point of view, the policy of the Trudoviki was correct; a revolutionary situation would be created. But the Cadets
opposed them at every step and defended the constitution. So the
Trudoviki subjected them to insults and accused them of treason, of
betraying the interests of the people, and of parliamentary cretinism.
A fundamental split was revealed between the two groups, the water-
shed between constitutional and revolutionary tactics. Had the Cadets taken their new position from the first, not only could there
have been no talk of betrayal, but those first false steps, which now
had to be corrected, would not have been taken. But the Cadets were
anxious to proclaim the "unity of the entire opposition," and for the
sake of this they adopted, on May 13, the sharp Trudovik tone. Now,
after having taken this stand, they had to contradict themselves and
retreat before its consequences. Of course, they changed this into
a virtue, as they had done on other occasions. Miliukov noted in
Speech on May 30 that

> The Cadets differ from the extreme Left, and at the same
> time they oppose the government. Their strength grows
> in proportion to the clarification of their independent
> political role. Of course, this strength lies solely in
> their moral authority and in the idea of organized strug-
> gle by parliamentary means, which they are making a
> reality.

But it was not so easy to break a pact once concluded. The
statement by Miliukov about emancipation from the extreme left at
once aroused the suspicion of the Trudoviki. Zhilkin regarded it as
a betrayal. I do not have his article, but on June 3 Miliukov replied
as follows:

> Citizen Zhilkin supposes that in speaking of our dif-
> ferences from the extreme left parties we betray our
> past and that formerly we spoke in a different manner.
> We said that as long as the chief enemy of the people is
> unconquered and not crushed, all opposition forces must
> unite into a common, threatening, indestructible force.
> We did say that formerly, and we repeat it now, and
> will continue to repeat in in the future. Does this mean

that we call for unity on the basis of tactics which forget
the chief enemy, or even worse, which make ourselves the
chief enemy....?

Citizen Zhilkin is bitterly sarcastic about our fond
hope for respect, about the Trepov and Goremykin com-
pany, and accuses us of raising our eyes above. We
have hardly deserved these insinuations and this tone.

But life took its toll. No matter how the Cadets tried to convince everyone that they were continuing their former policy, that it
had not changed, this was only a literary front. Thanks to their first
false step, they now had to hide the truth, pretend to be insulted, and
carry on negotiations without the knowledge of their allies.

Be that as it may, the Duma, that is the Cadets, were given
another chance to end ideological conflicts with the government and
attempt to work with it in the legislative field where they could prove
their superiority and their worth. Of all spheres of the Duma's activity this was the most suitable one. We shall see what use the Cadets made of this opportunity.

Chapter Nine

THE CHARACTER OF THE LEGISLATION

OF THE DUMA

As we know, the Duma's legislative work produced very meagre results. Only one government measure, regarding assistance in the distribution of food, was specifically examined by two committees, amended, brought before the Duma, and in spite of government objections to the amendments, adopted by the Duma in plenary session. The measure was then approved by the Imperial Council and confirmed by the tsar. It might be appropriate to mention that this episode indicates that the Duma was then far from being completely powerless, in spite of its complaints to this effect, and was not greatly troubled by the Imperial Council.

However, this was the only law carried to its completion. Also passed, by the Duma alone, was the declaratory and technically useless law regarding the death penalty. Apart from these, the Duma did not finish any business in seventy-three days of activity. There were several important reasons for this. As a matter of principle, the Duma did not want to engage in minor legislative matters, and when bills about "orange-groves" and "laundries" were introduced in the Duma, it was deeply offended. Yet major legislative projects require careful study and take up much time in an inexperienced institution like the Duma. But the main reason for the delay lay elsewhere.

The government brought before the Duma a number of bills, not only of great practical importance but also desirable from the Duma's point of view: bills dealing with local courts, extension of peasant landownership, peasant allotments, etc. The Duma could approve, amend, or reject them, but it preferred to disregard them altogether, without even turning them over to committees for examination. Only later, when two permanent committees, budget and finance, were established by decree, did the Duma begin to send the appropriate government bills to these committees; the rest remained neglected, resulting in obstruction of government activity.

I remember how Witte complained that the authors of the constitution did not foresee this abuse and did not set a definite time limit during which the Duma would be compelled to study a bill,

which would otherwise become law. Our constitution was not the
only one that did not foresee the possibility of legislative obstruction.
The slowness of parliamentary legislative work is a universal phenomenon, for which the West has sought special solution in the form of
decrets-loi (Orders in Council). With a little strain, our Article
87 could have been extended to cover such cases, but though it did
not endanger the rights of the Duma, the deputies indignantly protested against its use as a breach of their privileges.

However, the problem in the First Duma was not the natural,
temporary slowness of parliamentary work, but rather the delay
caused by the Duma's "inadmissible tactics." The Duma systematically held back government projects, though its main duty was to
examine them. In other countries the legislative initiative of parliament is of secondary importance, but that was not so with us. When
it was composing the address, the Duma already regarded itself as
the government and, later on, would not examine any projects but its
own. The ministry did not have its confidence, and the Duma refused
to work with it.

Because of this, the Cadets monopolized the legislative function
of the Duma, confining themselves to examination of their own bills.
It would seem that at least this could have been done quickly. The
Cadet measures had been prepared long in advance; they had first-
class politicians and lawyers in their midst; and the Duma was supposed to have unanimity of opinion. Legislative work could proceed
without obstacles. Nevertheless, nothing came from the committees'
work for seventy-three days. In order to understand this, we must
examine the conditions that the Duma stipulated for its work.

As with everything else, the Cadets blamed the government for
their own delay, claiming that the government intentionally created
a constitution that prevented the Duma from showing its capabilities.
Articles 55-57 of the Duma Statute dealing with the Duma's initiative
were, in their opinion, an artificial drag. This trite accusation was
tested in practice, since amendment of the articles was not prohibited.
On May 23 the Duma introduced a special measure for this purpose,
clear evidence of its objective. It went even further: without waiting
for the bill to become law, the Duma began, rather obviously, to use
its new rules of procedure. No one could prevent this except the
chairman, but he obeyed the Cadets and did not hinder them. Thus
an attempt was made at establishing the Duma's initiative. Let us
examine its consequences as an illustration of the Cadets' skill.

Those who compiled the Fundamental Laws were wise men
who understood that legislative work is not a simple matter. They
had no intention of interfering with the Duma's initiative, but merely
tried to make its work easier. A declaration by thirty members was
sufficient for initiating legislation, but since they could not be ex-

pected to draft the law, the constitution stated that the "basic proposals"* of the law were all that was required. The initiators should confine themselves to this simpler task and convey their "basic proposals" to the ministers concerned. If, after a month's waiting period, the Duma considered these proposals desirable, the text of the law would be drawn up by the ministry and brought before the Duma for final approval.

In case the government failed to share the views of the Duma as to the desirability of the "basic proposals," the constitution provided a safeguard for the Duma's initiative by permitting it to draft the law by itself, putting the matter in the hands of a special committee. Article 40 of the Duma Statute provided that the Duma could obtain any information and help it needed for this task from the government.

This was the pattern of work established in the Duma committee in which a new legislative measure was being drafted. The drafting of a law is, of course, not the work of a committee. As a group they can examine, but not draft. Still, the task of such a committee was facilitated because, in the first place, the measure had already been initiated; and second, because the Duma tentatively accepted the "basic proposals" from which the committee was not supposed to deviate. Thus the Duma could count on government support for its initiative in legislative work, if the government agreed with the Duma, and it had the right to draft and pass a law even if the government rejected it.

Certainly the Duma should have appreciated such a procedure, which made its work easier. It was helpful to initiators of legislation from whom only "basic proposals" were required; and it assisted committees of the Duma that were not burdened with the task of drafting a law without any guidance. What better basis could there be for profitable cooperation between the Duma and the government that still preserved the independence of both? Preliminary debate on the "basic proposals" was open to the Duma and public opinion, and could provide the basis for understanding and agreement.

This procedure proved so convenient that it stood the test of experience and was not tampered with following the period of the First Duma. There was some suspicion that the government might abuse it, by agreeing to draft a measure without doing so, by replying with obstruction to the Duma's obstruction tactics; but there was never any evidence of this, and these suspicions proved unwarranted.

Nevertheless, the Duma was dissatisfied with this procedure. It would not admit that it needed the help of "rotten bureaucracy." So the Cadets introduced a measure to change Articles 55-57. Vinaver

----

* The principles underlying the measure, which were to be embodied in a bill. [M. B.]

spoke in support of it in these words:

> The proposals made at the time of the establishment of the
> Duma no longer conform to the conditions under which
> the Duma is working now. I am convinced that our mea-
> sure will receive the support of the whole Duma, which
> is anxious to get on with its work without needless waste
> of time. The earlier measure was adapted to the con-
> ception of the Duma as a helpless, speechless infant. A
> month's experience has shown that we can draft legisla-
> tion and discuss it intelligently. The Duma has proved
> to be a mature child, not an infant, able to speak dis-
> tinctly, and even able to show its teeth.

As was to be expected, the Duma applauded vigorously.

How did the Duma intend to speed up legislative procedure? In
the first place, the monthly time limit for the minister's reply was
replaced by a weekly one. Of course, it was not the monthly limit
that delayed the Duma, since it spent more than a month on speeches
about "direction"* of legislation. With an abundance of work to be
done and the slowness of the Duma, the monthly time limit passed
unnoticed. The speed-up consisted of doing away with the system of
double discussion--the consideration of the desirability of the basic
proposals, and then the judgment of the completed bill. The initiators claimed that the preliminary discussion about the desirability
of the basic proposals was unnecessary, so they proposed that the
completed bill be presented to the Duma rather than the "basic proposals."

This procedure was immediately put into practice, and we had
an opportunity to judge the technical maturity of the Duma, its attempt
to improve on the constitution, and its ability to speed up the work.

Let us examine, for example, the first in order and importance:
the agrarian bill. Cadet specialists worked on it for two years, and
it was ready even before the convocation of the Duma. All that remained to be done now was to introduce it which the Cadets did on
May 8 in the first session following the address of the Duma. The

----

* The practice of "debates on direction" was introduced by the Cadets in the first days of the Duma's activity. The Cadets supposedly
saved the Duma from the inaction to which the government condemned
it, in order to compromise it in the eyes of the impatient people. No
vote was taken; it was merely the preliminary exchange of opinion and
clarification of the essential points of a project, to serve as a guide
to the committee that would receive completed bills with instructions
to examine them. In reality, the Duma discussed the law itself.
[M. B.]

126

whole Cadet press rapturously acclaimed this as evidence of Cadet preparedness for their task.

Had the Cadets followed the prescribed, lawful way, they would
have formulated and introduced only the "basic proposals" of this
measure, and after a month's wait, deliberation and voting on the
desirability of these proposals would have taken place, with the ministry's participation. If the government refused to draft the bill after
the Duma approved the "basic proposals," the Duma could do so itself, entrusting the work to a special committee. Such a committee
would not have had to start its work blindly, since it would have before it the proposals approved by the Duma's plenary session.

Even "basic proposals" might be so complex or controversial
that the Duma would not want to discuss them in a general meeting,
without preliminary examination by a committee. Creation of such
a committee was the Duma's prerogative, and following the report
of this committee, the vote on the desirability of the "basic proposals"
would have taken place. By this time the constitutional monthly time
limit would be over. This procedure became the normal course to
follow in subsequent Dumas.

But the Cadets did not want to follow the constitutional path of
action. In accordance with their decision to present to the Duma
completed bills rather than "basic proposals," they introduced their
agrarian measure. However, instead of the complete agrarian measure, which was beyond their competence, they really introduced
only the "basic proposals." In order to dispense with their approval
by the Duma, and to avoid the ministry's cooperation in drafting the
bill, they entrusted the drafting to a committee of the Duma. Their
measure concluded with these words: "We propose the election of
a committee of thirty-three which would elaborate and introduce to
the Duma a bill dealing with the agrarian problem, and we request
that all available memoranda be turned over to this committee, 'as
material.' "*

Could anything more cumbersome have been intentionally devised? Even if we disregard the fact that this was a violation of the
Duma Statute, it meant that legislative initiative was reduced to simply furnishing "material." Above all, what was the committee to
do? It did not have before it "basic proposals" approved by the Duma and so had no guidance in drafting the law from the variety of
material with which it was provided. Two weeks later the committee
received more "material" representing a Trudoviki legislative project, and its membership was increased to ninety-six. On June 6

----

*"Raw material" or "material": This referred to information
sent to committees without being approved or even discussed by the
Duma. [M. B.]

still another bill was introduced in the Duma, as "material, " and
by this time the Cadets were in despair: it was impossible to work
under such a system. Furthermore, the last proposal brought before the Duma began with the statement that "all private ownership
of land within the boundaries of the Russian Empire is abolished. "
This was such an extraordinary demand that the Duma could not
agree to turn it over to the committee. Yet this was inconsistent,
and Zhilkin, quite correctly, asked whether handing over the first
two measures to the committee in any way signified their approval,
since the Duma did not discuss them at all. Why, then, make an exception of this legislative project? Still, the Cadets rejected it even
as "material" and did not turn it over to the committee, which was
unimportant, for its supporters in the committee would bring it up
themselves in the course of their work.

Is it any wonder that when an inquiry was made on June 26 as
to the progress made by the agrarian committee, its chairman had
to report that "the committee had examined the categories of lands
which were to be transferred to the working population, but beyond
that it could not give any positive information"?

Naturally, under such a system, everything ended up in committees. Handing matters over to committees absolved the Duma
and the initiators of the project from all work and responsibility, and
provided the classic "first class funeral, " for what could be expected from the collective work of a committee ordered to invent
some legislative project?

The system might have worked had the committees been small
and consisted of experts and technicians, but since their work was
based on "raw material, " neither approved nor discussed by the
Duma, each committee, of necessity, had to be a cross-section of
the Duma, representing all shades of opinion found there. Thus the
agrarian committee consisted of ninety-six members, too large to
do any work and yet too small to replace the Duma. Our society,
supposedly better informed than bureaucracy on prerequisites for
collective work, as if on purpose chose the course that prevented
success.

Simultaneously with the imposition of law drafting on committees,
the Cadets introduced the practice of "debates on direction, " which
was a record waste of time. Turning a matter over to a committee
either signified the Duma's acceptance of the "basic proposals" of
the bill, in which case they had to be discussed and voted on,[1] or it
did not signify acceptance and the bill was sent to the committee for
careful and complete examination, in which case no arguments about
direction were necessary. Business procedure in the Duma differs
from a meeting because idle talk is not permitted there; each discussion must be based on a definite proposal that is to be voted on.

But this Duma acted differently. Under the pretence of "debates on direction," it discussed the actual law, though no vote ended the discussion; thus the sessions were transformed into meetings. After a few days, the deputies themselves realized this and took steps to oppose such a procedure. The hall emptied during each debate, and speakers who had signed up to speak were entreated not to participate; those who agreed were warmly applauded. Such was the sorry result of Cadet planning and organization.

This ridiculous procedure was later justified by the excuse that the Cadets invented "debates on direction" to save the Duma. For a few days the plenum of the Duma had nothing to do, and the Cadets suspected the government of stifling the Duma by condemning it to inaction, and of compromising it in the eyes of the impatient population. From this danger, the Cadets supposedly saved the Duma. Vinaver called these debates "an act of self-defense in the struggle between the newly-born yet active institution and the hopelessly stupid and evil government." Even if this were the case, surely the Cadets could see that a few days of inactivity would not be as compromising as the meaningless debates! In this case, the cure was worse than the disease--hardly a credit to the physician's skill. One more appropriate observation: the Cadets introduced this scheme (debates on direction) surreptitiously, like conspirators. Vinaver tells us in his Conflicts how this happened:

> In the very first session in which we decided to implement the plan intended to end the Duma's inaction and provide it with important legislative work, contrary to government intentions, our chairman and the leaders of the Party of Popular Freedom, who devised the plan, had to speak repeatedly to straighten the careening wagon, lurching now to the right, now to the left. Our position was undoubtedly precarious, and the slightest miscalculation could topple the whole structure; we had to cover a certain distance as quickly as possible, to establish a precedent. I remember how we (Novgorodtsev, Nabokov, Petrazhitski and I), followed with bated breath the innocently questionning remarks of Count Heiden, Aladin, Kuzmin-Karavaev and the nonparty peasant Zhukovski, each seeming to threaten our slender skiff. Nervously we jumped on the podium to try to placate them whenever possible, to stop further pressure, and how we sighed with relief when both the Duma and Count Heiden admitted that "it is always permissible to talk about and clarify the essential points of a project."

However, the results of this ruse were not particularly gratifying. Most surprising was the part played by the chairman, who could
not fail to understand that Count Heiden's admission made a meeting
out of the Duma. Yet he yielded to party politicians and backed up
their decision with his prestige as chairman. While attempting to
reassure Count Heiden, he went so far as to give the following explanation (May 12): "No vote will be taken; this is only the preliminary exchange of opinions regarding election of a committee, which
I dare say will be useful to the committee." Instead of the committee
being useful to the plenum of the Duma, in speeding up its work, the
Duma exchanged opinions designed to be useful to the committee.
Muromtsev's silence would have been preferable to concealing disorder in this way.

Any experiment becomes particularly convincing when it is
successfully repeated; this was accomplished in the Duma by the Cadet bill on Assemblies. I shall not speak of its nature, except to
mention that it resulted in the most serious clash between the Cadets
and their supporters, but the procedure in effecting its passage was
curious. The bill was introduced on May 30, after the Duma discussed changing the articles of the Duma Statute dealing with the examination of new laws. Both bills were supported by the great Cadet
figures, Vinaver, Shershenevich, and others. They applied the new
rules to the bill about Assemblies, furnishing proof of the effectiveness of the new procedures.

The measure was even introduced in the new fashion, in completed form rather than as "basic proposals"; fortunately, it was
not complicated, having only twelve articles. It would have been
infinitely more difficult to introduce a proposed law all at once had
the problem been more complex, but since the initiators proved that
they were able to handle the matter, so much the better. The new
procedures were being tested in a favorable atmosphere.

Since the bill on Assemblies was introduced in completed form,
there was no longer any need for two examinations, nor for government assistance in drafting the measure. Omitting the intermediary
stages and time limits, the committee was to examine the completed
bill and present it to the Duma for its approval. The measure was
formulated as follows: "Presenting for the Duma's consideration
the proposed law on Assemblies, together with explanatory memoranda,
we request recognition of the urgency of our proposal, and election of
a committee for its examination." [2]

The bill was introduced on May 30, 1906, and the discussion
started on June 16, before the expiration of the monthly time limit.
It is interesting to note that while the Duma considered the monthly
limit too long, and a week's delay sufficient, it delayed the bill for

three weeks in "debates on direction." It is quite evident that the
Duma's complaint about the monthly limit was not in earnest. Those
who dabble in fine legal points might wonder what would have happened in case of a conflict between the Duma and the government over
this unconstitutional action of the Duma. While adopting its bill, the
Duma infringed on the government's rights by nonobservance of the
time limit, by elimination of discussion on the desirability of "basic
proposals," and by denying the government its right of drafting bills.
Yet the government would have been powerless to prevent the Duma's
actions. Whether or not a legislative measure adopted by the Duma
was approved depended on the Imperial Council and not on the government. And if the Imperial Council accepted it and presented it
to the tsar, was it likely that he would have refused to confirm it
because of the failure to observe the correct procedure? Thus the
violation of the constitution might have been sanctioned by a deliber-
ate action. However, this did not occur and common sense triumphed.
      Debates on "direction" opened on June 16. According to the
authors of the new regulations, the debates were concerned only with
the creation of the committee that would receive a completed bill
with instructions to examine it. The Duma would decide the fate of
the measure after receiving the committee's report. Thus the work
would, indeed, be speeded up.
      But matters turned out quite differently. Though the completed
bill on Assemblies rather than "basic proposals" was introduced in
the Duma, nevertheless, in the explanatory memorandum accompanying the bill, the authors considered it useful to point out the principles
underlying the measure. In other words, the "basic proposals,"
rejected by the Duma, appeared in disguise in the explanatory memorandum. When the debates began on June 16, supposedly about the
transfer of the bill to the committee, the deputies were actually
arguing about the desirability of the "basic proposals," that is, they
were back to the original step, prescribed by the constitution and
formerly rejected by the Duma. Very interesting debates, in which
the best Cadet forces participated actively, continued for three sessions, June 16-20. Kovalevski joined the Trudoviki, who considered
that the "basic principles" of the bill were so bad that they proposed
to reject it without sending it to the committee at all. This revealed
the deep gulf between the Trudoviki and the Cadets, and the bill was
saved only by the intervention of the right-wing majority on its behalf. Finally it was agreed to send the bill to the committee, thus
approving its "basic proposals." So experience made a mockery
of the Cadet speed up of procedure, and restored the Duma to the
order established by the constitution. The double examination of a
bill remained, though under a different name, with this difference:
that while in reality the deputies voted on "basic principles" of the

bill, according to form, the vote was concerned only with the transfer
of the bill to the committee. This procedure created ambiguity, leaving room for disputes.

I shall not labor the point any longer. There was now convincing evidence that those who drew up the constitution were more skillful in organizing the Duma's work than our brilliant lawyers. The
Cadets would have gained much had they attempted to implement the
constitution intelligently, instead of correcting it at the outset. It
is no wonder that the Duma had little to show for two months of work.
On May 23, when Vinaver defended the measure changing legislative
procedure, he made a pun about the Duma no longer being an infant,
and showing its teeth. There was bitter truth in it: the Duma could
not work as yet, but it tried "to show its teeth" on every occasion.

Chapter Ten

THE CHIEF LEGISLATIVE PROJECTS

OF THE DUMA

However characteristic of Cadet faults the legislative procedure that they wanted to introduce may have been, it was less important than the nature of their legislative measures. These might have revealed the Cadets' political understanding. Miliukov wrote about them on May 30 as follows: "Everyone without exception is amazed by the lack of planning on the part of the government and the orderly plans of the Duma."

The task before them was clear and definite. In some periods of history everything converges on one main reform; the rest is tacked on. Thus in the 'sixties there was a struggle for "liberation" in the 1900's--for a constitution. After the "liberation" the decadent bureaucracy was able to rebuild Russian life on the basis of new principles and created the epoch of "great reforms." After the proclamation of the constitution, a similar rebuilding should have taken place through the collaboration of liberal society with the government. Liberalism won certain rights and was no longer limited to giving advice from the sidelines, or occupying itself with irresponsible criticism, as it had to do previously. It could propose and pass definite legislation and introduce organic reforms, concerning all segments of national life, intended to bring about the "restoration of the morality of the Russian land." This could not be done all at once, but as this lengthy work continued, the Duma could, without waiting for its completion, remove some particular evil from which the people undoubtedly suffered.

Let us take an example from an earlier period. On the accession of Nicholas II, in the period of "hopes," Russian society with one voice, the Imperial Council included, petitioned for the abolition of corporal punishment of peasants. The tsar could permit this, even while continuing to consider as nonsense the zemstvo dreams of participation in the central administration of the country. The one did not exclude the other. The Duma correctly followed the same course, when, in addition to outlining the general plan of complex reforms, it wished to abolish the death penalty by extraordinary

132

procedure. There were many such individual and simple but very
tangible reforms. The Duma had to follow both courses consciously,
the course of organic reorganization and the path of immediate removal of a particularly glaring evil. Let us see how it handled both
these tasks.

In the opinion of the Duma, the reorganization plan was outlined
in its address. I have already pointed out that, unfortunately, this
was not a practical plan; it resembled a journalistic article in which
everything is mixed up. But the Cadet party also prepared for real
legislative work. Its specialists had pored over various legislative
projects long before the opening of the Duma. These measures were
elaborated in party committees and were discussed by party congresses,
and some of them were brought forward for the Duma's consideration
at its opening. On May 8 the agrarian law was introduced, and on May
15 the law for "equality of rights." This speedy presentation was regarded as a triumph for the Cadets who thus proved greatly superior
to the government with its ridiculous "orange grove" and "laundry"
projects. But let us see how the Cadets approached these problems.

First let us consider the major problem of "equality of rights."
Who could question the necessity of this reform? It was not yet fifty
years since the abolition of serfdom, when some Russian citizens
sold others. Inequality still remained in the customs and character
of national life and these were supported by the existing state system,
which could not have been maintained without peasant subordination.
The Cadets, who had been preoccupied with this question for several
years, could introduce in the Duma a series of concrete proposals
that would gradually rebuild the life of the country.

They did introduce such a law, but on closer examination one
would find it rather perplexing. Could such legislation have been in
earnest? The Cadets understood very well that it was not a question
of writing some one law. The title of the legislative measure read:
"Basic Proposals for Laws on Social Equality." The text began with
the words: "We propose that the State Duma undertake the elaboration of a series of legislative measures...." The initiators added
that the "elimination of inequality by means of a single legislative act
appears impossible..." and proposed "to divide the legislative work
intended to establish social equality in the country into four categories
of laws."

I shall not insist that this was formally incorrect and contradicted
Article 55 of the Duma Statute. But what sense was there in introducing
a legislative proposal if it had to lead to the elaboration of four categories of new laws? Those laws might be unrelated and the attitude toward them would vary. Supporters of the Jewish equality of rights
would not necessarily need to support equality of rights for women.
What was there in common between them? To whose advantage was it

to lump these problems together? The classic method of obstruction is well known--to prevent adoption of a law it is made intentionally complicated and amended; it is then found to be inadequate and consequently unacceptable. This is a cunning procedure and it often attains its goal. But why did the Duma do all this?

Besides, how could the committees cope with such an indefinite, vast, and it may be added, incomprehensible task? The initiators based all categories of the future new laws on one thesis: all citizens of both sexes are equal before the law. This was not by any means a general statement of a law, but a declaration, or more simply, a phrase. It either signified nothing or suggested more than it wished to do. It was a mere platitude, if it meant only that no one can be above the law, that laws are binding on all. If, however, this was a way of saying that, supposedly, all citizens are subject to the same laws, it was not true. In the naive eighteenth century this idea could be proclaimed in the Declaration of Rights, but in the twentieth century such an absolute statement was inaccurate. Surely we would not deny the effectiveness of social legislation that defends some classes of people from others, special laws for the protection of women and children, and many others? To create a committee and entrust it with the elaboration of four groups of laws on such a basis was literary, not legislative, work.

The initiators of the law should have taken the trouble to think things through and to do a little preparatory work. They should have pointed out concrete evidences of the inequality that they criticized and the principles guiding their proposals to eliminate it. These had to be drawn from experience and from Russian legislation. The Cadet specialists had enough time for this, and had they brought before the Duma the results of such work, it would have been a significant contribution, on their part, to legislative initiative. As it was, however, their proposals could only serve as material for magazine articles or resolutions at meetings. They merely hindered the legislative work of the Duma.

As a result of such initiative, a large, multiparty committee was created and instructed to do the work that the initiators were unable to accomplish. Such a system of legislation meant an off-hand attitude toward the work of others. Instructions such as ''to devise a law'' were formerly given by superiors to their subordinates. But in the bureaucratic world the subordinates were specialists. In the Duma they were inexperienced and subordinate to no one, and the committees to which the initiators gave such instructions inevitably bogged down. Meanwhile, the initiators reserved for themselves the public interest, in both the general meetings and debates on direction; they made lofty speeches on questions that were undisputed, in view of the composition of the Duma. This came to be called legislative initiative, simplifying but completely distorting earnest legislative procedure.

In the debates on direction concerning the law on equality on
June 5, 6, and 8, Count Heiden pointed out all these shortcomings in
a thorough and business like manner. This brought all the Cadet
lawyers to their feet with vehement retorts. Petrunkevich, Kokoshkin, Rodichev, Vinaver, and lesser deities accused him of contradictions, pettiness, inconsistency, obstruction, inability to understand
the ideal heights of their law, and of course, of lack of sympathy for
equality. It was an explosive party controversy. Why was the discussion so heated when the question was purely technical, one concerning a more correct and speedy way to carry out the reforms whose
meaning was not disputed? It is impossible to understand this if we
do not admit the sad truth that the Cadets had not elaborated any legislative measures about equality. If their legislative procedure were
considered unacceptable, it would soon become clear that the highly
praised, orderly program and the preparedness of the Cadets were
pure bluff; that at the party's disposal there also were either liberal
"orange groves" and "laundries," or "Declarations of Rights" that
were 125 years too late. The Cadets could not be blamed for this,
for it was the job of the government to prepare legislative projects,
but they should not have contrasted their preparedness with the want
of talent of the corrupt bureaucracy, since conclusions were drawn
as a result of this contrast.

The legislative measure on "equality" demonstrated the bar-
renness of the Cadet legislative equipment. It was easier, of course,
instead of working on a positive law, to declare a general principle
and instruct a committee to transform it into a whole series of new
laws, and then claim that the measure on equality had been prepared
earlier. Why was this done? The Duma did not evade work, but it was
even more fond of effects and sonorous phrases, even if the results of
the work suffered. The ideal of the leaders of the Duma was not a
working parliament, toiling on positive legislation, but an "Assemblée
Nationale," on the model of 1789, hurling "principles" into the world.
But that National Assembly had the historic mission of achieving revolution, not reorganizing a nation peacefully.

To what extent Cadet specialists proved unprepared for practical
legislation can be judged from the very same measure on equality, in
so far as it concerned the peasant problem. Equalization of peasant
rights to bring them in line with other classes had long been a platitude in the liberal program. But the position of the peasants in Russia was so singular, and yet so interwoven with all of the country's
past, that the inspiration of the West and America was not enough for
the solution of the problem. It was necessary to study the subject with
the utmost care. And if the Duma was wrong when it tried to find a
common solution for quite different problems, it was no less wrong
when it broke up the basically interlinked peasant problem.

More than once, in my presence, did Witte bitterly reproach
the First Duma for not taking an interest in the peasant question. Such

a reproach seemed blasphemy, for the Cadets took pride in the fact
that they were the first to raise the issue in earnest. The reproach
was indeed unjust, for the Cadets earnestly desired a solution. But
in spite of their love of the people, they not only were unable to cope
with the peasant question, but they did not even master its peculiarities. They saw in it only an aspect of the question of equality, along
with the feminist, national, and other questions. But this was not the
crux of the matter, since all aspects of the peasant problem in Russia
were closely linked with one another. Witte understood the complexity
of the problem better than the Duma; and all measures bearing the imprint of his hand always raised the general peasant problem, notably
the Special Conference on Agricultural Industry and the ukase of
December 12, 1904. Traces of this point of view also appeared in
the declaration of May 13, which he prepared, though it had already
been read by another. But the Cadet legislative measure on equality
did not take any notice of this and separated the peasant problem artificially into various compartments.

Social differences among the peasants in Russia were a most
glaring phenomenon because they affected the majority of the population. But the peculiarity of these differences lay in the fact that
peasant privilege stemmed partly from the basis of their inequality,
the exclusive right of peasants to allotment land. This peculiarity
was adopted in the interests of the peasants. In order to safeguard
the newly liberated peasant communities from losing allotment land
through sale and individual peasants from landlessness, allotment
land was declared inalienable, and belonging not to individuals but
to the whole peasant community. This resulted in the creation of a
peculiar class isolated from the rest of society, though the arrangement was beneficial in its time. However, it had other aspects: it
brought about the isolation of the peasant class, created special conditions for entering and leaving it, formed a tie between allotment
land and social hierarchy, and placed communal land ownership outside the jurisdiction of ordinary law. A section of society obtained
special rights over some of its members; a form of peasant self-
government developed, including peasant courts; a peculiar order of
inheritance, and much else. All this made the peasants a state within
the state and, as though to make up for it, special responsibilities
benefitting the whole state--the chief and most unjust being the obligation of compulsory army service--rested on peasant society. Such
was the historic foundation on which the peasant problem rested in
Russia.

How could this Gordian knot be untied from the point of view of
equality alone? The most ardent supporters of this principle would
not have been willing to declare immediately the freedom of allotment
land, put an end to the commune, or even substitute the principle of
inheritance based on labor for that of blood relationship. How could

the country get along without the "natural obligations," including
police duty, imposed on the peasants alone and only at their expense?
All this remained outside the field of vision of the First Duma, for it
was impossible to solve the problem merely by abolishing limitation
of rights. Peasant class legislation could, however, be destroyed
and replaced by social legislation, creating a class of small peasant
landowners and protecting them from powerful ones. Here was a fertile field for the creative genius of our populists and rural experts;
but to put this question on one level with feminist and Jewish rights,
snatching out of it only this trait of inequality, was an absolutely
superficial approach to the question.

The government's declaration presented this question more logically than did the initiators of legislation in the Duma, but even the
government was unable to deal with the full scope of the problem. I
can judge from my own experience and observation how far removed
the Cadets were from understanding all the peculiarities of the Russian peasant question. I was, in this respect, as little prepared as
all the rest; the principle of equality seemed to solve for us the whole
complex question. Witte, incidentally, related in his Memoirs that
he, too, at first was not interested in the peasant question. It was
because of the general indifference that the situation remained unchanged for so long. Everyone was so used to the condition of the
peasants that few realized what was involved and what surprises
were in store for those who approached the problem.

I had occasion to come in contact with this question, accidentally,
in 1916. The "Progressive Bloc" decided, for "demonstration purposes," to put on the agenda the government measure on peasant equality introduced in 1907 to replace Stolypin's law of October 5, 1906, *
which had been passed in accordance with Article 87 of the Fundamental Laws. I was appointed to report on this. It was a new subject
for me but the report did not present any difficulties. The law of
October 1906 had been in effect for a long time and no one questioned
it. Its confirmation by the Duma seemed a mere formality. The office clerk brought for my signature a short report that he had prepared. Such a method of work was quite accepted then among the
deputies. I am glad that I was not tempted to confine myself to his
report and worked on the question myself. Though the work was in
vain, I became aware of the complexities of the problem.

Naturally I decided not to restrict myself merely to the confirmation of the existing law, but to try to extend its application to areas
to which the law did not appertain at that time. The situation was delicate but rewarding. If the amended legislative measure were rejected
by the Imperial Council, then even the measures that had been in effect

----

* One of a series of land laws (August, October, and November,
1906) which ended serfdom in Russia. [M. B.]

since 1906 would cease to exist. It would be difficult for either legislative chamber to undertake such a responsibility. If the Duma went
too far with its amendments, and on its account the laws were rejected,
the responsibility for the loss of a former achievement would rest on
the Duma. A similar responsibility would rest on the Second Chamber
if it proved intractable. A compromise was essential. When my report was adopted by the Duma and sent to the Imperial Council, A. S.
Stishinski was appointed to report on it there. He understood the
difficulty of the situation and came to bargain with me, bent on reaching an agreement with me without fail. The revolution prevented us
from learning how this would have ended.

I do not intend to explain this episode, as I have too many personal
memories connected with it. I merely want to establish one thing.
While I was familiarizing myself with the literature on this question,
I could see, as was natural, that the literature did not present a plan
for practical action. This was beyond its competence. But even the
preparatory work of the Cadet legislators, who intended to solve the
peasant problem in a practical manner, added nothing in this regard.
Lack of experience was evident in this. How little the Cadet party
understood the practical solution of the peasant problem was shown by
the amendment introduced in the Duma during the discussion of the law
of October 5, proposing to include Jewish equality in the peasant law.
This conformed to the general principle of equality, but the worst
enemy of the Jews could not have thought of a more fallacious, and
for the Jews a more harmful, step, to run the risk of defeating all
peasant equality on this amendment. I, as the speaker, had to oppose
my own party. This violation of discipline passed without serious
consequences for me, particularly because the party leadership was
then abroad (spring, 1916). During the discussion of my report, I
had the pleasure of getting full support from one of the few experts in
the Duma on the peasant question, A. S. Postnikov. I recall the address of thanks I received from the peasant deputies in the Duma, and
many other things about which I shall remain silent, so as not to break
the thread of the story.

While making a study of this question, I could not fail to see
that in Russia there was one basic peasant problem. It would be beneficial to present a summary of it and outline a plan for its gradual
but complete solution. This was new work which no one delegated to
me and which apparently was beyond my powers. I decided at least
to put the question before public opinion at large, and gave two reports on this subject to the legal societies of St. Petersburg and Moscow. Incidentally, I spoke in Moscow on the very day of Rasputin's
assassination. My report was later published in the December, 1916,
and January, 1917, volumes of Viestnik Grazhdanskago Prava (Jour-
nal of Civil Law). But I sought help from legal circles in vain; there,

too, there were few people who had thought about this question. One
of the few experts, A. A. Leontev, welcomed my report for raising
this question, in which, according to his observation, learned lawyers showed very little interest. Apparently our liberal society had
to work and learn much more before grappling self-confidently with
the peasant problem. The experience of the bureaucracy would have
been very useful, for it knew the problem and made constant efforts
to solve it in a practical manner, though it followed the wrong road.
Nowhere could cooperation between bureaucracy and mature social
thought have been more productive. But this was the very thing that
society refused to recognize, preferring to solve the entire problem
at one swoop and unaided.

But if the Cadets did not evaluate correctly the legal aspect of
the peasant question, merging it in the abyss of general equality, they
believed that, at least, they solved the problem of land ownership. To
this day many people suppose that if the Cadet agrarian legislative
measure had been adopted in time, there would have been no revolution. This opinion is an example of the origin and persistence of
legends. I spoke in the previous chapter about the procedure employed
in connection with this measure; let us now examine it in detail.

This project did not, of course, deserve the categorical censure
it received in the declaration of the Council of Ministers, but the criticism referred not to the project but to the address of the Duma. The
government's opinion of the Cadet bill was expressed in the session of
May 19 by Stishinski and Gurko, who did not declare it "absolutely
inadmissible." However they presented serious, or at any rate quite
relevant, objections against it.

To evaluate this measure, it is necessary first of all to realize
that it did not solve the general peasant agrarian question. For the
time being, everything about peasant landholding remained unchanged,
with no hint of improvement. The measure proposed using expropriated land to set up (in Cadet terminology) a special "area of state
land" and outlined the method of using this land; according to Trudovik
terminology (Project 104), the same thing was called the "public land
fund." These special lands were set aside for the peasants by the
Cadets, but for all "workers" by the Trudoviki. Even in such a limited
matter, the two projects proposed different approaches. The basic
feature of both plans was that these lands were not transferred as
property but only for limited use. According to the Cadet project,
the allotment should not exceed "the production norm," taking into
consideration the consumers, but according to the Trudoviki, the
basis was to be the "labor norm." Lands received in such an allotment could not be transferred to others, and if, because of changed
circumstances, the receiver was found to have more than the norm,
it could be taken away from him.

I do not want to go into detail about these fantastic land schemes. Like all who denied private landownership, the authors of these bills established the most flimsy claim to the land for all peasants receiving allotments, and in this way they started a dangerous concentration of land in the hands of the central authority. The Bolsheviks realized this later, adding to it a number of their other "achievements."

But the important thing was that all these projects concerned only newly expropriated land. Apart from these, however, the very same peasants had allotment lands acquired by the commune, involving special rights, and comprising the bulk of their possessions. What improvements did the Cadets propose for them? None. The project did not touch on the ancient form of peasant landownership, and yet, its improvement, in particular, was the most urgent and important task.

The authors of the bill understood perfectly that they did not raise the general land question. Hertsenshtein explained on May 18, "We spoke of the supplementary allotment as of a part, and a rather insignificant part, of the agrarian question." But prior to securing new lands for peasant use, it seemed necessary to correct at least some of the defects of the peasant economy that caused the low productivity and were not connected with lack of land. Even the Bolsheviks thought of that and, as compensation, introduced agrarian industrialization. Even though they exchanged former defects of the peasant economy for a multitude of new flaws, at least they raised the question. But the First Duma, knowing how badly off the peasant economy was, still started with the liquidation of the more profitable private landownership. At the same time it transferred land to peasants under even worse conditions than those under which peasants held allotment land. This was equalization to the lowest level.

Why was this approach used in dealing with such an important question? The Duma was strongly influenced by the idea that the expropriation of private lands must not be delayed any longer, and the agrarian measure was introduced, supposedly to preserve order in Russia. It is true there were many instances of agrarian unrest, but they did not in any way justify the proposed measure. What the Cadets proposed in 1906 was equivalent to saying that, because of the occupation of a few factories in France in 1936, a bill should have been introduced for immediate compulsory nationalization of private industry, destruction of the privileged class, and turning over the factories to the workers. Judging by the Cadet speeches in 1906, it was not the time to think of improvements in peasant landownership. On May 19, replying to Stishinski and Gurko, Hertsenshtein said:

It is impossible to propose now measures calculated to last a long time; special measures are necessary, and the compulsory expropriation is a special measure [pro-

longed applause]. We are passing through a period when
immediate action is an urgent necessity. Is it not enough
to have the experience of last year's May illuminations
when 150 estates were put to the torch in the province of
Saratov, almost all in one day?

What a testimonial to lawmakers afraid to undertake permanent measures. This was not legislation but panic. How mistaken was Hertsenshtein in this respect! The people did not rise, no matter how
much this was predicted after the dissolution of the Duma. And when
Stolypin introduced the law of November 9, intended for long-term
effects, it found among the peasants themselves an unexpected, sympathetic response, in spite of its shortcomings. Had it not been for the
war, this law, not the Cadet project, would have saved Russia from
revolution.

In his alarm Hertsenshtein was sincere, and this was his justification. Otherwise it would be a crime to justify a law this way.
What a weapon the Duma's tribune handed to revolutionary agitators,
who could now say that even in the opinion of the Duma "illuminations"
are useful to the peasant cause!

Careful examination of the Cadet agrarian bill as it was presented to the Duma reveals that it was dictated by purely political
motives, showing little concern for the welfare of the peasants themselves. The reform ignored the improvement of the peasant economy
and stressed the expropriation of land, on a larger or smaller scale,
from private owners. This seizure of land was, in fact, if not the
will of the people, then an ancient dream of the peasants. It was a
deserved Nemesis for the legal condition in which the ruling classes
kept the peasants, and thanks to which the peasants could see in the
landowner the former master. That is why the agrarian plans of the
Cadets, in so far as they started with expropriation, won them, for a
time, popularity among the peasants. Of course, the Cadets could
not compete with revolutionary parties on this basis and very soon
lost their popularity in the peasant circles. At first this project was
intended to win popularity not for the party but for the constitution itself. While elaborating the agrarian program as an aspect of the
Liberation Movement, its authors, Hertsenshtein and Manuilov, insisted that only in this way could the peasants be attracted to the constitution; Witte threatened to play a similar land card against liberalism in favor of the autocracy.

Later the stakes were lowered. On the eve of the Duma's convocation, political leaders openly pointed out that to achieve success
in the inevitable conflict between the Duma and the monarch, it would
be necessary to arouse a conflict over the land question, which was
the only one disturbing the peasants. Thus the Cadet agrarian project
was inspired not by the welfare of the peasants, but by politics; first

the struggle for the constitution, and later the preservation of the
existing Duma. In this respect the plan played into the hand of revolution, not pacification. As always, the Cadets sat on both sides of
the fence, first arousing revolutionary feelings and then proposing
their measures to calm them.

There wan another equally harmful aspect of this policy. The
Cadet agrarian project widened the gulf between them and the non-
revolutionary liberal parties, since it threatened to destroy the landowning class, which was melting away quickly as it was. The ordinary course of events, which transferred to the peasants the lands of
their former landowners, could not be stopped and was generally
sound. This process could be hastened by encouraging the transfer
of lands into peasant hands, by the imposition of a progressive tax on
land, by putting an end to unlawful exemptions on the mortgaged land
of the landowners, and so on. Such action would have been sufficient
to accelerate the transfer of land to those who could use it so that it
would not lie idle. This would have been a natural and therefore useful process.

There might be, of course, isolated critical instances when it
would have been imprudent to wait for a general improvement. In
such cases, resort to expropriation would be wise; for example, in
instances where the peasants' shortage of land compelled them to
rent, and where the landlords exploited the peasants by excessive
charges. To cope with such situations a rental law could be introduced, as well as purchase of land for the benefit of the renters. Such
an arrangement would be just as natural and lawful as the purchase of
land occupied by urban settlements that still remained under private
ownership. Purchase would also be beneficial in correcting some defects and abuses of 1861, when cross-strips and other analogous
traps were intentionally created to ensure the economic dependence
of liberated peasants on landlords. Furthermore, wherever no free
lands remained to be acquired either by purchase or expropriation,
resettlement could be encouraged. Such a policy could mitigate critical conditions and, by following the channel of natural development,
save the country from that ordeal to which the mass destruction of
private landownership would have led it. Why was it necessary to
destroy the class of private landowners by an accelerated method,
by political action, instead of letting it die a natural death?

The revolutionary parties might consider the disappearance of
the landlord class a blessing since they regarded it as their political
enemy, which would be playing politics rather than solving the agrarian
question. But why was this disappearance essential to the Cadets, the
better half of whom came from the ranks of the landlord class? After
the agrarian bill came the rift between the Cadets and the landlord
class, which broke away from them. This, in turn, reduced the chances of a peaceful reorganization of the state. And if the Cadets really

intended to halt the agrarian revolution by their legislative measure,
they were naive. The agrarian law would have been the first step to
revolution. It would have been difficult enough to take the land away
from the landlords; but to divide it among the peasants, without increasing dissatisfaction and avoiding throat-cutting, would have been
impossible. Maintaining order would have required such an effort
on the part of the government that no trace of liberalism would have
remained. In so far as the revolutionaries considered it useful to lead
Russia to revolution, the Cadet agrarian project was useful to them.
Since liberalism could not have implemented a reform such as the
Cadets planned, this would have turned out to be one more step in the
direction of revolution.

    With all their tactical shortcomings, the Cadets were a liberal,
not a revolutionary, party. Only because of tactics, foreign ideas
inspired by revolution--namely, the Constituent Assembly and the
agrarian project--appeared in their program, contradicting the nature of the Cadet party. Neither of these two issues was actually a
plank in the Cadet program; rather both were employed for demagogic
appeal.

    It was profitable, of course, to contrast the wealth of large land-
owners with the crying misery and need of the peasants, since the
main reason for this inequality was the unjust attitude of the state toward the peasants, who were forced to work and pay for others. And
in so far as the peasants' want arose out of the policy of the state and
was dictated by the selfishness of the privileged classes, this policy
had to be changed radically. But it did not necessarily follow that
private landowners should be liquidated as a class and their land expropriated. Why, then, did the Cadets in their attempt to solve the
agrarian question agreee to this? Indeed, social inequality no less
glaring and shocking existed outside landownership, in factories and
mills. However, the Cadets understood that there had to be a gradual
development of social legislation to combat this inequality, and even
the demand for the eight-hour day would be limited in scope. The
Cadets did not propose any one measure calling for nationalization of
all enterprises, or destruction of capitalists as a class. Even without Bolshevik experience they understood that ideal conditions cannot be introduced in the economic order by command.

    Why did the Cadets forget all this in their agrarian project? In-
stead of social legislation for the peasant they proposed only the seizure of land from private owners and the destruction of large-scale
economy. Seizure alone did not solve the question at all. The Cadet
project was merely a political maneuver, a combination of revolutionary ideology and Cadet tactics.

    Even now one can meet enthusiasts of the Cadet agrarian reform
who insist triumphantly that European post-war policies justified them,
for they point out that many countries carried out the same expropria-

tion measures with complete success. This is an interesting question but too complex to examine in passing; it is premature to speak of complete success. But how characteristic of the Cadets is this comparison!

It is generally inconsistent for champions of a legal order to fall back on the unexemplary laws and customs of a postwar period. Often they are a negation of every right except that of force, which may do anything it wants, and such force may be the state as a whole or only a temporarily victorious social class. To deny these sad manifestations is as useless as to deny wars and revolutions. But to seek in them lessons for peacetime legislation, especially when the task of the moment was to strengthen in Russia the principles of justice and to substitute law for the will of the autocracy, meant that the liberals were lowering their banner.

There has been, in post-war Europe, a strongly marked tendency of transition from large-scale landownership to small holdings, and it has continued with increasing tempo. Generally this process is natural and sound. However, experience already makes us doubt whether this is a final process, in view of the fact that the use of agricultural machines requires large economic units for profitable operation. The solution of this contradiction may come from the establishment of a cooperative system, or from a rebirth of large non-collective units--that is for the future to decide--but it will be determined by experience, not theory. Meanwhile only the liquidation of large economic units is taking place.

Special measures for such liquidation are not required to hasten this process. Nowhere is this going on more normally than in England, where tax pressure is used to bring about the desired results. That is why this process has had such a wholesome character there; the liquidation begins with the least profitable units, which come into more ambitious and skillful hands.

The same process started in Russia long ago. The shortsighted policy of our government tried to hinder it and safeguard large units artificially, but the increase in small holdings has continued. What might have happened had the authorities changed their policy and encouraged by means of progressive taxes the transfer of land into the hands of the peasants? Natural selection would have been assisted; the large units that could not meet the tax would have fallen into the hands of small owners, automatically or through state institutions, and the profitable, progressive units would have remained and have been of benefit to the state.

When there is an acute shortage of land in the country, such a policy cannot be implemented. Then special measures are justified. During a war personal possessions and homes are requisitioned; bread rationing is introduced and unnecessary courses are forbidden at mealtime. All such measures, which under normal conditions would have seemed inexcusable, are then accepted as necessary.

However, this necessity did not exist in Russia with its vast untouched
reserves of land, which should have been used to encourage settlement or internal colonization. Easier acquisition of the neighboring
landlord's land and destruction of efficient households was the negation
of such a policy.

The allusion of present-day Cadet supporters to post-war European agrarian legislation is instructive in another way.   Examination
of this legislation reveals that, even in Europe, the reason behind
many agrarian measures was political. This was particularly notice-
able in the newly-established states, where large-scale landholdings
proved to be in the hands of national minorities. Thus liquidation of
all large-scale economic units under cover of agrarian reform was a
concealed form of internal struggle. In other instances, with the formation of democratic states on the ruins of former autocratic empires,
the struggle with large-scale landholding was the consequence of victorious social revolution dispatching old social enemies. This, in
fact, determined the specific character of post-war agrarian legislation in Europe. Cadet agrarian reform was unnecessarily inspired
with the same revolutionary ideology. It could be understood and
justified as a beginning of social revolution and an attempt to destroy
Russia's former ruling class; but this could not be the task of liberalism in Russia. The Cadets, while unconsciously serving this
aim, presented their reform merely as an agrarian measure, directed
towards the welfare of the whole state. They were cloaking revolutionary aspirations in supposedly just and harmless forms. Herein lay
the basic sin of the Cadet tactics.

I shall not pause any longer on organic reforms, the solution of
which proved beyond the capacity of the Duma, but turn to the incomparably easier task: their efforts to remove individual evils not connected with any general reforms. The most characteristic example
of this was the fight against the death penalty.

In contrast to most legislative projects of the Duma, the law
concerning its abolition was completed and voted on in the Duma in a
particularly speedy manner. The Duma was very proud of this law,
as this put Russia ahead of the rest of Europe. But it is not difficult
to see that the Duma could not pass even this simple law properly.

The death penalty has opponents, in principle, all over the
world. A declaration to set the world an example could have been
stated abstractly as a principle. But this would have meant shutting
one's eyes to conditions in Russia, where the death penalty was not
merely a matter of principle. Here, the death penalty had become a
daily occurrence, employed in a shocking and unjust manner, and it
was necessary to struggle against it in a practical way before giving
the world lessons in theory.

Why was there, at that time, such an enormous number of executions, unheard of until the coming of the Bolsheviks? It was not
because of the severity of our courts or our criminal laws. On the

contrary, they were more lenient than others. Executions were carried out only because Article 18 of the Exceptional Regulations, which
were applied almost everywhere, gave the administrative authorities
the right to exclude any matter from the jurisdiction of regular courts
and hand it over to the military courts for trial according to martial
law. Here were two typical Russian defects. First, the arbitrariness of the administration, which is inadmissible in a constitutional
state. Cognizance of a matter was determined not by the nature of
the crime nor the character of the accused, but by the discretion of
the administrative authority in each individual case. Equally intoler-
able was the procedure of judging, in military courts according to
martial law, crimes committed by civilians in peacetime. This was
simply abuse of authority. Repeal of the Exceptional Regulations
was the monarch's prerogative and did not depend on the Duma (Article 15, Fundamental Laws). Nor did the severity of military courts
and military laws depend on the Duma; this was the province of
"special military legislation" excluded from the Duma's competence
(Articles 96, 97). But the Duma could, through its own initiative,
change the Regulation on Security and annul the dreadful Article 18
of the Exceptional Regulations. Here was a legal course open to the
Duma, a way so simple and nonprovocative that speedy results might
have been achieved.

    What did the learned authors of this legislative project do in-
stead? On May 18 they introduced in the Duma a law consisting of
two parts, the first of which stated: "The death penalty is abolished."
Thus they did not raise a concrete issue that the administrative authorities could not defend, as for example, the death penalty imposed
at the discretion of governors. Instead, the death penalty in general
was being questioned, which complicated matters. It was proposed
to send this project to a committee for elaboration, but though no one
in the Duma defended the death penalty, nineteen speeches were made
"as to direction," taking up twenty-one pages of a stenographic report. To speed up matters, the Trudoviki proposed nonobservance
of Articles 55-57 regarding the monthly time limit and immediate
adoption of the bill without waiting for the ministerial reply. The Cadets opposed this proposal and it was rejected, but the chairman of
the Duma was instructed to take steps to receive the ministry's reply
before the legal time limit.

    If it had been only a matter of repealing Article 18, Regulations
on Security, the only department concerned would have been the Ministry for Internal Affairs, and the problem would have been so simple
that a speedy reply might have been expected. But this practical way
out, virtually abolishing the death penalty, seemed insufficiently effective to the Duma. In the first place, annulling one article might
imply tacit consent or recognition of the rest. Secondly, even if no
further death sentences were imposed, the death penalty still would

have remained on paper, and there would be nothing to boast of before Europe. So the Duma undertook a job worthy of its greatness
and abolished the death sentence as a matter of principle. This created one special difficulty, for such a clause would have abolished
the death penalty even in a theater of war. One may be an opponent
of the death penalty and yet not go so far. During a war, under conditions of organized legal murder, when many innocent people are
killed, humanitarian objections to the death penalty seem hypocritical.
In no state had the death penalty been abolished in such circumstances.
The solution of such a question in a hasty manner would be evidence
of thoughtlessness unworthy of the government. By presenting the
question this way the Duma itself provoked a refusal, and received
it. The departments concerned proved to be not only the Ministry
for Internal Affairs, as would have been the case regarding the repeal of Article 18, Regulations on Security, but the Ministries of
Justice, Army, and Navy. A week later their reply was received,
couched in similar language. They stated that

> In view of the fact that the Duma's proposal concerns the
> abolition of the death penalty not only in connection with
> ordinary criminal laws, but also in regard to existing
> military and naval codes and laws operative in wartime,
> the problem appears to be extremely complex and requires
> the most detailed study. Consequently, the ministers can-
> not give their reply before the legal time limit.

The government was right. It was not difficult to abolish the death
penalty on paper. In 1917 this was done "forever" by the Provisional
Government, which immediately restored it at the front. The second
time it was "finally" abolished by the Bolsheviks. The government
did not want to act so lightly in 1906 and the Duma had to submit, as
the law was against it. After twenty-four speeches, the Duma consoled itself by adopting the following formula of transition:

> Further execution of death warrants resulting from the
> delaying tactics of the ministers, at the time when the
> government itself has already approached the solution of
> the question, will be a violation of basic moral principles,
> and will be regarded by the country not as an act of jus-
> tice, but as murder.[1]

This declaration was perhaps terrifying but it frightened no one.
     When the monthly legal limit passed, discussion started on the
fundamentals of the bill, or the desirability of its "basic proposals."
The speaker, Kuzmin-Karavaev, made a very long speech defending
the measure that no one in the Duma questioned. For some reason,

by the way, he pointed out that in his personal opinion the death penalty was absolutely unnecessary, even in wartime. These words, of
course, aroused prolonged applause. However, he immediately added that the death penalty exists in wartime in all European military
penal codes and, because of this, the committee decided not to raise
this question now. This was wise but it was now impossible to say
that every kind of death penalty was abolished. The ministers replied for their departments. The spokesman for the Army Ministry,
Pavlov, was prevented from speaking by whistles and noise, but the
representative of the Naval Ministry pointed out--and this was in-
structive--that the death penalty imposed according to the military
and naval penal codes could be repealed only by special procedure of
military legislation which was beyond the Duma's competence. Thus
a legal barrier was erected in the form of Articles 96-97 of the Fundamental Laws.

The question was now clear. The orators vented their indignation, extolled their conduct toward Pavlov, and promised to deal
with him in a similar manner in the future; but what more could they
do regarding the death penalty? It was decided, in view of the answer
of the ministers, to transfer the matter immediately to a committee
to elaborate the bill. This was an empty formality, for the bill did
not consist of "basic proposals," but was a completed text. Debates
of great interest followed.

The law consisted of two clauses. The first stated: "The
death sentence is abolished." The second read as follows: "In those
cases where it is established by law, it is to be replaced immediately
by the punishment next in severity."

What would be the results of such a measure? Let us suppose
that it should be adopted by the State Duma as well as by the Second
Chamber and confirmed by the tsar. It would then become law. But
since it did not repeal Article 18, Regulations on Security, the governors would retain the formal right of handing over individual cases
to military courts to be judged by martial law, and what could military courts do in such cases? They had to be governed by military
law, which remained unaltered under Articles 96-97. The highest
legal authority, the Supreme Military Court, would clarify the meaning of the law to the military courts and its elucidation would be
binding on them. No wonder the speaker himself announced, in the
name of the committee, that the Duma's bill did not touch on the
death penalty in wartime. So it would be perfectly legal for the courts
to continue to condemn to death, in spite of the new law.

Thus, the law that had promised so much would not save a single life. Deputy Sholp drew the attention of the deputies to this
thoughtlessness or hypocrisy. He pointed out that misunderstandings
would be unavoidable in military courts, and proposed inserting in
the second clause the exact names of the laws, among them military.
Then all would be clear.

He was right and a lawyer like Nabokov could not fail to understand this; but Nabokov understood something else, too. To do as
Sholp proposed meant endangering the whole bill, since Article 96-97
of the Fundamental Laws did not permit such editing. Besides, if
the law were proclaimed in this form, the death penalty would have
been abolished even in wartime, which the committee itself did not
want, as Kuzmin-Karavaev announced. What was the solution? None
that was seemly. Nabokov proposed leaving the text of the bill unchanged, saying nothing about the Articles of War, but instead adopting the decision that "In the opinion of the Duma this law applies to
absolutely all cases when active legislation calls for the death penalty."
The Duma could not take such a petty and unworthy stand; the committee yielded, and Sholp's amendment was adopted. The Duma approved
a law the like of which "had not been seen in Europe." The death
penalty was being abolished in a theater of war and in wartime, but
all it meant was that the fate of those who were at the discretion of
the governors would still be tried by martial law. The Duma showed
no concern for the condemned whom it might have saved from execution. It preferred the effective but useless declaration to their rescue.
Such were the Duma's tactics.

These activities of the Duma, rather than the obstruction of the
government, the monthly time limit for a reply, or the complex nature of the legislative procedure, were the main reasons for the
fruitlessness of the Duma's legislation. The procedure invented by
the Duma was more difficult than the one established by the constitution. The Duma was hampered most because it renounced the constitution and did not understand the difficulty of the work that it undertook so bravely; it was handicapped because it preferred showy phrases
to practical achievements, complicating simple problems for effect.
In its haste to introduce projects on which it found no time to work,
the Duma set impossible tasks for the committees. However, the Duma must not be blamed, for legislative work was new to it; it would
have learned in time. The only trouble was that the Duma did not
want to learn and considered that it could teach all others.

Chapter Eleven

THE DUMA'S CONTROL OF ADMINISTRATION

The second business task of the Duma was control of administration, which was realized mainly by means of interpellations. The
Duma made the most of this right. If the Duma's efforts proved fruitless in the field of legislation, it broke all records in the sphere of
control. During thirty-nine sessions, it introduced, examined, and
adopted more than three hundred interpellations. Almost all of them
as well as the accompanying transition formulas were adopted unanimously. Thus, on the surface, it seemed that this activity of the
Duma was successful.

Yet, in reality, this work did not lead to anything. The members of the Duma themselves admitted this with bitterness. They
did not prevent any lawlessness and did not save anyone, but what
was even worse, by their method of investigation they killed interest
in interpellations on the part of the press, and in the Duma itself.
Before long, the Duma tried to combat this practice; restrictions
were devised to eliminate interpellations and transfer them without
debate to the committee, setting certain days and later even hours
for their discussion. When interpellations were to be discussed, the
hall would begin to empty. Everyone realized that this activity became a waste of time. The Cadets, of course, blamed the constitution
most of all for this failure. It is surprising to learn all the petty reasons which, in the opinion of the Duma, led to such a result. The
failure of interpellations was ascribed to the fact that the constitution
strictly limited the rights of the deputies. The Duma could question
only the irregular activities of the authorities; the ministers were
given too long a time (a month) for replying; finally, the interpellation could come only from the Duma and not from individual deputies.
All this diminished the deputies' rights.

It is amusing to recall these and similar accusations. On the
basis of experience it may be said that when a particular interpellation
aroused interest, the government did not wait for the monthly limit,
and sometimes it even replied before the interpellation was adopted.
The government did not hide behind the narrow interpretation of conforming to the law. Furthermore, no parliament is obliged to spend
time listening to interpellations if it does not wish to do so. In France,

for example, any deputy may demand an explanation of a matter, but the day for hearing interpellations without debate is set by parliament, and in this way they may be rejected at once. It is curious that the clauses dealing with interpellations were not limited by the Fundamental Laws, and although the desirability of some legislative change was pointed out in passing, nothing was done.

The chief objection to interpellations was that they were without sanction; supposedly, that was why they were fruitless and interest in them was soon lost. This objection was characteristic. There really was no sanction for interpellations; Article 60 pointed out one particular possibility, that of bringing disputes between the Duma and ministers to the attention of the tsar. But this article, transferred from the Bulygin Duma, was never applied because it did not fit in with the role of the monarch in a constitutional country.

In general, what kind of sanction could have been made regarding interpellations? It was impossible, of course, to give the Duma the right to reject decrees that it censured; this would have led to anarchy. The only other possibility was the resignation of the minister criticized by the Duma. In a parliamentary constitution this is self-evident and need not be stated. However, since we had no parliamentarianism, such a sanction for interpellations alone would be an inconsistency and even a distortion. Parliamentarianism is introduced into a constitution by practice and custom rather than by special laws. The introduction of the rights of interpellation into our constitution practically opened the way for the establishment of parliamentarianism, if the Duma could have taken advantage of this course of action.

The Duma complained about its limitation of rights without appraising correctly the precious right it was granted: the right of interpellation, which changed the country's atmosphere. No wonder that no absolutism ever permitted it; neither the autocracy nor bolshevism nor present-day totalitarian states permit interpellation. Even if encouragement is given to what is now picturesquely called "self-criticism" in the USSR, it may be exercised only in the direction and within the limits prescribed by the authorities, and must correspond to the views of the government. But so long as the Duma retained the right of interpellation and investigation was unrestricted, society conserved ammunition for the struggle with the government. But this was not all. The government was obliged to reply to the interpellations. In an old ukase of Peter the Great, senators were required to formulate their opinions publicly, in order that, as the ukase frankly stated, "each one's folly be evident to all." This was now considered to be the duty of the authorities, giving the Russian parliament an opportunity of showing all society, friends and foes alike, its superiority over the government in efficiency and understanding of state problems. The contrast between the old order and

the new one now established by the constitution was no less striking
than the difference between the pre-reform injunction court and the
competitive public process. The truth could not be concealed for
long and telling falsehoods publicly was dangerous to the ministry.
Thus, gradually, the way was actually opening toward responsibility
of the ministry to parliament. Such was the ammunition that the Duma now possessed.

But in order that interpellations might bring results, certain
condit'ons were essential. If the Duma were to expose convincingly
the unlawful activities of the authorities, it had to stand on a firm
basis of law itself. The tendency of the liberalism of that day to
imagine itself in a "revolutionary situation" and regard formal legality with contempt destroyed the force of interpellation and resulted in the same distortion as Muraviev's Committee of Inquiry in
1917. A revolutionary government need not speak of legality. The
idea of establishing a committee of inquiry to investigate the defeated
old régime was a sound one, providing the committee did not pretend
that it was prosecuting the former authorities for lawless actions.
Muraviev's contrivances to bring such activities under the jurisdiction
of criminal clauses of old laws were repulsive in their deceit and deprived his conclusions of conviction. It was fortunate that the committee remained only an historic relic and did not come before society's judgment. So, too, in order to be convincing, the Duma's
control over the legality of the actions of the authorities had to rest
on a basis of lawfulness and devotion to a legal order--that is, to the
existing constitution.

There was another condition, too. In order that the interpellations might justify the claims for responsibility of the ministry to
the Duma, it was essential that in evaluating the actions of the authorities and the explanations of the ministers, the Duma maintain at least
a semblance of objectivity; that it show, on its part, good faith, and
be a judge, not a warring party employing every available weapon
against an enemy.

Given these conditions, interpellations might have become a
powerful weapon in the hands of the Duma; without them, they ceased
making an impression or even arousing interest. This is what happened to the mass of interpellations that were presented to the Duma;
it almost seems that the Duma intentionally did everything to destroy
the weapons it was given. I shall mention a few examples to illustrate
this point.

One subject of the most impassioned, if not the most frequent,
of such interpellations was the death penalty. Its application aroused
the indignation of the Duma, which strained all its resourcefulness in
struggling against this practice. I pointed out in the previous chapter
how the Duma tried, unsuccessfully, to abolish the death penalty by
means of legislation. Let us see how the Duma fought against it by
using the right of interpellation.

This was a more difficult course, but it was not hopeless. The application of Article 18 of the Security Regulations was always the basis of a death sentence. This article permitted the administrative authority to transfer a particular case to a military court for judgment under wartime laws. The formal right of transfer was indisputable, but since the meaning of conformity to law is broader than the meaning of formal law and presupposes agreement with the aim of the law, it was possible to prove that in a number of cases--and this would have been the truth--use of this article was not in agreement with either a legal order established by the constitution or with the aim of the Exceptional Regulations. In short, abuse of power was involved. Such an interpellation could have been directed to the Minister of Internal Affairs about the irregular use of Article 18. But from the moment the case came before the military court, except in case of acquittal if guilt were not proven, the death penalty was unavoidable. The military court laws, with an explanation by the supreme military court and instructions from the Ministry of War, did not permit the court to reduce the punishment. Herein lay the horror of Article 18 on Security: the disposition of the administrative authority predetermined the court outcome; it was itself the sentence, imposed by the action of the administrative authorities rather than by the court.

This showed what the Duma could do and what it could not. It could ask the Minister for Internal Affairs why the administration under him deviated from common law in a given case, and then question the legality of this deviation. But it could not direct an interpellation to the Ministry of War asking why the military court pronounced the death sentence, and particularly why it was carried out.

The Cadet lawyers knew all this, but they did not wish to follow the constitutional course and would not agree to make abuse of Article 18 the subject of an interpellation. The motives were the very same in this case as those which prevented the repeal of the article by legislative means. So the Duma adopted as the basis for interpellation not the abuse of Article 18 but the death penalty itself. What constituted illegality in this case? In the opinion of the Duma illegality was involved because the Duma denied the right to impose the death penalty and was preparing to abolish it. It is difficult to believe that the Duma, in its right mind, would have chosen such a basis for an interpellation; nothing could have been more prejudicial to successful results. Nevertheless, the Duma chose this course of action, varying the wording from time to time without changing the sense.

A glance at the formulation of a few interpellations reveals the obstinacy with which the Duma clung to this unfortunate idea.

On May 12 the first interpellation regarding confirmation of the death sentence was directed to the chairman of the Council of Ministers. It read as follows: ''Having in mind that the State Duma, in its address in reply to the speech from the throne, stressed the necessity

of halting execution of death warrants... has telegraph communication
been made with the Baltic Governor-General about halting the execution of the above mentioned death warrants?''

On May 24 the following interpellation was made: ''In view of
the firmly expressed attitude of the State Duma, does the government
intend to adopt extraordinary measures to forestall execution in the
Nepliuev case?''

On May 26 during the discussion of the Duma's bill concerning
the abolition of the death penalty, the Duma adopted the following
formula of transition: ''Taking into consideration the fact that further execution of death sentences, at the time when the government
itself has already approached the solution of this problem, is a violation of fundamental moral principles, and will be regarded by the
country not as an act of justice but of murder... demanding suspension
of death sentences, the Duma is passing on to the next order of business.''

This formula of transition implied a new reason for considering
the death penalty unlawful in the future: it contradicted a formula
adopted by the Duma.

Such interpellations merely showed that the Duma considered
its will, even its intentions, above the law. It was still possible that,
in view of the Duma's wishes, the Minister of Internal Affairs would
order the governors not to use Article 18 prior to reviewing the Exceptional Regulations. This would be within his rights. In the Second
Duma, Stolypin did so with the courts-martial. Having heard the debates in the Duma on March 13, 1907, he announced:

> Having reviewed this matter, the government has come
> to the conclusion that the country expects from it an evi-
> dence of faith, not of weakness. Gentlemen, we hope to
> hear a conciliatory word from you. In expectation of this,
> the government will take measures to limit this severe
> law only to the most exceptional cases of the most shock-
> ing crimes, so that when the Duma directs Russia to-
> wards peaceful activity, this law would lapse through
> nonconfirmation by a legislative assembly.

Stolypin kept his word; the law about courts-martial was no longer
applied; it was not introduced in the Duma and lapsed. This was accomplished in the Second Duma, the fate of which was determined at
its election. It would have been much easier for the élite of the
country, the First Duma, to win such a concession. But when the
Duma maintained that, in view of its expressed desire, the execution
of death sentences effective according to law was not to be permitted,
and demanded that the government halt them by telegraph, submission
to such a demand meant recognizing the Duma's desires as above the

law. Even in the address, the Duma did not contest the fact that the
suspension of death sentences could be made only by the Supreme
Authority. It stated: "In expectation of this law, the country awaits
the suspension of all death sentences now, by Your Imperial Authority." The tsar did not reply to this and did not suspend the sentences. Yet, the Duma still considered that, because of its expressed
desire, the suspension had to be made by the governors, and by telegraph, too! The desires of the Duma were to supersede the lawful
rights of the tsar.

By stating the interpellation in this manner the Duma itself
built the scaffold for the condemned. It changed the question of the
death sentences of a few persons into the question of what governs
Russia: the law or the wishes of the Duma? This interpellation
was so defiantly unlawful that both the chairman of the Council of
Ministers and the Minister of War could have replied bluntly, pointing out to the Duma its constitutional place, but this was not done.
The usual procedure was followed, and on June 1 the Minister of War
replied, through the Chief Public Prosecutor, to the interpellation
addressed to him regarding the actions of the military authorities.

From the legal standpoint, the minister's reply was irreproachable. Once a matter was turned over to the military courts for trial
according to martial law, these courts had to fulfill their duty, and
applying the compulsory interpretation of the law, they could neither
fail to sentence to death nor halt the execution of the sentence. The
law did not permit the Minister of War to interfere, and the Duma's
expression of its negative attitude towards the death penalty was, likewise, insufficient.

The Minister of War could not give a different reply, but what
did the Duma say to this? A specialist on military law, Professor
Kuzmin-Karavaev, did not deny that the law was not violated: "If
we considered [he said ironically] that the government has acted and
is acting contrary to law, would we have formulated our interpellation
in this way?... We would have asked, has the Governor-General been
brought to trial and has he already been executed?"

A witty joke from the lips of a man who only recently argued in
the Duma that the death penalty should not be applied under any circumstances. But if everything was done according to law, then why in the
world would the Minister of War interfere with the process of law?
Kuzmin-Karavaev continued:

> The highest legislative organ of the empire expressed its
> opinion on the death penalty. The Duma pointed out, in
> the address in reply to the tsar, the necessity of immediate
> suspension of death sentences. What was the reply? The
> Minister of War screened himself behind the law which
> does not permit him to interfere.

Such was the sad, and for the supporters of a legal order, the shameful argument of the State Duma when it left constitutional ground.
Apart from the bombastic claim that it was the highest legislative
body and so above the law, it did not in any way prove the unlawful
actions of the military authorities. Consequently, it had to turn its
eloquence into a different channel; many powerful and moving and
also some rude speeches were made that day, thundering against the
death penalty in general. It was an inspiring theme and the Duma
had many splendid orators, but the common defect of all these speeches
was irrelevance. The Duma did not want to discuss what it could and
should: the worthlessness of Article 18 or at least its abuses. The
orators preferred to be indignant because the Minister of War dared
to put the law above the wishes of the Duma, did not consider its mood
and, in the words of Vinaver, "He did not wish to submit to the sovereign will of the popular representatives." The Duma strengthened
this pretension by its transition formula, in which it pointed out that

> The Minister of War screens an obvious unwillingness to
> satisfy the demand of the Duma by a formal excuse, citing
> the fact that he has no right to "interfere" with the de-
> cisions of the Governors-General, while such interfer-
> ence was imperative in the present instance, both because
> of the unanimous decision of the Duma and the extreme
> urgency of the situation, which the government stubbornly
> refuses to see. Expressing its profound indignation re-
> garding the content and form of the reply of the Minister
> of War, the Duma is going on to the next order of busi-
> ness.

This finale revealed the impotence of the Duma, but failed to
induce it to follow a different course in order to get results. Next
day the Cadet press rejoiced over this new "victory."
Miliukov wrote in Speech on June 2:

> Another début, and what a début! The lawyers answered
> Mr. Pavlov in the name of justice. The priest in his cas-
> sock answered him in the name of conscience. Mr. Pub-
> lic Prosecutor disappeared immediately after his speech,
> without waiting for the destructive blows which were
> showered upon him. Had he remained, he would have
> had to prepare a different reply, longer and more to the
> point. Kuzmin-Karavaev, Lednitski, then Vinaver, proved
> to him that the excuse of incompetence was hypocritical
> and false; that besides the fact that the government was
> never embarrassed by interference with the law, in the
> present case, it was only a question of conscientious

application of the executive authority. The government
received a terrible blow and a terrible lesson.

This was the way they recorded history and fought for justice at that
time.
    Whom, except their own adherents, could such an interpellation
convince or dissuade? Meanwhile the Duma continued its successful
tactics after the "new victory," presenting the same type of interpellations about death penalties, occasionally changing the editing but
not their nature. Before long, the interpellations deteriorated into
a formal correspondence and the Minister of War began to answer
them in the same routine manner. Thus on June 30 in reply to seven
interpellations directed to him in the same form, the Minister of War
cited the explanation he had given previously. Nabokov replied wittily:
"If the replies are identical, then the indignation the Duma feels
is also identical." However, his remark, rewarded by prolonged
applause, was not sincere, for there could not be much indignation
now; it was too strong a feeling for the red tape into which the Duma's
arrogance transformed the interpellations.
    The second largest group of interpellations was based on the
use of powers that were granted to the administration by the Exceptional Regulations. Imprisonment without a statement of guilt,
searches without warrants, exile without cause, insecurity of jobs
and dismissal--all the defenselessness of the citizen in the face of
state authority flowed like a torrent through the Duma. Such concrete cases, when seen with one's own eyes or when they are por-
trayed by artists and writers, make a profound impression, but when
introduced en masse and stereotyped, they are only boring.
    The struggle with this evil was also completely within the Du-
ma's competence, while the uselessness of the Exceptional Regulations was openly acknowledged by the authorities. Review of these
regulations was more important than the law about the inviolability
of personal freedom, because the existence of the Exceptional Regulations rendered this law ineffectual. Legislative initiative in the
field of Exceptional Regulations was barred to the Duma by the Fundamental Laws, but their content, the scope of the rights of the administrative authorities, the establishment of responsibility for
abuse, or the method of control and self-defense--all these were
within the Duma's competence. It would have been a profitable task
to combat the government from this position, having shown how these
regulations were implemented. Their use in cases where no policy
was involved was so widely known that the government itself would
not have dared to defend the former procedure. This was a course
which should have been followed to obtain results.
    The Duma rejected such a course because it wanted the complete
destruction rather than the correction of the Exceptional Regulations.

It recoiled from the idea of introducing safeguards concerning them, as confirmed pacifists do from an invitation to humanize war. In the explanatory memorandum to the bill on the inviolability of personal freedom, it was pointed out that "all laws which by their very nature contradict the principle of inviolability of personal freedom are repealed simultaneously; these include existing laws concerning measures for the preservation of national order and social tranquillity." In its address the Duma also spoke only of the abolition of the Exceptional Regulations, not their review.

Of course, the Exceptional Regulations should not have been a normal condition, as it was with us. But the question immediately arises: was the Duma sincere in its insistence that no exceptional powers were needed by the authorities? Did it really believe that the country could be governed merely by implementing the law of inviolability of personal freedom? It is difficult to believe such assertions, if only because the Duma itself acknowledged the existence of an epoch of civil war. During the discussion of the law on assemblies, the Cadet orators, Vinaver and Kokoshkin, reminded their audience of the enormous powers vested in British officials, which might be used against assemblies that threaten social tranquillity. Vinaver added: "There are different kinds of assemblies. We who have lived through the horrors of the last few years, who have witnessed meetings of persons with flushed faces, preparing to start pogroms, we shall not close our eyes to the possibility of such meetings in the future."

This was characteristic; the Cadets understood the danger of impotence when they themselves suffered from it. Though the discussion was about assemblies, the question was raised about exceptional powers generally. Might they sometimes become necessary, even though they did contradict the law of inviolability of personal freedom?

The same day Vinaver was saying this, on June 20, the Duma adopted a laconic interpellation introduced by the Trudoviki and Social-Democrats. It was formulated thus: "A pogrom is starting in Batum following the murder of a Cossack. The population is in a panic. Special measures are required. What action does the chairman of the Council of Ministers intend to take to prevent a pogrom?"

Apparently not only was the population in a panic but also the authors of the interpellation. Otherwise they would not have spoken of preventing a pogrom which, according to their words, had already started. But it is still evident from the interpellation that the authors admitted the necessity of extraordinary measures, and therefore extraordinary powers. It is impossible to prevent a pogrom among people in a panic merely by implementing the principle of inviolability of personal freedom.

It is not worthwhile laboring this point. The Duma did not deny, in principle, the necessity of exceptional measures and sometimes called for them itself. It criticized the methods used and, above all, the reasons that the government used for applying them. In this case, there were two lawful courses open to the Duma: either to undertake a legislative review of the Exceptional Regulations, which conflicted with revolutionary ideology; or to accuse the government of abuse of these regulations by applying them unlawfully and contradicting the aim of the law. The latter course was even less to the liking of the Duma because it still implied tacit consent to the legality of the Exceptional Regulations, so long as they were not repealed, to say nothing of the fact that this required more familiarity with the factual side of each case than the Duma could acquire. So the Duma followed a third hopeless course. It simply found that their very application was unlawful and so provided a reason for an interpellation.

But why did the use of these regulations suddenly become unlawful? The Duma's lawyers did not bother with proofs. As far back as May 13, Kokoshkin considered that the Exceptional Regulations were repealed by the Manifesto of October 17. Others found that they contradicted Witte's report, which the tsar ordered to be adopted for guidance. Later the Duma began to insist that the regulations were unlawful because the bill to repeal them had been introduced in the Duma. Such arguments were futile because they were all irrelevant and could not be sincere. Invariably the Duma concluded with the customary cry, "resign," which might have satisfied the Duma itself but could not be regarded as asserting control over the administration.

It is evident that in accusing the government of unlawful actions, the Duma was putting itself on an unlawful basis by considering its own wishes as law, and itself above the law. Thus the interpellations lowered the prestige of the Duma, not of the government, and revealed what a menace the introduction of a parliamentary order might be. There would then be no legal order but merely autocracy in reverse, the autocracy of the Duma's majority.

Now let us look at the Duma's side of the argument. The preservation of even an appearance of objectivity by the Duma was as unlikely as the maintenance of an objective attitude towards the enemy in war time, and every page of the stenographic reports confirms this. What kind of control could there be under such circumstances? Two interesting interpellations may serve to illustrate the existing conditions.

The most interesting interpellation made by the Duma, as to content, was announced on May 8, "concerning incitements to pogroms, printed in the police department." It unmasked the crying evil in the very center of the administration and threw a revealing light on the

methods of the old order. There was one weakness in it: it referred
to December, 1905, when there was no Duma; and concerned the government anarchy when both the old régime and revolution were plotting against Witte and October reforms. At that time the Minister of
Internal Affairs was Durnovo, not Stolypin, so the latter had every
right to decline to reply to such an interpellation.

He did not wish to do so, however, because he still had hopes
of working with this Duma. He had nothing to conceal from it and
decided to use the interpellation to dissociate himself from the past
and clearly define his position. He declared on June 8, "I permit
no reservations and recognize no half-measures." After this introduction he painted a picture of what went on in the police department
at that troubled time. He told about the incitements to pogroms that
were printed there; the dismissal of Rachkovski, and Budakovski's
reprimand, although the latter simultaneously received the tsar's
praise for other activity. Having exposed the past, Stolypin clearly
expressed his attitude toward such practices. He admitted that these
actions were wrong and promised that the ministry would undertake
the most energetic measures to prevent their recurrence. He said:
"I can guarantee that there will be no such repetition."

What more could be demanded of a minister who was not responsible for the actions of his predecessors? The early Stolypin was a
person in whom even opponents showed confidence, and in this very
session, Urusov, Rodichev, and Kovalevski declared their personal
respect for him. This minister made a public promise and it was
necessary to support him and wait for further development, though
the Duma might have pointed out the conditions necessary to enable
him to keep his promise. This was the crux of the problem. Stolypin undoubtedly exaggerated his importance as a bearer of authority,
as the Cadets overestimated theirs as the representatives of the will
of the people. Both adversaries could manifest their real strength
only through agreement and cooperation with each other. Stolypin's
appeal to the Duma, while exposing past practices, for which supporters of the old order never forgave him, was in fact an endeavor
to bring about the reconciliation of the government with liberal society, which was necessary to both for success in the common cause.
Prince Urusov summed it up this way in a remarkable speech.

In the First Duma there were few remarkable speeches in a
national sense. Urusov's speech was one of these. History has recorded only the concluding, rather poorly worded statement about those
who "are sergeants and policemen by upbringing and pogrom-makers
by conviction." His speech deserved more than this brief mention.

Urusov, like Stolypin, belonged to that pleiad of liberal bureaucrats who, by their position and connections with the ruling class,
could permit themselves the luxury of independence. Such men were
not few in number and the Cadets needed their help to reorganize

Russia in a peaceful way. Unfortunately, society could use them
only when they broke with bureaucracy. Urusov, thanks to his bureaucratic experience, understood the situation. He had no illusions about
everything going well once the Cadets were in power, and he warned
of this as follows:

> I maintain that no ministry, even if it be chosen from the
> State Duma, could secure order so long as obscure per-
> sons or evil forces, standing behind an impenetrable
> barrier, have an opportunity to grasp separate parts of
> the state mechanism. [Indeed the evil lay here. Urusov
> warned Stolypin that his ministry alone would be power-
> less to cope with them.] The chief inspirers exist,
> apparently, outside the sphere of influence of the Min-
> istry of Internal Affairs, and that is why, without direct-
> ing my words against the ministry or against individual
> ministers, I can still maintain that the categorical an-
> nouncement made here today has no sound basis. [This
> was an approach to the crux of the problem. Who were
> these dark forces and, above all, wherein lay their
> might? Urusov was more experienced than Stolypin and
> understood this better. He did not attack Stolypin per-
> sonally.] I am completely confident that the Minister of
> Internal Affairs gave us all the information he could give;
> I am certain of the sincerity of his information and I do
> not doubt that under Minister Stolypin no one will decide
> to use the ministry's building and finances to organize
> pogroms and establish underground printing presses.

But unfortunately Urusov drew no conclusion from all this. He
pointed out the evil correctly but he proposed no means for its correction, since the Cadet tactics of the period did not permit this. That
is why Stolypin did not understand him. He replied proudly: "I must
say that when I took over the management of the Ministry of Internal
Affairs, I received at the order of the Tsar Emperor complete authority, and I am completely responsible. If there were ghosts which
would have interfered with me, they would have been destroyed, but
I do not know of any."

Experience proved later how unwarranted this self-confidence
was. "Dark forces" not only murdered Stolypin, they also ruined
Russia. Urusov was right, they were not overcome.

But it was not enough to recognize these forces prophetically,
as Urusov did. It was necessary to realize wherein lay their might.
Of course, their strength was not the result of their being "sergeants
and pogrom makers," as Urusov concluded in the midst of an unceasing

thunder of applause. Unfortunately, their strength lay in the fact that
liberal society, by its tactics, created a favorable basis for their
intrigues and their consolidation. By opposing agreement with the
government, liberalism weakened the whole state. The revolutionaries of the right who made pogroms on Jews; the revolutionaries of
the left whose state wisdom contrived pogroms on landlords; the ter-
rorists who murdered Hertsenshtein and Iollos, and those who shot
down policemen at their posts--all these were the scourge of the
land. In a sound state organism neither the one nor the other exists,
and such phenomena are only individual crimes. Their contagion
disappears in a healthy, legal atmosphere. It was not so in Russia.
The left Acheront became the ally of liberalism and liberalism could
not make up its mind to repudiate it. So the right Acheront found its
support in the government, including the tsar himself. Both ruinous
Acheronts nourished one another. The Duma thundered against right-
wing pogrom-makers while demanding amnesty for its own supporters
who were guilty of "murder and all kinds of agrarian crimes." The
tsar refused the Duma's request for an amnesty, and instead pardoned
"his own" at the intercession of the Dubrovin gang. The comparison
of the two may seem blasphemy morally, but politically they resembled one another as a negative resembles a photograph. No wonder
it was often impossible to distinguish the revolutionaries from the
reactionaries, and the revolutionaries, having won power, showed
their reactionary side. The increase of the revolutionary bacteria
was one of the consequences of the autocracy. The proclamation of
a constitutional monarchy might have become the beginning of a recovery, but to bring this about, agreement and cooperation between
the government and the Cadets, as leaders of liberal society, was
essential. Only such agreement could save them both from their
dangerous Acheronts. This was the task and the guarantee of restoration of "morality" in Russia.

But when Stolypin came before the Duma with criticism of the
right Acheront and the promise that while he was in office it would be
kept in check, how did the Duma receive him? It did not understand
that its interest lay in supporting Stolypin's newly-promised policy.
As if on purpose, and for the benefit of "dark forces," the Duma set
out to hinder Stolypin. Vinaver thundered eloquently against the former ministry and its deceitful attitude towards Rachkovski and Budakovski, and made caustic remarks about Trepov (who at this time
was negotiating with Miliukov about a Cadet government). Rodichev
claimed: "There was a time when the ministry might have solemnly
declared to the country that it foreswears the old ways of violence
and arbitrariness and repudiates deceit, but it did not do so. Now,
only by leaving their ministerial posts could the ministers fulfill their
duty to their native land. [Stormy applause, voices: 'resign, resign.']"

Aladin ridiculed Stolypin's speech saying: "He appealed to us with a touching tremor in his voice and meekly begged us to forgive them for the sins of the past because they repented in the present."

Ramishvili mocked Stolypin because he, supposedly, admitted that "All evil and abominable things ruining Russia were done consciously. Whether he asserted it or mentioned it inadvertently, he spoke from the heart; forgive the past, nothing like this will happen in the future."

In the formula of transition adopted by the Duma it was stated that "Only the immediate resignation of the existing ministry and transfer of authority to a cabinet enjoying the confidence of the State Duma can lead the country out of the great and rapidly increasing difficulties." This was the Duma's reaction to Stolypin's frank and manly speech.

Next day Miliukov's delight was expressed in Speech, June 10:

> The resolution adopted yesterday by the State Duma in
> connection with the reply of the Minister of Internal Af-
> fairs clearly stressed the moral of the new lesson that
> the Duma gave the ministry, proving that the ministry is
> unable to understand its duty to the country, that it is
> powerless to fulfill it, and therefore must yield its place
> to a ministry armed with real strength and moral authority.

The conduct of the revolutionary parties in this session of the Duma was understandable. They tried to hinder agreement with the government and heighten the revolutionary mood. But how can Cadet tactics be explained? How could they speak of impartiality and objectivity after such a session? Whom, except their adherents, could the Duma's formula of transition convince?

It is enlightening to compare this interpellation directed to the Minister of Internal Affairs with another to the Minister of Justice. The St. Petersburg justices of the peace suddenly remembered that, according to the decrees of 1864, they had the right to check prisons and free those who were detained unlawfully. For a long time not one of them thought of exercising this right, but they tried to do so after the promulgation of the constitution. As could be expected, it was found that many of those arrested were held without documents to justify their detention. This was immediately corrected; the required documents were furnished and legality triumphed. The Security Regulation made this correction very easy. But the interpellation was not interested in the actions of the Ministry of Internal Affairs, which blandly kept arrested persons without warrants, but in the activities of the court authorities and the Ministry of Justice itself. The Duma wished to know why the justices of the peace and

the public prosecutor were inactive all this time, and what was the
attitude of the Ministry of Justice in regard to this inactivity.

On June 30 the deputy minister, Senator Sollertinski, replied on
behalf of the minister. If his words could be accepted without prejudice, one would have to admit that the Ministry of Justice did all it
could under the constitution. Sollertinski confirmed the sad fact that

> Although the powers of justices of the peace and the public
> prosecutor are limited, consisting almost exclusively of a
> formal review of the documentary correctness of the con-
> finement, we must confess that even these powers have
> their sorry history, confirming once more the fact that
> individual laws not in agreement with the general political
> régime are not practical.... These laws, outlined in the
> judicial statutes of 1864, have fallen into disuse over a
> period of years and had been so thoroughly forgotten that
> when the urban justices of the peace remembered the ex-
> istence of these statutes, and appeared in the prisons, they
> caused some alarm. This alarm extended not only to
> prison wardens who had not seen any justices of the peace
> in their midst until then, but also to public prosecutors
> who responded to this by the narrowest interpretation of
> these powers, and consequently of their own. In the course
> of his supervision the Public Prosecutor of the St. Peters-
> burg Court Chamber reported the decision of the justices
> of the peace to the joint session of the Governing Senate.
> This was not all. I must admit that the Governing Senate
> meeting in joint session, having repealed by its decision
> of June 8 some details of the general competence of the
> Congress of Justices of the Peace, recognized the question
> of limiting their right to visit prisons as so new in court
> practice that it decided to transfer the problem to the gen-
> eral meeting of the Governing Senate. *

----

* This institution was established in 1711 by Peter the Great with
extensive administrative and judicial powers. During subsequent reigns
its functions were altered and it became primarily concerned with the
promulgation and execution of laws. In 1857 there were twelve departments of the Senate, located in St. Petersburg, Moscow, and War-
saw. By the end of the nineteenth century the Senate was further re-
organized into six departments: general administration; peasant
administration; legal department; heraldry; and Courts of Cassation,
one for civil and one for criminal affairs. An Ober-Prokuror presided
over each department. The Minister of Justice, as General Prokuror
and the highest officer of the body, presided over plenary sessions.
Members of the Senate were appointed by the emperor. The Senate
was abolished by the Soviet Government, November 24, 1917. [M. B.]

Such was the confusion in the capital, in the prosecuting magistracy of the St. Petersburg Court Chamber, and in the Senate, the second month of Shcheglovitov's term of office. What did the new minister do when he found out about it? Sollertinski continued:

Before the decision was made by the general meeting of the Senate, and even prior to the June 8 joint session meeting, the Minister of Justice, trying to meet the urgent need for establishing the fundamental principles of the legal reform of November 20, repealed the order of the Public Prosecutor of the St. Petersburg Chamber as incorrect, and ordered him to inform prison wardens immediately that justices of the peace have the right to enter, without hindrance, all places of confinement. At the same time he sent a circular letter to public prosecutors of all district courts, ordering them to investigate immediately, personally or through their subordinates, the justice of detaining prisoners whom they were holding, and henceforth carry out without fail Article 10 of the Statute of the Criminal Code. As for prison wardens who negligently permitted prolongation of the prison term, the Minister of Justice instituted disciplinary measures to deal with them.

What else could the Minister of Justice do? The determination with which he came to the defense of judicial legality recalled the memory of the Shcheglovitov of former days. Later he became an enemy of the constitution and court independence and one of the leaders of reaction, but at this time he was at his zenith. Also edifying and honest was Sollertinski's reference to the "withering of laws that are not in agreement with the general political order." Was he not correct in making this observation? To illustrate the point: when Alexander III ordered the abolition of justices of the peace because they were harmful, and Katkov referred to court regulations as "court republic," would not the attempt of public prosecutors to establish control over gendarmes, or of justices of the peace to free prisoners, have led to a further limitation of their powers? Everyone in Russia knew that the reforms of the 'sixties, the beginning of our restoration, were halted chiefly because they were "not in agreement with the autocracy," which struck at the courts and the zemstvo alike. For this reason, even the Liberation Movement with its slogan "Down with the autocracy" included not only revolutionaries with their utopias but also liberalism, which wanted only the extension of the "great reforms." A new political order was granted in 1906 and a new form of government was established. Henceforth, the methods of government had to be acceptable to the new order, not to the autocracy. It was time for other, obsolete laws to fall into disuse, even before their formal repeal.

How did the Duma react to Sollertinski's declaration? No
one doubted the sincerity of this honest man. Rodichev paid tribute
to him in his opening remarks: "The colleague of the Minister of
Justice spoke subjectively not only the truth but the whole truth."
Then began an eloquent attack against the Ministry of Justice for its
past: for having become, long ago, the servant of the Ministry of
Internal Affairs (applause); for the impotence of court authorities in
prosecuting officials (though the bill dealing with this had been introduced by the new minister more than a month ago and had been left
tabled by the Duma). Rodichev also thundered against the illegal
actions of the former minister, Akimov, and some criminal actions
involving the office of the Chief Public Prosecutor, Shirinski-Shikhmatov,
unnamed by the speaker and still unpunished. Of course, all this might
have been quite true, but what did it have to do with the interpellation?
Zhilkin ironically questioned Sollertinski:

> Who helped to distort so completely the Statutes of '64?
> We know that you come from the social circles which ac-
> complished this distortion of the law; and if you did this
> in order that all legality might vanish, how dare you come
> here and offer to cooperate with us? You punished yourself
> once, let it be your last appearance; do not come here any-
> more [applause]. If you have any understanding of the
> present situation, all you can do now is fulfill the demand
> of the State Duma to go and make way for a real cabinet.
> [burst of applause].

Even Vinaver, who was quite familiar with court procedure and
people associated with it, had some satisfaction from ridiculing Sollertinski:

> It seems that over a forty-year period the law was for-
> gotten, and when it was revealed it caused alarm--first
> in prison offices, then in the prosecuting magistracy.
> The public prosecutor hastened to halt the implementation
> of this newly-revealed law, and when the matter reached
> the Senate, the Senate was perplexed and turned to the
> general meeting to decide what to do with the newly-found
> law. The Ministry of Justice explains this strange pro-
> cedure by the fact that a law not in conformity with the
> political regime falls into disuse....

This may have been witty, but people who live in glass houses
should not throw stones. The law was forgotten not only by the prison
authorities and the prosecuting magistracies but by the justices of the
peace, by lawyers, and by enlightened society itself as well. What
prevented them from remembering this law after October 17 and

demanding its application? While unnecessary stupid articles were written, declaring that after October 17, supposedly, no new laws could be proclaimed, when the monarch's right to promulgate the constitution was being questioned, it would have been easy to send justices of the peace to examine the prisons, and if they were refused admittance, shout about an actual act of lawlessness. But no one did this because these laws "not in conformity with the new political order" were actually forgotten even by our liberal society.

Those who remembered this law and caused a salutary alarm deserved public gratitude. However, the Minister of Justice, who used his authority to restore the law and did not try to prove that the latest security regulations repealed it, had the right to expect more than ridicule. Under such circumstances it was necessary to distinguish friends from foes. Tactics that insisted on confusing them might be successful only if it was a case of asserting the principle: all or nothing. Furthermore, such tactics convinced the government that those of its members who wanted to work with the Duma found themselves in a worse position than those who openly ridiculed it.

This was illustrated by the sad fate of another interpellation concerning the printing in the Pravitelstvennii Viestnik (Government Gazette) of reactionary telegrams addressed to the tsar.

I have pointed out in previous chapters that the enemies of the constitution concealed themselves during the first days of the triumphant opening of the Duma. But the Duma's address was the signal to come out into the open and attack. The reactionary leaders merely followed in the footsteps of the "liberators" and their address, telegraph, and banquet campaigns. The reactionaries, in turn, began to create the impression that they represented public opinion, sending telegrams to the tsar from various parts of Russia. They accused the Duma of plotting to seize the government, acting in a revolutionary manner, humoring foreigners, conspiring against the unity and integrity of the Russian Empire, and so on. The tsar was urged to abolish the Duma and preserve his unlimited autocracy. These appeals were, of course, tactless in themselves, but it was quite improper to print them in the official Government Gazette. By doing this, the government not only expressed its solidarity with them, but it allowed the linking of party appeals with the name of the tsar. It was difficult for the ordinary citizen to believe that this printing could have taken place without the tsar's permission: in fact, this was so unlikely that the Duma was provided with splendid grounds for an interpellation. Not only could it accuse the ministers of encouraging unsuitable attacks on a constitutional institution, but it could also attack the government for unworthy implication of the tsar's name in party quarrels. The blow intended by Goremykin against the Duma could be turned against himself.

But the Duma was prevented from profiting by this favorable position by its earlier statements and the very text of its address. No matter how exaggerated the telegraphic accusations were, the Duma did give grounds for them; it was the first to attack. But the government, by its encouragement of the telegrams, surpassed the Duma and gave it a chance for revenge. However, even on this question, the Duma failed to take advantage of its position and managed to surpass the tactlessness of the government.

The authors of the interpellation considered that the telegrams published in the Government Gazette constituted "an audacious dis-respect to the highest legislative institution." "Audacious disrespect" was the authentic phrasing of the famous Article 128 of the Criminal Code. But this article spoke of "audacious disrespect" only in refer-ence to the Supreme Authority, not in regard to a group of people in a given legislative institution. It was an arrogant and unfortunate idea to employ these sacramental terms in relation to the Duma, to compare respect for it with respect for the Supreme Authority, and to consider attacks on it as treason. It was not up the members of the Duma to demand respect from the population under threat of capital punishment. There still was nothing criminal in the completely improper telegrams and no court would condemn them.

The chief accusation against the government should have been based on the claim that publication of such telegrams involved the tsar in party quarrels. The interpellation apparently intended to do that, but it turned out to be something altogether different. It stated: "The publication of such testimonials above all undermines the dignity of the person to whom they were directed. What did this mean? Did the Duma consider that some telegrams from irresponsible persons could undermine the dignity of the tsar? Stakhovich and Heiden ob-jected with moderation and restraint to these unfortunate words, while Nabokov tried to defend the wording without success. He declared: "Even if in the final analysis these telegrams do not undermine the dignity of the tsar, generally speaking that is their aim. Undoubtedly, if the tsar followed these invitations and proposals which were directed to him, he would by doing this undermine his dignity."

This is to go from Scylla to Charybdis. To say that, as a result of some actions, the tsar would undermine his dignity, is simply a rhetorical twist, inadmissible in relation to the person of the divine tsar. Nabokov evidently sensed that he was tangled up, and rejected this statement. But with the omission of this point all accusation vanished from the interpellation. All that remained was the Duma's indignation because it was shown "audacious disrespect." Thus, in-stead of condemning the activities of the government, the interpellation took the form of a series of questions about the procedure and aims of publishing telegrams addressed to the tsar. This is the way the inter-pellation was phased:

1) What procedure is used to determine the printing of
   telegrams directed to His Majesty? What institutions

or persons are responsible for the choice of telegrams for publication?

2) Was the publication in this case made with the knowledge and consent of the chairman of the Council of
Ministers?

3) If the publication of such messages [above all undermining the dignity of the personage to whom they are
directed] was made with the knowledge and consent
of the chairman of the Council of Ministers, with what
aims in mind was this done?

From the last point, as I already pointed out, the bracketed
words were omitted.

The interpellation, in this form, threatened no one and released
Goremykin from responsibility. This was not an accident. Unfortunately, it was inappropriate for this Duma to defend correctness of expression regarding organs of the constitution, or to express jealous
regard for the dignity of the tsar. But Goremykin did profit by the
Duma's formal mistake. In the wording of the interpellation he discerned, not without reason, the application of Article 40, not 58, of
the Duma Statute, which permitted requests for explanations only if
they directly concerned matters examined by the Duma. Goremykin
replied, not without irony, that he could not discern which one of the
matters being examined by the Duma concerned the urgent interpellation . Then the chairman of the Duma committed a blunder. He
might have replied to Goremykin that the text of the interpellation
pointed out the unlawfulness of certain activities of the authorities,
which were under the control of the Duma, whether or not they concerned matters examined by the Duma. Muromtsev did not do this
and acknowledged and confirmed the direction of the interpellation
according to Article 40. Wishing to match Goremykin's irony, he
made public in the Duma, on May 26, Goremykin's letter and his own
biting reply.

I consider it my duty to declare that anxiety about the
defense of the dignity of the highest state institutions,
whole existence rests on the Fundamental Laws of the
Empire, from criminal attacks circulated through official
organs of the government is a matter of constant concern
and interest to government institutions. [At this point the
chairman's reading was stopped by applause and cries of
"bravo." He continued.] I conveyed to Your Most High
Excellency the urgent declaration adopted by the Duma
questioning the publication in the Government Gazette of
various testimonials, which constitute an audacious disrespect for a legislative institution and arouse one part
of the population against the other.

The Duma was so pleased with this letter that it immediately adopted as the formula of transition, "approving the actions of the chairman." Because of the demand of one of the deputies, they added to these words the word "completely." In voting on this formula, the Duma followed strictly parliamentary procedure, the chairman being replaced by the deputy chairman, since the formula concerned the actions of the chairman. Its adoption was greeted with prolonged applause. The Duma's satisfaction with the effectiveness of the reply concealed its defects.

In the first place, even the Duma following the chairman's lead now considered that this was not an interpellation, but a reference to Article 40. Secondly, no reply was given to Goremykin's formal objection; it was not a question of what was "an essential subject of constant concern of government institutions," but what business connected with the interpellation was at the time being examined by the Duma. After all that the Duma said and did regarding the Fundamental Laws and the government, it was strange for it to pretend to be concerned about the "defense of the dignity of the highest state institutions whose existence rests on the Fundamental Laws of the Empire." This lofty tone rang false from the lips of the organ of revolutionary upheaval.

Muromtsev's letter gave Goremykin an opportunity for further and more obvious derision. On June 2 Goremykin replied: "I am compelled to inform you that the concern you mention about the defense of the dignity of the highest state institutions, whose existence rests on the Fundamental Laws of the Empire, guides my actions in as great a measure as the solicitude revealed in this regard by the State Duma." This hit the nail on the head. Goremykin's mockery was apparently directed not even so much against the interpellation of the State Duma as against the bombastic letter of its chairman.

The Duma found itself in a foolish predicament; then it remembered that it had the right of interpellation, so for the third time an interpellation was sent to Goremykin. The concluding point was formulated as follows: "Have the guilty persons been prosecuted?" After the correspondence that had already taken place this question was ridiculous. Unwilling to compete with the Duma in further sarcasm, Goremykin ended the correspondence on June 30, finding it impossible to give a different reply. The Duma meanwhile conforted itself by declaring, in the transition formula, that it saw in this refusal a new violation of the duties imposed by law on the executive authority.

The Duma might have noticed, in this instance, the difference in attitudes toward it. The Ministry of Internal affairs and the Ministry of Justice answered the interpellations fully and did not hide behind defects of form. But in its relations towards those who wanted to work with it, the Duma adopted an exaggerated tone of impenetrable indignation. It hounded Stolypin and Shcheglovitov with cries of "out" and "resign," and then it was short of ammunition for the chief enemy; for Goremykin, who undermined it and ridiculed it openly, the Duma had only caustic remarks. This was a sad lesson to both friends and foes. The Duma's political stand, which did not correspond to its constitutional role, rather than lack of ability prevented the Duma from handling properly this exceptionally promising task. Furthermore, the Duma's conduct in this interpellation could not in any way have contributed to the introduction of a parliamentary order in Russia.

Chapter Twelve

THE INFLUENCE OF THE DUMA'S WORK

ON THE COUNTRY

Experience showed that no favorable results could be expected
from the legislative work of the Duma, since it consistently rejected
cooperation with the government. The Duma did not examine government bills, sending only its own to committees, either as "raw material" (the agrarian project and the bill on equality), or in finished
form (the law on Assemblies). Nor did it invite representatives of
the ministry to such committees. The government could either participate in debates "on direction" (as did Stishinski and Gurko in connection with the agrarian bill), which was mutilating the constitution,
or wait until the bill was returned by the committee and then propose
changes in the general debate. The legislative procedure took on the
appearance of a Versailles Conference, where the Allies quarrelled
among themselves for a few months but Germany was given a week's
limit for study and objection. By this system the Duma eliminated
the possibility not only of agreement with the government, but also
of coordinated work with it.

In the field of control it was no better. The interpellations, it
is true, were directed to the government and replies were discussed,
but the interpellations were presented in such a way that no reasonable
answer was possible. What reply could be made to the Duma's pretension that its expressed wish be placed above the law (the death
penalty), or its stubborn assertion that the Exceptional Regulations
were already repealed by the Manifesto? When the Deputy Minister
of Internal Affairs, Makarov, tried, in answer to the interpellation,
to analyze and justify each individual case, he was interrupted at
every word, and at the end of his speech, Ramishvili threateningly
asked: "How dare they come to us with such explanations?" Makarov's
reply was, of course, absolutely unnecessary if it were a crime to
use special powers for security reasons. Teamwork required a community of interests, and since the Duma did not recognize the existing
constitution, there could be none between the Duma and the government. The government's hope that once the Duma got down to business, agreement with the government would be facilitated, was
doomed to failure.

The government could not be so blind as to fail to understand
this, but the country began to understand it, too. A different policy
was expected from the Duma by the citizens who regarded this institution as a vital part of the new order; not just a parliament, but evidence that the supreme authorities had finally become concerned with
the needs of the people. If the revolution was now over, the time for
reforms had arrived. But there were no reforms in sight and a semblance of revolution continued. Involuntarily the question was asked:
was it possible that what was going on in the Duma was the much
vaunted constitutional order? The Duma's stand confused everyone.
If it had told the whole truth, that its rights were based on laws that
the former authority established, and so were limited; that there was
a second chamber with the very same rights as the first; and that control of administration remained in the hands of the former authority,
then the citizens, no matter how impatient they might be, would not
have expected a miracle. They would have understood that the restoration of "the morality of the Russian land" would proceed slowly
through the coordinated efforts of the Duma and the government.

But the Duma did not speak this way about itself. It asserted
that, supposedly, it alone expressed the will of the people, which was
above the law, and that the ministers were obliged to submit to the
Duma. So the citizen was perplexed: why then did everything remain
as of old? This was not all. Though the newspapers constantly blared
about the new victories of the Duma over the government, no less than
the Bolsheviks do about their "achievements," what was the practical
result of these victories? The Duma's tactics struck a blow at the
idea that a constitutional order would prove to be Russia's salvation,
and yet this very idea brought victory at the polls. These tactics
also compromised most the supporters of a legal order, whose impotence was openly revealed to all and whose prestige was shaken.

It was quite evident who would benefit from such a state of
affairs. In the first place, those reactionaries whom the Liberation
Movement almost destroyed again appeared on the scene. Their
warnings that Russia was not yet ready for a constitution were apparently being realized. The Duma was uselessly agitating and ex-
citing the country, and adherents of the old régime ridiculed liberal
bureaucrats who betrayed the "legacy of history" and put up ridiculous stakes to get agreement with the Duma. Now they could admire
the fruits of their policy. At first this was only whispered about, but
the trend would be intensified in the future and become liberal bureaucracy's most dangerous enemy, thanks to the tactics of the Duma.

Also triumphant was the left-wing camp, which did not believe
in the possible success of the constitution, and did not want it. For
this camp, the promulgated constitution was a "premature peace."
"As a state institution the Duma is powerless," they said, "but it
is irreplaceable as a weapon of revolution." The Duma would break
down and destroy the old order, personifying the supreme will of the

people in contrast to the broken debris of the traditional state authority.
Everyone had to realize where the real power lay. When the Duma
called itself the legislative authority to which the ministers must submit, when it declared unlawful the subordination of military courts to
laws and not to its wishes, these pretensions were not opposed by the
government as they should have been. Such subtle tactics could not
be understood by the country as a whole. Even if the victories of the
Duma did not go beyond the walls of the Taurida Palace, no matter
how the press extolled them, yet the broad and peaceful masses almost
daily received a different object lesson from the Duma. Seeing the
ministers appointed by the emperor defamed, insulted, and ousted by
the Duma, and discovering that this was considered quite normal, was
an unexpected revelation for people not yet used to such an attitude;
for the unenlightened masses the Duma's conduct became convincing
proof of the impotence and impending doom of the government.

    I recall an episode of a much later period. On April 27, 1917,
there was a gala session of all four Dumas to commemorate the opening of the First Duma. I had to speak to Prince Lvov, who sat in the
deputies' seats, and while chatting with him, I sat down on the arm of
his chair. A. F. Kerenski upbraided me, saying that such familiarity
detracted from the prestige of the chairman in the eyes of the public
that could see us from the gallery. I do not think that this incident
would have had any effect on the prominent people who obtained admission tickets for this session, but this is unimportant. His remark
was characteristic and significant; perhaps it would be better not to
permit such familiarity. But in the period of the First Duma it must
have been clear to left-wing people that the attitude adopted by the
Duma was striking a major blow at the prestige of traditional authority.
To undermine faith in pagan gods, St. Vladimir chopped down the
idols in Kiev. The Duma's actions had a similar effect. What the
Duma did to the ministers was spread across Russia in minute detail
by newspapers, which are always particularly interested in scenes of
this kind. In this manner, not by earnest words and deeds, the Duma
strengthened its popularity, as Purishkevich did later. Interest in
sessions of the Duma increased so much that again, as in wartime,
crowds of children stood along the railway tracks and shouted
"papers!" All Russia was learning what villains our ministers were
and what the Duma was doing to them.

    Had these been individual pranks or rare scenes, they could
have been regarded as accidental, but such scenes became so frequent
that they were regarded as an inseparable part of the Duma session.
The Duma's tone was continually growing more shrill. The Cadets
themselves, of course, did not resort to this; this was the specialty
of their friends and allies. Usually, however, the Cadets did not
oppose them, and Muromtsev, by his conduct, implied the approval
of the entire Duma.

S. Muromtsev's conduct in this respect was enigmatic. Scandals and violence in the Duma were deeply repugnant to his placid, correct, and stately figure, to say nothing of his passion for dignity in parliamentary sessions. Yet he permitted them. It must be admitted that although Muromtsev had the reputation of chairman by God's grace, he could not restrain passions. He was a suitable chairman for triumphant days, not for down-to-earth ones; for the chosen few, not for the throng. He reminded one of a master of ceremonies rather than of a leader. If the Duma had not been dissolved so soon, he would probably have become, even as chairman, one of the first victims of his faith in social maturity, as did Prince G. E. Lvov later as chairman of the Council of Ministers. This was not the kind of Duma and Russian parliament that Muromtsev had pictured to himself in the past; he could grieve about this, but he could neither cope with it nor even struggle against it.

I shall relate a few examples of the conduct of the Duma and its chairman to help us understand the atmosphere of the First Duma.[1]

During the session of June 12, in connection with the food distribution question, Aladin burst forth with this tirade in the presence of the ministers:

> Every time when multimillion expenditures are needed,
> the ministers appear in good time, and we know the results
> of their appearance; three-quarters of the money will re-
> main in the wrong hands, beginning with the ministers and
> ending with the last... [burst of applause]. Gentlemen
> ministers, you have never been too late to plunder the
> Russian people. The starving need help and we will help;
> we have our own committee of eleven; I think that the most
> effective way to help the people is to take the business of the
> people into our own, as yet unstained, hands.... [And the
> speech concluded with these words:] Gentlemen ministers,
> when will you find enough decency and honesty to get out?
> [Loud applause from the center and left wing; voices:
> "Go away, resign!"]

Perhaps too much should not have been expected from Aladin, but what did the chairman do? He made no comment. Stolypin could not stand this tone. Having answered other speakers regarding the nature of the question under discussion, he replied to Aladin's tirade: "I say to their slander, their threats, their... [noise, shouts, 'enough'...] threats to seize administrative authority, [noise, shouts, 'enough'...] that the Minister of Internal Affairs, the bearer of lawful authority will not answer them [noise, shouts...]."

In comparison with Aladin's speech, Stolypin's reply was very reserved; but left-wing deputies considered themselves insulted.

Zhilkin spoke indignantly: "We saw the flushed face, the threatening
gestures directed at the Left; the word 'slander' was flung in our
faces. Can we listen to this with indifference?" It was not the chairman but Count Heiden who reminded Zhilkin that the Duma also
listened to the "unparliamentary" expressions used in regard to the
ministers, which might outweigh the Duma's protests now. The
chairman spoke after Count Heiden. It was to be hoped that, even
belatedly, he would liquidate the incident fairly, but he spoke only of
the formulation of the question, and the Stolypin incident was closed
in silence. Next day, new attacks were showered on Stolypin for the
same statement. Nedonoskov exclaimed: "He cannot justify himself,
no matter how loudly he shouts, beats his breast, and declares his
honesty and his lawfulness. He cannot justify himself with the word
'slander,' which he dared to utter here."

A week later, on June 19, an incident occurred in connection
with Pavlov's speech. There could be no friendly feelings toward
Pavlov among the political defenders of my generation. He personified for us "the death penalty." He demanded that judges impose it,
removed lenient judges, quashed sentences that did not call for the
death penalty, set time limits for appeals--in a word, he did everything to prevent any culprit from escaping the gallows. What he was
guided by, I do not know. Later we saw that assassins, on whose
conscience there was more blood than on Pavlov's, were regarded
as people with hearts of gold; that former freedom-loving people
applauded them, and the agent-provocateur and executioner became
honorable callings. However, one did not have to see all this to
admit that a man's soul is complex and his motives are varied. Fanaticism does not resemble fawning, but the results of both may be
the same. It is best to refrain from moral judgment of our opponents
so long as we do not know them well, and no one knew Pavlov's inner
self. He was simply an enemy, outspoken, dangerous, and merciless. Enemies must be fought, but we have no reason or right to
insult them.

Nevertheless, when Pavlov rose to the tribune on June 19,
during the discussion of the bill dealing with the death penalty, a
row started; the stenographic report is laconic and presents the
incident as follows:

> Chairman: On instructions from the Minister of War
> [noise] the chief military public prosecutor... [noise].
> Voices: "Down."
> Chairman: Gentlemen, if you do not wish to break up
> the session, I ask you to stop... [noise].
> Voices: "Adjournment, enough, we do not want him...."
> Chairman: "The session is adjourned for an hour."

But this is what Vinaver writes: "As soon as Pavlov appeared on the tribune, the hall resounded with unheard-of shouting, whistling, desk thumping, and hundreds of disorderly exclamations." Here is another excerpt from Lokot's book: "I could not take my eyes off an almost completely white old man sitting in the ranks of the party of Popular Freedom. He banged his desk violently, jumped up, shook his fist and shouted: 'Get out, murderer, executioner, out!'..."

It is easy to understand and justify people who lost their equilibrium; this is a reflex. But it was the clear duty of the chairman to protect speakers from insults, maintain order in the Duma, and bring to justice those who violated it. Muromtsev should have done what any chairman does under similar circumstances. On re-opening the session he should have expressed regret about the incident and appealed to the deputies for calmness. Besides, Pavlov had left in the meantime, so the Duma won an inglorious victory. When the deputies reassembled, all the ministers except Pavlov were present. The chairman gave the floor to another minister without any reference to the incident which took place, or a word of regret about the scene all had witnessed.

But the members of the Duma were not at all embarrassed and returned to the incident. Anikin declared: "We can examine the law without any interference on the part of any of these gentlemen, whom we have just driven out of here [applause]." The chairman remained silent. Count Heiden objected to Anikin's rudeness: "We have met here in the name of freedom and every violation of freedom, from my point of view and that of my colleagues, is inadmissible and undesirable. A new order must be introduced by new methods, a profound respect for the law and even for the person of one's enemy [applause]." The applause showed that not everyone regarded the Duma's physical superiority as a moral victory.

However, two Cadets unexpectedly objected to Heiden. Vinaver declared:

> We are also safeguarding the legacy of respect for freedom, but there are limits beyond which patience is exhausted. The State Duma, while it must be jealous of its dignity as an institution, has the right to demand a more respectful attitude toward it and its clearly expressed wishes. All persons who openly oppose the wishes expressed by the State Duma should not appear here on the instructions of ministers.

So this was not an uncontrollable reflex that was regretted; it was a pattern of behavior which the Duma considered it had a right to adopt and even justify morally, as protection of the "Duma's dignity."

The elegant and invariably correct Petrazhitski came to Vinaver's
defense. Here it may well be said: and thou, too, Brutus! He spoke
as follows: "I intended to say what comrade Vinaver said, so I give
up the floor." Is it any wonder that Aladin drew a logical conclusion
from this and proposed a new method of struggle between the Duma
and the government. ? Henceforth the Duma would not give the floor
to everybody, but only to selected persons. These are his words:

> The floor is to be given to those who have a minimum of
> decency and honesty, who can look an honest man straight
> in the eye. Those who do not meet this minimum, never--
> neither today nor tomorrow, nor the day after--will they
> have the opportunity to speak from this tribune. I declare
> in the name of the Labor group that we are most willing to
> listen to any representative whatsoever of the War Ministry,
> but Mr. Pavlov will not say one more word from this tribune.

The chairman remained silent. Next day, June 20, Vinaver, speaking
in regard to another matter, referred to the previous day's scandal
as a "refreshing storm that cleared the atmosphere and should have
shown the difference between friend and foe."

The last incident occurred on June 22. Deputy Siedelnikov had
been subjected to a police beating and an immediate interpellation was
initiated. Stolypin, without waiting for the interpellation to reach him
officially, announced that he had received telephone information from
the chief official about the "regrettable fact," and that he immediately
took steps to investigate the incident. The information he received
differed from the Duma's account, so as soon as he was provided with
unprejudiced facts, he would make a statement. What reply did he
receive from the Duma? Aladin declared:

> If ever again any one of our deputies is touched under
> conditions similar to the Siedelnikov case, not one min-
> ister will ever speak a word from this tribune. If by
> chance any deputy should be killed, not another minister
> will appear here. We disavow the responsibility for their
> immunity. Do not forget that we alone are restraining
> the revolution, that we would not even have to give orders,
> we would only need to say that we are able to do no more,
> and you would disappear not only from these benches, but
> from the face of the land as well. Tell that to your min-
> isters. Do not forget that the time has already come
> when the army's weapons bow before the people's repre-
> sentatives.

And here is his reply to the minister's desire to investigate
the facts first:

Woe betide ministers who ever dare to doubt the words of
deputies. We advance a constitutional principle. Whatever evidence may have been received from corrupt police
and spies, one word from our deputy Siedelnikov is enough
to remove any doubt from the minister's mind; this constitutional principle, I am sure, will be supported by the
Russian people.

The chairman was again silent and suffered all this, including
the declaration of the wonderful "constitutional principle." Individual
deputies protested against Aladin's unnecessary loquacity. Count
Heiden objected and this time, Nabokov as well. He noted ironically
that should he, Nabokov, be beaten or killed, he requested deputy
Aladin to continue "to admit to this tribune both the Minister for Internal Affairs and his cabinet colleagues." However, this mild remark
did not pass off lightly. The Trudoviki became indignant, and Lokot
wrote the next day: "There was no need for such statements by the
Cadets against the Trudoviki. The Cadet remarks in this case were
completely unnecessary, unreasonable, and ill-considered. The Duma need not be preoccupied by Cadet good manners or Cadet 'parliamentary' tactics."

In a commemorative article about Kokoshkin, Vinaver speaks
of the atmosphere of his beloved Duma. He sees in it "the undying
flame of enthusiasm, the soaring of the soul, dignity and straightfor-
wardness," adding to these virtues "the captivating gentleness" by
which the activity of the First Duma "will be imprinted in the memory
of posterity." These words indicate how difficult it is to judge oneself.
As for atmosphere, it is impossible to perceive in the scenes of which
I have given a sample either "dignity" or "gentleness." The Duma
could not regard itself objectively, but the country watched it and was
learning.

Ugly scenes of insults and violence are not a rarity in parliaments; but the indecorum of the Duma had a peculiar character. In
parliaments, clashes involving party differences occur, and deputies
of different parties insult each other; ministers also suffer insults
as party members. But those insulted always find protection, not
only from the chairman but also from the party supporters. With us
it was different. The deputies, generally with little education, addressed one another with particular courtesy in the First Duma. The
chairman observed this very strictly and did not permit insults to the
Duma itself or to individual deputies. In this regard he approached
the ridiculous. His famous phrase, that it is not permissible to utter
criticisms from the tribune for "the Duma is above criticism," became his line of conduct. He decreed that no one may criticize decisions of the Duma or even express regret about them and checked
a deputy for saying "empty appeal." Examples of his strict censor-
ship are numerous. But when ministers were slandered and insulted

he did not protect them and did not extend to them the rules of good
manners that he established. As a result, the impression was created
that while individual deputies were not guilty of excesses, the whole
Duma as an institution was free to defame and revile unhampered the
government appointed by the tsar. Figuratively speaking, the relations of the Duma and the government had the aspect of a war with a
foreign enemy, not of a lawful dispute between different institutions of
the state. This war between the Duma and the government lasted two
months.

It is impossible to recall without wonder the conduct of the members of the government themselves. They did not defend themselves
and did not protest; they permitted, without objections, unconstitutional
claims of the Duma which they, as ministers, were duty-bound to deny; they did not even rebuff insults. When Pavlov was driven out, and
the deputies, the Cadets among them, considered it necessary to declare that they would do the same thing again, the representatives of
other ministries re-entered the hall after the break and, as though
nothing happened, continued their explanations to the Duma. Whether
this was merely a desire for peace, or a secret contempt for the Duma whose uproar could no longer insult, I do not undertake to judge.
In any case, the masses did not understand this. In the Duma, the
government reminded one of a military detail sent to a place of popular unrest and forbidden to use firearms. Usually the soldiers'
patience serves only as provocation to the mob, for it is interpreted
as weakness or fear. At the time, Prince Lvov confided to me his
impression that the government feared the Duma to distraction. If
Prince Lvov thought so, the masses believed this even more strongly.
That is why the boisterous revolutionary fervor, which V. Rozanov
spitefully christened in his witty pamphlet, Kogda Nachalstvo Ushlo,
(When Officialdom Departed, grew stronger. Such fervor is never
in earnest; it is born of confidence of impunity and disappears at the
first serious shout of authority, but as long as the authority does not
assert itself, it makes an impression. At this time the clamor expressed itself in sympathetic telegrams to leaders of left-wing parties;
in the appearance in the Duma of numerous village representatives
with the promise of support and help in case of a clash with the government. This, in turn, nourished the militant mood of the Duma.
The revolutionary spirit of the Duma and the growing revolutionary
mood of the masses nourished and bolstered one another. Local authorities began to realize that they would not be supported from above;
but all revolutionary elements were certain, and they were not mistaken, that the Duma would take their side immediately if anyone dared
to touch them. A telegram sent to one's left-wing deputy would immediately, without any verification, become the basis of a unanimous
interpellation. In this respect the Duma believed all that it was told.

When the military court hearing into the attempt on the life of
General Nepliuev began on May 24 the Duma presented an interpellation declaring that "there is good reason to believe that among the
accused there may be some who are innocent of the matter." This
was proven by the fact that among those summoned was B. V. Savinkov,
whose innocence had been established by "the published declaration of
the Central Committee of the Social-Revolutionaries!"

The Trudoviki received this telegram from a well-known peasant
demagogue of that period, Shcherbak: "The Moscow Chamber ordered
my arrest for attending the Congress of the All-Russian Peasant Union
in Moscow, on November 6-11, 1905. The Chamber has refused to
grant me a postponement. I demand an immediate trial or bail. The
whole bureau of the Peasant Union was freed. I appeal for help to the
State Duma." The telegram became the basis of an interpellation proposed on May 23: "What reasons prevent the fulfillment of the request
of Anton Shcherbak for bail?" Even the venerable Kovalevski rose to
Shcherbak's defense. He said: "I know Shcherbak personally, having
met him as an auditor in a Paris university. He is a very moderate
man, and I absolutely cannot understand how such a man can be the
subject of some exceptional prosecution." In the session of June 9
Kovalevski returned to the Shcherbak case and certified before the Duma that "Shcherbak is kept in confinement only because he shares the
same views that were expressed in literature by Henry George, Iolles,
and other writers recognized and respected by all. These writers, as
far as I know, never were and are not now in prison...."

By chance, I was present as a visitor at the session of the Peasant Congress in November, 1905, and I shall never forget it, particularly Shcherbak's speech. At the end of the session Shcherbak emerged
triumphant. This was the form of his propaganda: he advised the peasants not to pay taxes or debts and to demand payment of their deposits in
full and in gold from all savings banks. He considered himself master
in his province. "The peasants," he said, "will follow me as one
man, no matter where I call them." Such demagogues were useful to
the revolution. Criminal prosecution might be considered useless
against them; perhaps it was better to trust the good sense of society.
But how could Kovalevski consider Shcherbak a "moderate theoretician?" Could it be because he was a poor judge of character, as indicated by his belief that another of his protegés, Lunacharski, was
a champion of "freedom and democracy?" The police department
probably laughed a good deal at this intercession.

Thus, the Duma's work as a revolutionary organ continued, and
various governors reported that if the Duma's existence were prolonged, they would not be responsible for maintenance of order. The
revolutionaries' appreciation of these activities of the Duma is revealed by Vinaver in his Istoriia Vyborgskago Vozzvaniia (History of

the Viborg Appeal). After signing the appeal, Cadet leaders met
with the leaders of the Social-Revolutionaries and the Social-Democrats, who until then reviled the Duma and Cadet tactics. Strange to
say, they extolled them now. Vinaver recorded these impressions:
"The flame of fervent enthusiasm flashed in the eyes of Chernov when
he mentioned the name of the First Duma; the cascade of sonorous
phrases resurrected before his listeners its virtues. All this was
too unexpected to be allowed to go without a reply...."
     The reply was indeed forthcoming. Particularly successful
was the bitterly sarcastic speech of V. Gessen, which reminded
Chernov of the comparatively recent past, and wittily expressed "our
amazement at the very sudden conversion of such confirmed heretics."
Why was Vinaver so surprised? The left-wing parties were consistent. If the Duma's task, as they assumed, was not the strengthening
of the new order and passing reforms beneficial to Russia, but the
strengthening of the revolutionary mood; if the Duma was praised for
serving this aim, and such praise did not embarrass the Cadets, then
why were they surprised that the revolutionary deputies still reviled
the Cadets? It was done because this abuse, sometimes pretended,
served the same purpose for which the Cadets were now praised.
These were only different aspects of the very same policy, that of
strengthening dissatisfaction in the country.
     But if the Duma consciously led to this result, one might ask:
What did it think of the future? What did it hope to gain by heighten-
ing the revolutionary mood? The answer is not difficult to find. The
Duma had no faith in the government and put its hopes in the Acheront.
The left-wing deputies appealed to it, to the unfathomable popular
masses, from the Duma's tribune. Revolutionary elements seemed
to have inundated everything. They were found in the peasant circles, long justly dissatisfied with their position and convinced that
the landowners' property should belong to them. The countryside
was terrifying in its certainty of getting justice, in its habit of acting
as a mob, long deprived of its rights and without the stabilizing influence of lawful authority. Skillful demagogy of Shcherbak's kind
was assured of success there, if not for long then for a while at
least. There were even more revolutionary elements in the labor
circles, where self-sacrificing revolutionary agitators had worked
persistently for a long time and dissatisfaction with the economic
conditions could easily be directed against the government. It was
not difficult to call a strike in factories; an energetic, aggressive
minority is stronger than a passive majority. It it true that the
masses did not know themselves what to expect of the revolution;
they reasoned like the peasant who dreamed of becoming tsar in order to steal one hundred roubles and run away. But to the agitators
it seemed most important to rouse this mass; the rest would be
achieved by inertia. Agrarian pogroms and general strikes were

favorite methods of this period. The government's only recourse
against them was military force, but was it dependable? Here, too,
propaganda was going on. Aladin significantly predicted: "The time
has come when the weapons of the army will bow to the popular representatives." Pogroms in the countryside, strikes in the city, an
armed uprising resulting in the collapse of frightened authority and
the establishment of a Provisional Government that would summon
the master of the Russian land, the Constituent Assembly--this was
the program outlined but not fully realized in 1905. It was carried
out in its entirety in 1917 with undisputed success. All left-wing
parties were in agreement with this program; surprises and disap-
pointments were to come only later. Meanwhile they had to rouse the
Acheront and adjust the Duma's actions to its understanding, taste,
and progress. There was something deeply distressing in the fact
that the Cadets, the élite of the land, the cream of Russian society,
and the illustrious First Duma which, for the first time in Russian
history, received a share of tangible state authority, exchanged it
for the Acheront, seeking its support and approval and dragging at
the heels of demagogy. But having chosen this course the Duma
could not act otherwise.

How did the Cadets regard this policy? What did they expect
from it? Their left wing reasoned as did the revolutionary parties,
preferring the risk of revolution to the slow recovery of state authority. After the collapse of traditional authority under the blows of
revolutionary upheaval would come the time for the Cadets to realize
their plans. This group thought that the revolutionary explosion
would bring them to power, as it actually did in 1917. But the right
wing of the Cadets thought differently. They did not believe in the
possibility of a complete collapse of the government and had enough
sense not to want it, either. Besides, the government was still too
strong to collapse at once, and much work had yet to be done to accomplish this. But the Cadets wanted to weaken and frighten the
government and bring matters to such a state that the government
itself would call on them and their program as saviors. Then it
would be possible to demand conditions that the government now rejected; then would come the time for agreement. This was a wiser
and more realistic tactic, but in order to implement it successfully,
vigilance and tact were required. The Cadets had to recognize the
opportune moment when it presented itself, avoid going to extremes
and burning their bridges behind them. Let us examine this phase
of the State Duma's activity.

Chapter Thirteen

NEGOTIATIONS OVER THE FORMATION OF A

MINISTRY WITHIN THE DUMA

Wartime negotiations with the enemy are unlawful and treasonable. The Duma regarded negotiations with the government in approximately the same manner. The leaders of the Duma eliminated all possibility of contact with the ministers, and yet such contact was essential for carrying on coordinated activities. They tried to show that the Duma was in a special position, a new world to replace the old, with which it had nothing to discuss.

Count Kokovtsev recalls that on the day of the Duma's opening the ministers received an invitation to Taurida Palace for the religious service. The Duma was master there, the government a guest, and the masters did not consider it necessary to be courteous. Count Kokovtsev relates the following incident:

> At the end of the service we all stood in an isolated little
> knot and no one came near us, except Count Heiden who
> knew me when he served in the Office of Petitions. He
> was the only one who greeted a few of us but he, too, did
> not stop to chat, and having stood around for a few minutes
> we all began to disperse, each in his own direction.[1]

This was unimportant but it was symbolic. It is true that the Duma already knew the contents of its address and its intention immediately to demand the resignation of the ministers. It might have seemed inconsistent to the Duma to chat with them politely prior to making such a demand; but it was even more inconsistent to invite them to the religious service. In all probability the invitation was not extended by the Duma but by the appropriate government office, as a matter of routine, and by its conduct the Duma disavowed the gesture.

The Duma elected a chairman through whom normal relations with the government could be established. But, as S. Kryzhanovski tells us, Muromtsev did not consider it necessary to call on members of the government, supposing, probably, that they should have approached him. Stolypin, who for some reason wanted to see Muromtsev,

had to ask Kryzhanovski to arrange their meeting. I recall a similar
episode that started many rumors at the time. The St. Petersburg
City Duma decided to arrange for an official reception in honor of
the State Duma, but with the exception of a few deputies, the Duma
did not attend this function. Whether it considered it beneath its
dignity to accept such an invitation from a "restricted" Duma or
whether there were other reasons, is not known, but the Duma consciously sustained the impression of an institution at war with everyone.

Such an attitude of course hampered agreement. The Duma
and the government behaved like enemies who may not meet openly,
though it was impossible to carry this idea to its logical conclusion.
So communication between them, of necessity, took the form of secret meetings that occurred without the knowledge of the Duma or
the chairman of the Council of Ministers. It is difficult to say how
many there were, but from observation and experience in the Second
Duma, I recall that the deputies were eager to attend them. At
these sessions I heard about similar activities in the First Duma.
It is useless to recall that now, and impossible to guarantee the ac-
curacy of the stories, but in the final analysis, these meetings are
of no interest. I shall touch only on the one that more or less came
into the open and dealt with the possibility of forming a Cadet ministry. Various memoirs have clarified this event and the secret
episodes fill in the picture of the activity of the First State Duma.

The first episode consisted of conversations between Miliukov
and Trepov. In many ways they have remained a riddle to this day,
since the main participant, D. F. Trepov, died long ago and carried
the real secret of the talks to his grave. Miliukov has referred to
them several times and has now related them in greatest detail in
his Russian Memoirs. But Miliukov did not know all aspects of the
situation himself, and imagined much that was incorrect. It is now
impossible to restrict ourselves only to his story. Even in 1921
Miliukov maintained in Three Attempts that

> There were two centers of negotiations for a cabinet
> chosen from the majority in the Duma: the first was at
> court, the second in the ministry. Only the first initia-
> tive, that of Trepov, was in earnest. Trepov's direct
> appeal to me was the beginning of negotiations. Our
> meeting, which I described in detail in Speech, was se-
> cret, and for a while its secrecy was preserved. I sur-
> mise that as a result of our conversation further negotia-
> tions were transferred to several ministers, etc.

Miliukov has not renounced this conjecture to this day, even
though memoir literature has shed new light on the subject. In his

Russian Memoirs he confirms his deduction about the connection
between the Trepov conversations and the later entry of the ministers
into the discussions.

> Following Trepov's first contact, amateur conversations
> about a ministry continued on direct instructions from the
> tsar. I did not expect at that time that my talk with Trepov
> would so soon reach the ear of the tsar, and did not con-
> nect this particular conversation with the events that fol-
> lowed. I was the first to get an invitation from S. A.
> Muromtsev to meet at his home with Ermolov and others.

Thus, even in 1921, Miliukov was convinced that the negotiations
with the ministers, which were carried on in accordance with instructions from the tsar, were the result of his first meeting with Trepov.
Yet the memoirs of A. Izvolski and Count Kokovtsev make it clear
that this was utterly wrong. As a result, an erroneous evaluation
was made of all that was taking place. How the negotiations with
the ministers actually started we learn from the memoirs of Izvolski,
which established without any doubt that the ministers knew nothing
of Trepov's activities at that time. The two initiatives of which Miliukov speaks were not only independent and unrelated, but completely
different in character and mutually exclusive. However, since both
were secret, it might have seemed to Miliukov, who participated in
both, that the second negotiations were merely a continuation of the
first. This is not just a factual error that he now repeats; it is a
misunderstanding of which he was guilty even then, and it had disastrous consequences for the second negotiations. Because of it,
Miliukov did not evaluate the significance of the new negotiations and
took a stand that was not justified by the circumstances.
Another fallacy of Miliukov, closely connected with this one,
was his conviction that only Trepov's initiative was important. On
the contrary, it, in particular, was not and could not be important.
How did these curious negotiations start? Gessen's memoirs
give us a vivid description of their origin.

> The intermediary in these negotiations was a mysterious
> individual. Foreign newspaper correspondents, who ap-
> peared daily to orient themselves with the political situa-
> tion and exchange opinions, were then permanent guests
> in the editorial office of Speech. The most active and
> nimble among them was Lamark, a man who did not in-
> spire confidence. (Ganfman was very hostile towards him,
> because he was suspiciously close to bureaucratic circles).
> Lamark's proposal to Petrunkevich that he meet with
> Trepov was categorically refused because Petrunkevich

considered that he had no right to enter into negotiations with representatives of the government without the party's consent. This did not prevent Lamark from appearing a second time with an invitation to Petrunkevich to come to the restaurant, Kiuba, where Trepov was already waiting. "What do you mean waiting? Did I not tell you distinctly that I refuse to meet him?" exclaimed Petrunkevich. "That is what I conveyed to Trepov," calmly replied the cunning intermediary, "but he still requests you to come to Kiuba."

When this trick failed, Lamark turned to Miliukov, who accepted the invitation.

Why the journalist, who by the irony of fate was the namesake of Lamark, Mirabeau's friend who arranged his first negotiations with the king, was chosen to be the intermediary, is quite easy to understand. Trepov was far removed from liberal society and not many would conduct negotiations with him, as was shown by Petrunkevich's refusal. Trepov needed intermediaries, not necessarily earnest people but alert ones. Who can say whether or not the very thought of a meeting was born in the minds of intermediaries, just as matrimonial plans are often born in the minds of match-makers.

This role of Lamark is also confirmed by Miliukov in his Memoirs. He adds that in agreeing to talks with Trepov, he had no idea of how close Trepov was to the tsar. This declaration is rather amazing, and I am inclined to consider it a self-suggestion of a later period, for everyone was aware of Trepov's position in 1906. And if, by some miracle, Miliukov alone did not know it, why should he have started talks with him? However, this is unimportant, particularly because later Miliukov even exaggerated Trepov's influence in the negotiations. Something else is more important: what was the tsar's attitude to Trepov's initiative?

Trepov might have started negotiations on his own account, without the tsar's knowledge, depending on the sovereign's confidence in him and knowing he would not be blamed for his desire to reconnoiter the camp of the enemies. And of course, this was the fact of the matter. Had the tsar known of the negotiations between Trepov and Miliukov when he instructed several ministers to conduct such negotiations with the same people, he could not have failed to say something to them about what had been done previously by Trepov. Yet he said nothing about it to anyone. Izvolski who was abreast of the latest negotiations, categorically insists that even if Trepov conducted some negotiations, it was without the tsar's knowledge.

But if Trepov turned to Miliukov only for information, he did not limit himself to that. After the talks, Trepov came to the conclusion that a parliamentary Cadet ministry was highly desirable.

He presented this plan to the tsar, apparently even with the list of
ministers. Miliukov recalls in his Russian Memoirs that he himself
was excluded from the list, which is not significant. However, it is
most interesting that the result of restaurant talks between Trepov
and Miliukov was at a certain time presented to the tsar. Undoubtedly, it met no sympathy whatever from him and, when it became
known, objections against it arose on all sides.

  Kokovtsev recalls that just before the dissolution of the Duma,
A. F. Trepov came to inform him of his brother's mad plan and
begged Kokovtsev to take measures to prevent this plan from being
carried out. Kokovtsev promised to speak about it in his next report
to the tsar, but this was unnecessary. Four days later, A. F. Trepov
returned and informed Kokovtsev that D. F. Trepov contacted him
from Peterhof and told him that he had the impression that his project was
unsuccessful and that the tsar did not speak of it again. Some time
later the tsar himself told Izvolski about Trepov's plan, which,
apparently, was presented to the tsar about the time the ministerial
discussions of a quite different plan were taking place. Originating
from different sources and with different aims, both plans reached
the tsar at the same time, and Trepov's was rejected. After this,
Trepov's influence weakened: he lost the tsar's confidence and soon
died--of disappointment, it was said. Thus he became the chief
casualty of his meetings with Miliukov.

  What was the nature of the plan with which Miliukov successfully tempted Trepov, who was unsuccessful in tempting the tsar?
Periodicals that published Trepov's views have given an insight into
the matter, and Miliukov's latest references in Russian Memoirs
have confirmed what we already knew. Of course, no matter how
Trepov conceived his desire to speak with Miliukov, the latter regarded the action as proof that the government was impotent to halt
the revolution and was willing to make big concessions to obtain
reconciliation with the Duma. Thus Miliukov's expectations were
becoming a reality; the tactic of unity with revolution was bearing
fruit. Now it was possible to put forth the Duma's conditions. Of
course, he did not repeat his error of 1905 and demand a Constituent Assembly. It was too late for that, but true to his program
and his public announcements, he demanded a parliamentary, that
is a Cadet party, ministry. This is always done in really parliamentary countries: the leader of the opposition is instructed to form
a cabinet.

  Then discussion started about the program of the future government. Miliukov presented the Cadet party program, including
full amnesty, Cadet agrarian reform, and the review of the Fundamental Laws. Trepov noted all this in his notebook, without objections.
Miliukov was surprised, but came to the conclusion that "further
negotiations on this basis are possible." Before long, he received a

partial reply to his demands from Trepov's interview with Reuter's
agency. I am not familiar with Trepov's statement, but their divergence of opinion is revealed in Miliukov's article in Speech on June
30. In the interview Trepov definitely expressed himself in favor of a
Cadet ministry and Miliukov praised Trepov for his foresight. But
Trepov thought that a Cadet ministry was possible without implementing the full Cadet program. He was against expropriation[2] and
complete amnesty. However Miliukov warned: ''If so, we might as
well stop talking about a Cadet ministry. The party will agree to a
sacrifice in taking over the government on one condition: that the
party will remain the same as it was at the polls.''

In his Memoirs Miliukov says nothing about the Cadet concession.
Apparently, they would break with the revolution, which would no
longer be needed once they themselves were in power. The fact that
there would be no Trudoviki in the Cadet ministry was an illustration
of the new attitude of the Cadets to revolution. On June 18 Miliukov
wrote an article in Speech under the expressive title, ''Is There a
Basis in the Duma for a Cadet Ministry?'' He proved that not only
was such a ministry possible, but that it was the only one possible.
No coalition ministry would be necessary and the Trudoviki were not
acceptable.

> Not only because there are not enough people prepared for
> this role among the members of this group, but also be-
> cause its leaders would hardly want to change their posi-
> tion to the less favorable one that they would have to accept
> in the ministry. The Cadets are assured of a safe majority
> even without them. The ministry will be safer and stron-
> ger if it will not be a coalition but a purely Cadet one.

If Miliukov could convince Trepov of the soundness of this plan
in a restaurant, it was of course, on his part, a victory over Trepov.
But like the majority of Cadet victories it was self-deception. We
can evaluate this plan better now.

In 1921 Miliukov wrote in Three Attempts that a Cadet ministry would be the first hurdle that would halt the revolutionary process. Why would a Cadet parliamentary ministry be a more serious
obstacle to revolution than agreement between the Duma and the government; better than a common plan of action on the part of the wise
section of the bureaucracy and the cream of liberal society? Why
did the Cadets reject the attempt at agreement with the government
and prefer a purely Cadet ministry? At the time when all this was
taking place, they might still have nursed the illusion that they knew
everything and could do everything, and that the people would follow
them. But how could this still be repeated in 1921, after our unfortunate experience? What should have been done to halt the revolu-

tionary process? First and foremost, reforms needed by the nation
as a whole had to be introduced. The bureaucracy understood this
as well as the Cadets and had much more ability and experience in
drafting laws. Indeed, we had seen the results of the Duma's attempts
at independent legislative action. The Duma preferred dramatic effects to realistic accomplishments and considered declarations superior to legislative output. To achieve these aims, the Duma end-
lessly complicated the simplest questions. It put first on the order
paper whatever revolutionary demagogy prompted--amnesty, confiscation of land from private owners--but not the country's needs.
The Cadets could not deviate from these artificial demands, for their
allies would not have permitted it. Thus, any reforms that they might
have introduced would of themselves result not in forestalling but
rather in hastening the revolution.

But above all, how would they have halted the revolutionary
process? Did they really expect that the revolutionary parties would
lay down their arms because they had confidence in the Cadets, and
would be pleased to see them as the government? Their ministry
would be received by the left-wing parties as treachery to the "opposition bloc" and betrayal of the national welfare for the sake of
ministerial portfolios. This theme of the future treachery of the Cadets had been developing for some time. All the malice and accusations, which until now were directed to the ministerial benches,
would be heaped upon the heads of the Cadet traitors. The concession
made to the Cadets by the traditional authority would merely have inspired the destructive energy of the revolutionary parties. It is ever
thus. This was shown in 1917 when the revolutionary parties began
to "deepen" the revolution after the fall of the monarchy and the creation of the Provisional Government with its liberal program. So,
too, in 1936, particularly after the victory of the Popular Front
under the ministry of L. Blum, France experienced the intensified
occupation of factories and an upsurge of Communist financial and
international demagogy.

The Cadets, of course, would have been superior to Goremykin
in replying to verbal attacks in the Duma, and debates would have
assumed an earnestness and interest that they rarely had in the First
Duma.. But it would not have been merely a question of speeches in
the Duma. The country would have witnessed the spontaneous upsurge of the masses--pogroms of estates, general strikes, armed
resistance, terror, and finally insurrection. What would the Cadets
have done to cope with this? We can answer this now because we
saw them in action before and after. In December, 1905, we merely
heard their advice to the government to abolish the Exceptional Regulations and withdraw the troops. But in 1917 we saw them in power
and observed their actions; they hastened to destroy the police, remove all governors, and submit to the will of the people. Herein

lies the basic weakness not only of revolutionary governments but of
liberal governments, which, by their origin, are indebted to revolution. Without betraying themselves and contradicting their whole
ideology and their recent past, they are unable to fight revolution
with force. The Cadet ministry, too, could not have dealt with such
a task. Its position would have been even more difficult than that of
other parties. The tsar had no confidence in the Cadets and would
have permitted them fewer privileges than he would permit others;
yet the revolutionary masses would have demanded more concessions
from the Cadets than from persons not connected with them in the
past.

Thus a Cadet ministry would not have become an obstacle to
revolution, but the first step towards it. The year 1906 would have
anticipated what 1917 made a reality. Of course the government was
stronger in 1906, the people incomparably less revolutionary, and
the troops were not occupied at the front. Revolutionary excesses
could be easily crushed by force in 1906. This was possible, but it
would not have been done by the Cadets, by the liberal parties, or by
liberal measures. It would have been done by the old régime and,
at least for a time, it would again have triumphed not only over revolution but also over liberalism, which had compromised itself. Forming a Cadet ministry in a period of struggle against revolution was
like playing a losing game. The winner would have been either revolution or the old order, which would have found strong defenders in
the presence of danger. There could be no hope for the triumph of
liberal principles. They had to be served differently, not as the
First Duma wished to serve them.

In 1906 the Cadets did not yet understand this. They had not
yet learned the real lessons of history. But Miliukov's assurance
that his plan convinced not only Trepov, but also through him the
tsar, had disastrous results. Miliukov was convinced that the tsar
agreed, in principle, to the Cadet ministry, and under the impression of this conviction, he later talked in an irreconcilable tone with
Stolypin, Count Heiden, and Muromtsev, when they spoke to him
about something altogether different. That was why he was so indignant, later, at the ambitious courtier, Stolypin, who supposedly
undermined his Cadet ministry.

This was obvious. But what was Trepov's role in this picture?
The memoirs of Izvolski throw an unexpected light on the matter.
In our recent history Trepov was the personification of contradictions.
Liberal society considered him its chief enemy, remembering his
notorious phrase, "do not spare the ammunition." Trepov's removal was one of the first conditions laid down before Witte in 1905.
In June, 1906, when Miliukov was already conducting negotiations
with Trepov, Vinaver, in speaking about underground printing
presses in the department of the Ministry of Internal Affairs, accused

Trepov in particular of pogrom work. Witte told and wrote about the
fateful influence wielded over the tsar by Trepov, in the capacity of
Court Commandant, and his opposition to Witte's liberal course.
This was one facet of his personality, but there were also others.
In the conference on the Bulygin Duma, Trepov defended from right-
wing attack Article 49, which prohibited presentation to the tsar of
bills rejected by a qualified majority vote. He defended the clause
without soothing words, as others did, but with a blunt frankness, declaring that this was a limitation of autocracy but that it was beneficial for the state. Apparently he also advised granting autonomy
to universities. He was less restricted by routine than most others,
and was not afraid of new ways. However his devotion to the tsar
was so well-known that he could afford to do what others would not
have dared.

     This helps us to understand why Trepov, in particular, could
decide not only on a talk with Miliukov but also on the plan of the
Cadet ministry. The idea itself, as was proved later, occurred to
him even before his talk with Miliukov. Kokovtsev tells us that on
May 6, the day of the tsar's birthday, just after the address had
been received, Trepov surprised him at the reception by asking him
what he thought of a ministry responsible to the Duma, and of the
possibility of preserving a ministry dependent entirely on the monarch,
now that the Duma had come into existence? Such a conversation was
not timely and not in place, and Kokovtsev did not support it; but this
shows that, even before the negotiations with Miliukov, Trepov, in
some mysterious manner, was prepared for a responsible ministry.

     That Trepov later accepted this idea wholeheartedly is apparent
also from his interview with Reuter's, to which I referred earlier.
In it he categorically announced that "neither a coalition ministry
nor a ministry chosen outside the Duma would give the country peace."
The decisiveness of this conclusion is not surprising. Neophytes
often go further than those who have thought about certain questions
for a long time. Nevertheless, even if Trepov could think so on May
6, his state experience should have prompted him to realize the
impracticability of this plan now, when the mood of the Duma and
Cadet tactics were more clearly defined. He might have been able
to support a Cadet ministry, in spite of their inexperience in this
type of work, had the Duma and its leaders actually wished to
strengthen the constitution instead of "deepening" the revolution.
But the Cadets were doing the same thing in 1906 for which they
blamed "revolutionary democracy" in 1917. Trepov might have had
some illusions about the political sense of the Cadets, but only until
they presented the address and the resolution of May 13, from which
they could not retreat. But how could he support the idea of a Cadet
ministry after all that he saw? Or did he, a man devoted to the tsar,
regard the prospect of revolution with philosophic calm?

The memoirs of Izvolski give a curious reply to this question. Izvolski learned about the Trepov episode much later, which is why he erroneously placed it in the period following the dissolution of the Duma. It is very easy to confuse exact chronology in memoirs, but in reporting a conversation with Trepov, Izvolski could neither forget nor invent the explanations that Trepov himself gave for his action. Trepov told him that he understood perfectly the danger of a Cadet ministry and the risk of its hastening the revolutionary explosion. But, like Miliukov, he was not afraid of this, though for completely different reasons. In the conflict between a Cadet ministry and the monarch, he could not, at that time, doubt the monarch's victory, in which case the conflict would be only beneficial to the monarchy. While settling the score with the Cadets the old order could be, to a certain degree, restored. That is why a purely Cadet ministry seemed to him preferable to coalition cabinets in which moderate social leaders would participate. Izvolski himself advocated this at the time, but Miliukov rejected the idea.

Was this explanation, resembling an admission of provocation, sincere or invented to justify his plan in a roundabout way? Trepov was a very primitive politician, but he was neither a coward nor a provocateur, and the truth was self-evident. His interview with Reuter's agency quoted by Miliukov in Speech is quite to the point: "A Cadet ministry is connected with heavy risk, but the country finds itself in such a position that it is necessary to take this risk. If even this expedient does not help, then, and only then, will it be necessary to turn to extreme measures."

No attention was paid to these last words, and yet in them lay the whole solution. Trepov saw the other side of the situation more clearly than Miliukov. If the Cadets succeeded in the task, so much the better; this was the shortest route. But if their ministry failed and they were unable to halt the revolution, the government was still sufficiently strong to stop the revolution by physical force, even without their help. Then it would be possible to annul the constitution, which did not justify itself. Trepov would have no regrets about this. Miliukov did not convert him into a constitutionalist by conviction, and the right-wing's hope of gaining an advantage from a temporary triumph of revolution was not at all new. More than once it found supporters in various circles, and it was used in 1905 by Witte to justify his "weak" policy while alluding to Thiers's tactics with the Commune. The same hope was expressed by those who in 1917 refused to defend Kerenski's government from the Bolsheviks. To my amazement, M. A. Stakhovich also reasoned this way on one occasion in 1908. Trepov's interview also hinted at this reasoning, "if the Cadet ministry would not help, then, and only then, should the government resort to extreme measures."

Thus Trepov remained true to himself, but this whole escapade revealed the extent to which this attempt was removed from reality. It was not so much a political act as an entertaining subject for a movie. To Trepov, a restaurant meeting of two prominent enemies was an inspiring theme; both adversaries parried thrusts hoping to use one another to further their own aims, and as a result both failed. Trepov paid for it with his position, and Miliukov paid in a different way; the easy victory over Trepov blinded him to the real facts when the second, more earnest and realistic negotiations on the same theme began.

The second attempt at organizing a cabinet with Duma participation had an entirely different character from the first. They were in fact mutually exclusive. In the negotiations with Trepov, Miliukov wanted to exploit the revolutionary situation in order to create a Cadet ministry with a Cadet program. This would have been a complete victory of the Duma over the traditional authority.

That the second attempt had an entirely different approach[3] is now well known. The first to tell about it was D. N. Shipov, and Miliukov added some valuable information in his Three Attempts. In 1923 Izvolski's memoirs gave the finishing touches to the story. N. N. Lvov could have added more, but we know enough and on the main points all accounts agree.

This attempt, in contrast to the first, did not aim at victory over the government. It aspired to restore, by a joint effort, the relations between the government and the Duma, which were established by the Fundamental Laws, and to end the detrimental conflict between them. This was a belated but not hopeless attempt to return to the point of the Duma's departure from the constitutional course. In conformity with such a task, the second attempt emanated from a different sphere--not from the efforts of two political antipodes to outsmart one another. It was born in a circle of single-minded people, who considered the constitution as the basis of the new order rather than the violation of the rights of the people. Both camps were represented in this group: liberal bureaucrats who no longer dreamed of the return to autocracy; and those wise representatives of our society who did not consider it their calling, first and foremost, to "deepen" the revolution. Their common aim was to strengthen the new order by collaboration between the government and liberal society. Thus the significance of this attempt was not a search for a new form of revolutionary struggle but a return to the constitutional idea.

Characteristically, A. P. Izvolski was the initiator on behalf of the bureaucracy. Because of his past he was in close touch with Zemstvo circles, and the post of Minister of Foreign Affairs enabled him to understand better than anyone else the necessity of reorganizing the political order in Russia. He brought others around to his point of view, among them Stolypin. This was the beginning of his subsequent career. He was a truly national figure, a man of many talents, determined, very active, and able to make decisions. These qualities also accounted for his faults; he was impatient and some-times too quick to make decisions, and often forced his way when such action might have been avoided.

Liberal society was represented in this circle by N. N. Lvov: a man of left-wing opinions, a former contributor to the periodical Osvobozhdenie (Liberation), a member of the "majority" in the zemstvo congresses, one of the founders of the Cadet party and even a recent member of its Central Committee. He belonged to the group who, after the victory of 1905, could no longer understand Cadet tac-tics. He was not a political leader by nature and could diagnose bet-ter than he could point the way or supply methods of correction, but he could frequently penetrate a tangled situation. He was always carried away by some new idea and tried to find converts for it. He could rouse others to action but tried to remain on the sidelines in case of practical work. Thus do I remember him during the years 1915-17. Apparently he was the same in 1906. He was well-endowed with ideas and plans; in time of emergency he could find the appro-priate words to inspire his audience, while some of his speeches were events and provided excellent guidance; but he was not an achiever. Having observed the bacchanalia of the Duma during its early activity, he submitted a memorandum that Izvolski has now pub-blished in its entirety in his book.[4] It was characteristic of Lvov.

Lvov stated that with which all sensible people agreed: the sit-uation could not continue. The work of the Duma with the existing government brought only harm. He put the blame on both, or to be more exact, on the whole Russian past. Dissolution of the Duma would be dangerous because its prestige was still very great and much was still expected of it. Above all, the Duma was not hopeless, and its dissolution was not necessary because the sound elements in it understood the danger of the situation. Through them, normal relations between the Duma and the government could be established, but in order to achieve this, it was essential to change the ministry. Its relations with the Duma were strained to the limit, for which the ministry was to blame, but its removal was not to appear as capitu-lation to the Duma's demands. The change had to be brought about as an act of the free initiative of the monarch. It was quite un-necessary to introduce parliamentarianism in Russia, as the Duma demanded, or to create a party ministry, since there were not enough strong parties in Russia. This was Lvov's oldest and most earnest conviction. So the new ministry had to be nonparty, a coalition con-sisting of experienced representatives of state authority and wise representatives of the Duma. The union of former enemies in one cabinet was referred to as a "coalition ministry," whose task would

be the introduction of necessary reforms. The report did not propose any program because there was no longer any quarrel between
the government and society about the nature of reforms, and the
differences were only regarding details. Participation in the government by representatives of traditional authority and liberal society
was a guarantee that the lawful desires of both would not be forgotten.
Such a government and such a program would meet support in the Duma.

Izvolski included this memorandum in his earliest report to the
tsar, having made up his mind that he would resign in case of failure.
But there was no failure. The tsar listened to him attentively and
accepted the memorandum. A few days later the tsar summoned
Izvolski, and expressing general agreement with the memorandum,
he instructed the minister to enter into negotiations with prospective
members of the new cabinet. The tsar also asked that Stolypin be
brought into the negotiations and sent a personal note for him with
Izvolski. So this time the tsar himself joined the conspiracy, for
everything was still done in secret and many ministers learned about
this post factum.

Thus the matter was on sound foundations this time, in the
camp of the government. Finally deadlock could be overcome and
at least a small step forward made. It was now up to society, that
is the Duma, and in the final analysis, up to the Cadets. Herein lay
their political responsibility, for nothing could be done without them.
The most influential member of the party, its leader Miliukov, though
not a member of the Duma, was the chairman of the Central Committee and the editor of the official party organ. It was impossible to
circumvent Miliukov any more than the Cadets. N. N. Lvov admitted this in his memorandum:

> The attitude toward him in the Duma is characteristic.
> Though he is not a member of the Duma, his influence is
> very great, as much in the Duma as in liberal society,
> and in spite of all his faults, ambition, and inclination to
> intrigues, he is a man of clear insight and political un-
> derstanding. His participation in a ministry could be
> very useful, for he would then become its most energetic
> defender against the left wing. He alone could organize
> a government majority in the Duma under the existing
> difficult circumstances.

Thus began, on direct instructions from the tsar, genuine re-
connaissance among Cadet leaders. Negotiations with Miliukov were
undertaken by the ministers themselves: Izvolski, Stolypin, and
Ermolov. We do not know about the talks of Izvolski and Ermolov
with Miliukov. In his Three Attempts (p. 32) as well as in his
Memoirs, Miliukov mentions only that Ermolov told him that he

was carrying on the conversations on instructions from the tsar, and
that in his opinion, Izvolski was in earnest about the plan. But that
is all he says about them. We are much better informed about the
conversation between Miliukov and Stolypin, since both of them have
recorded it.[5] Their reports coincide, but they reveal the quid pro
quo, which would be very amusing if it were not such a serious matter.
        Stolypin's talk with Miliukov left him with the definite impres-
sion that Miliukov was not sympathetic to a coalition cabinet; instead,
Miliukov made it clear to him that he would not reject a commission
to form a cabinet himself. Such an unexpected turn of events could
only astonish Stolypin, for there was no question of Miliukov's premiership, either among the originating group or in the memorandum.
Now we can realize how this misunderstanding arose. Miliukov considered the talk with Stolypin merely a continuation of his conversations with Trepov, in which the formation of a Cadet ministry seemed
to him a settled question. The differences with Trepov were only on
matters of detail. Stolypin did not know about this, however, and he
was even more surprised when, according to Miliukov's own story,
the latter made it clear to him that there could be no question of his,
Stolypin's, participation in the cabinet.[6] Stolypin replied half-ironi-
cally to this completely incomprehensible and overconfident announcement "that the Minister for Internal Affairs is at the same time the
chief of the gendarmes, fulfilling functions to which the intelligentsia
is not accustomed." "Apparently," says Miliukov ironically in his
turn, "Stolypin was surprised when I answered that the elementary
functions of state authority are familiar to my followers." Of course
he was surprised; it was not a question of the theoretical knowledge
that even students have, but of ability, experience, and aptitude for
this work. At that time the opinion that "every cook can govern the
nation" was not yet prevalent. Stolypin was also surprised at
Miliukov's presumption in claiming this post for liberal society.
Miliukov, too, was very displeased with Stolypin; he stressed in his
story that Stolypin questioned him very superficially about various
points of the Cadet platform, while Trepov questioned him minutely,
trying to absorb details and noting everything in his notebook. Miliukov regarded his conversations with Trepov very earnestly and
thought that the tsar had already agreed, in principle, to the proposals
presented to Trepov. As a result of this misunderstanding, Miliukov treated Stolypin as though the latter was only concerned with
being included in the new cabinet. Finally Miliukov concludes,
"Stolypin's negative attitude to the subject under discussion became
clear from the moment he understood that there could be no question
of his personal participation in the cabinet." This is how history is
sometimes written. The whole thing was like an amusing vaudeville
act. Nevertheless, Stolypin was correct in his general impression.
Miliukov did not favor a coalition cabinet and would not assist its

formation; at the same time, he would not shun forming a cabinet of his own.

But Miliukov was also right, in his turn, when he sensed in
Stolypin the worst enemy of his own plan and understood that Stolypin would try to break up the Trepov combination. This should come
as no surprise.

When Stolypin understood from his conversation with Miliukov
that the Cadets demanded no more, no less than a Cadet ministry,
he frankly told the tsar the adoption of such a proposal threatened
Russia with ruin. Not, of course, because he would not be in the
cabinet; it would be unworthy to consider his attitude the result of
such personal reasons. But Stolypin understood the political situation better than Trepov, and he did not even consider Trepov's alter-
nate plan in case of the ministry's failure. Stolypin did not want the
repeal of the constitution and a return to the autocracy, but he understood that a Cadet cabinet was a dangerous adventure. Besides,
there was no question of that at all; only Miliukov hinted at it, without mentioning Trepov. So far, the tsar agreed only to a coalition
cabinet and only this possibility was being explored. Now the whole
plan was destroyed by Miliukov's unyielding stand. He would not
accept it and this was enough to undermine it; Miliukov's pretension
to become premier seemed merely amusing to Stolypin.

Could the plan for a coalition cabinet succeed in general? Not
likely, for it was too late. A false course is dangerous because, in
time, it leads farther and farther from the goal. Good intentions
are not enough to correct it and a sobering shock is necessary. The
coalition cabinet plan might easily have been adopted by the Cadets
in the early days of the Duma. At that time a constitutional majority,
which Miliukov later began to consider as the bulwark of his Cadet
ministry, could have been formed without any difficulty. This could
have been followed by a normal formation of a coalition ministry, in
which the presence of the members of the Duma would have prevented
the government from wandering off the new liberal road. But the
government did not do this in time, and the Cadets did much to make
such a course impossible. How could they support a coalition ministry after the generally anticonstitutional address, after they declared the Duma to be the legislative authority to which the ministers were supposed to submit? Having once turned in a false direction,
the Cadet leaders followed this course by force of inertia, unable to
change just because some of them would become ministers. The
cheap indignation of the left wing of the Duma and of society would
have descended on these ministers as traitors. Nor could they have
any guarantee that the government, seeing such an attitude toward
them, would listen to them; that dark forces might not vanquish them;
that they might not be cast aside when they were no longer needed.
What use would their entry into the cabinet be if, by doing so, they
would lose their influence over society?

After the preliminary exploration and conversation with Miliukov, the plan for a coalition ministry proved to have no basis. The Cadets did not want it, and without their support it could not exist. The plan was made impossible thanks to the tactics of the Cadet leaders and their ill-founded, grandiose hopes. With the failure of this plan, the chance of agreement between the government and the Duma vanished, but the matter did not end there. A curious reprieve occurred.

This was due to Stolypin's personal intervention. As a clever, far-sighted man, he drew the correct conclusion from his conversations with the Cadet leaders: no agreement could be reached on anything with the First Duma. It did not want a coalition ministry that might be its salvation, and continued to present demands that would ruin Russia. Continuing negotiations on this basis meant losing time and strengthening the growing disorder. To avoid risking a revolution it was necessary to take the offensive. This Duma, which had long ago gone off the tracks, had to be dissolved as soon as possible, and the work started anew. This was the only way to save the constitution; otherwise it was threatened with disaster. As a man of decision, Stolypin at once drew up his plan. He did not want the dissolution of the Duma to be the victory of the chief enemies of the constitution because he feared their excessive reinforcement. Furthermore, he feared that such a dissolution might be interpreted by the country as reactionary, and push the electors to the Left. Hence his personal, unexpected plan was evolved: the formation of a coalition ministry including popular social leaders, which would begin its activity with the dissolution of the Duma and new elections. For the post of chairman of such a ministry he proposed, and the tsar approved, the candidacy of Shipov.

That Stolypin could fabricate such a combination was excusable; he knew little about our liberal society, its sensitiveness and its scruples. But how Lvov could hope to attract Shipov, a man always more strongly influenced by moral than by political considerations, to support such a plan is a riddle to me. I can only explain this by the fact that Lvov recognized the hopelessness of correcting the Duma, and surrendered to the pressure of a stronger man, in this case, Stolypin, and as often happened with him, he was suddenly brimming over with enthusiasm. On June 26, when the unsuspecting Shipov came to St. Petersburg to the regular session of the Imperial Council, N. Lvov met him at the station, brought him up-to-date on the plot and asked him to go to Stolypin, who expected him. Shipov was indignant; he refused to see Stolypin and decided to return to Moscow immediately. But he had no chance to depart. Next day he received a summons to appear before the tsar. Since the issue could not be avoided now, he decided to see Stolypin first, and there he found Izvolski, too. He categorically rejected the proposed plan. In his opinion, there was no reason for immediate dissolution. Shipov

was displeased with the Duma in many ways; he considered the whole
tone of its address, as well as many individual speeches, improper.
But the Duma was not the only guilty party, and its strident speeches
related to the past. A new cabinet would not solve anything, and dissolution was no way to start liberal activity. Stolypin was displeased
with Shipov's reply but was unable to budge Shipov from his stand.

    Then Stolypin reluctantly returned to the old plan, which re-
ceived the preliminary approval of the tsar--the formation of a coalition cabinet, not to effect dissolution but to achieve reconciliation
with the Duma. Stolypin offered Shipov the chairmanship in such a
cabinet. While the first plan for a coalition ministry failed because
of Cadet opposition, the irreproachable Shipov, as chairman, might
overcome Cadet intolerance and be considered acceptable. This was
a new approach and Shipov seemed to have yielded. He promised to
explore the situation before going to the tsar. Naturally the very
same problem had to be faced: what would be the Cadet attitude to
Shipov's ministry? Would they agree to enter it and support it? Without them no ministry could count on the support of the State Duma.
Stolypin reported his previous conversation with Miliukov, which
promised little hope for the plan, but it was decided to approach him
once more. Count Heiden was sent to Miliukov and he received the
same reply: that Miliukov would accept nothing but a Cadet ministry
that he would agree to lead.

    So Shipov went to have a frank talk with his old friend S. A.
Muromtsev. He did not conceal anything from him. Shipov considered the coalition ministry, already accepted in principle by the
tsar, the best solution for the problem of the moment, but the opposition of the Cadet leaders appeared to be an obstacle to this.
Shipov tried to persuade Muromtsev to use his influence to convince
Miliukov and other leaders of the party not to hinder this attempt,
but his arguments were futile. Muromtsev did not object to this
plan in principle, but he considered it impossible to bring about a
change in the finally and completely defined Cadet attitude to this
problem. He said that Miliukov already considered himself premier,
and thereby strengthened Shipov's surmise that a coalition cabinet,
even under his chairmanship, would immediately bring him into conflict with the Duma. Muromtsev's pessimism went even further.
He stated that "No ministry would be able to satisfy this Duma: revolutionary outbursts would be unavoidable and the government would
have to take strong repressive measures against them and thus lose
the badly needed support of liberal society." So, in Muromtsev's
opinion, neither a coalition ministry to which the tsar agreed but
which the Cadets rejected, nor the Cadet ministry that Miliukov
wanted presented a way out of the situation.

    This was the negative baggage with which Shipov went to the
tsar. However, Shipov did not want to admit, even to himself, that
Stolypin was right, that nothing could be done with this Duma. What

positive proposal could be make to prevent the dissolution of the Duma? In spite of the hopeless mood of Muromtsev, who saw no way out for the Duma, Shipov decided to make an attempt before it was too late and propose Muromtsev as chairman of a Cadet ministry. He describes in detail his conversation with the tsar, and it is most interesting to note how far the tsar's compliance went at that time.

The tsar already learned from Stolypin that Shipov did not agree either to dissolution or to heading a coalition cabinet, but he asked to see Shipov personally and hear his objections. During the course of the conversation, when Shipov hinted at the possibility of the abolition of the constitutional order or a change in the election law, the tsar interrupted him both times with apparent displeasure, saying "there could be no question of that." This was true: after the dissolution of the Duma neither the one nor the other was done. This did not prevent Miliukov from maintaining in his Three Attempts that the tsar's displeasure with Shipov's words was explained by Shipov's "striking too close to the truth." I repeat once more, this is how history is sometimes written.

Having rejected the proposal made to him, Shipov put before the tsar his own plan. He proposed yielding to Cadet wishes and trying a Cadet ministry because the Cadets would not accept anything else. The only change that he recommended was making Muromtsev premier instead of Miliukov, whom he did not consider suited to this role. Miliukov should be given another portfolio, Foreign or Internal Affairs. Shipov added that he was confident that, once in power, the Cadets would behave differently from the way they behaved as the opposition, that they would moderate their program demands and would pay ten or twenty kopeks per rouble on their political promissory notes.

This proposal aroused the tsar's interest and he asked for clarification. He raised five questions in the Cadet program which confused him: the abolition of the death penalty; the agrarian question with expropriation; complete amnesty; equality of rights of all nationalities; and Polish autonomy. Shipov reminded the tsar that there was an Imperial Council which could amend and improve Cadet measures and projects, as it had already done in regard to the abolition of the death penalty. Regarding the agrarian question, Shipov assured the tsar that expropriation would apply only to absolutely necessary extreme cases. Instead of national autonomy for Poland, it would be possible to confine the problem to the extension of local self-government and greater Polish cultural rights. As for equality regardless of nationality or faith, Shipov foresaw no Cadet concessions in this respect, but in contrast to the other points, this question was already favorably regarded by the tsar, according to Witte's report accompanying the Manifesto of October 17.

This was Shipov's plan. The tsar did not express his opinion about it but thanked him for his frankness. However, his attitude to the plan soon became known to others. Izvolski, Stolypin, Ermolov, and later P. N. Trubetskoi reported to Shipov, the former with satisfaction, Stolypin with disappointment, that his report made a good impression and that his plan was receiving sympathetic consideration.

What was the attitude of the Cadets? Shipov first of all told Muromtsev of his conversation with the tsar. While he spoke Muromtsev agreed with everything, but he became upset when Shipov mentioned that he suggested himself as candidate for premier. "What basis and what right have you," he said to Shipov, "to touch on a question that must be decided by the political party alone?" This objection was unexpected, since choosing the premier is the prerogative of the head of the nation, not of a political party. If this is done sometimes now, it is a distortion of parliamentary order. As far as Muromtsev was concerned, it was a manner of speaking rather than a question of party rights. Shipov understood that Muromtsev regarded as the chief difficulty as the formation of a cabinet with Miliukov's participation. "It is hard for two bears to get along in one den," said Muromtsev. Miliukov himself indirectly confirmed this difficulty. He tells us in his Three Attempts that a few days later Muromtsev called him to his office and asked this question point blank: "Which of us two will be the premier?" Miliukov assured him that there would be no quarrel over personalities and that he would support his candidacy. "This reply," said Miliukov, "apparently made a good impression on S. A." We must conclude that while Muromtsev feared Miliukov's competition, he agreed in principle to accept the premiership, even though this contradicted the pessimism he expressed in his first conversation with Shipov.

Thus the Cadet ministry under the chairmanship of S. A. Muromtsev, improvised by Shipov during his audience with the tsar, once more appeared on the scene as a realistic plan, not merely a theme of restaurant conversations. And until the very dissolution of the Duma, Muromtsev expected the tsar to summon him.

This summons did not come. The Duma was dissolved first. But could there be any clearer indication than this improvised plan how hopeless the preservation of the Duma was at this moment?

What would have happened if Muromtsev had been summoned at this time? Official negotiations with the Cadets would have started. Would they justify Shipov's hasty supposition that they would understand that they were not the whole nation, and that their program was not only of no benefit to Russia, but it was not even the will of the people? Would they agree to pay ten kopeks per rouble on these promissory notes? This was impossible because they were too entangled. In Speech of June 27 Miliukov considered it his duty to disperse publicly the Trepov optimism regarding Cadet program concessions. Later, in 1921, Miliukov admitted in his Three Attempts that

> The party and the caucus of the party were in such an un-
> compromising mood that even my position, which seemed
> so stubborn to Shipov, appeared too conciliatory. I think
> that I would even have been forbidden to attend meetings
> for negotiations about the ministry if I had put the question
> formally before the caucus for a decision.[7]

It is difficult to dispute this because it was the only reply conforming
to the earlier accepted Cadet line.

But supposing we admit the unlikely agreement between the government and the Cadets, concessions made by one side or the other,
or compromise between them, what would have been the advantage of
this cabinet under the chairmanship of Muromtsev over a Miliukov
cabinet? As I mentioned previously, I am certain that Miliukov would
not have proved equal to the task; he would have been destroyed by
those revolutionary forces which he himself aroused in his desire
"not to extinguish the revolutionary flame. " But it would have been
even more difficult for Muromtsev to overpower them. His nature
rendered him even less suited for the role of a leader. Miliukov was
right when he said in his Three Attempts that Muromtsev enjoyed
"tremendous respect but he did not belong to the core of leaders of
a political group. " Even opponents could not help respecting him,
but he could not lead a party, did not want to do it, and did not even
try. Others would certainly become leaders behind the scenes.

At the same time, and this was another of his shortcomings,
Muromtsev was susceptible to the influence of others, not because
of individual weakness or lack of will power, but because he considered such submission the essence of democracy. He understood
many things more clearly and was more far-sighted than Miliukov,
but he could not display his true personality even as chairman. He
remained the "technician" and followed others on a course that he
knew was wrong and in whose usefulness he no longer believed, as
is clear from his frank talk with Shipov. Later he signed the Viborg
Appeal without a murmur, even though he was critical of it. As head
of the government he would have effaced himself behind the decisions
of the party and its executive. Even more than Miliukov, he would
have been a leader of the modern type: "Je suis leur chef, donc je
les suis (I am their chief so I follow them). " But at that time something entirely different was needed.

Besides, it was not enough for Muromtsev to have the Duma's
majority behind him; he would have had to have the tsar's confidence.
With the existing mood of the Duma, the one excluded the other. In
the new post, Muromtsev would have been subjected to savage attacks
and criticism of left-wing allies, and intrigues and circumvention of
the ruling class. His passiveness, stateliness, correctness, fastid-

iousness, and political honesty would have hindered him from struggling against them. Fate saved him from this ordeal, retaining for
him the scarcely deserved fame as the model chairman of the State
Duma.

Considering the direction that the Cadet party adopted in the
Duma from the very beginning, a Duma ministry was senseless,
whoever may have been chosen as its head. It might have been possible not as a compromise but only as a final transition to revolution.
Therefore, if the tsar did not want to yield to revolution as he yielded
eleven years later, he had no other choice except the dissolution of
the Duma. As a truly national figure, Stolypin understood this and
decided to act accordingly. It is not necessary to look for petty,
personal motives to explain his action. The Duma had to be dissolved
to save the constitution, just as, in 1917, the court revolution tried
to remove the tsar to save the monarchy and the dynasty. Stolypin
understood the necessity for dissolving the Duma and was able to
overcome the prejudice against it. However, the Duma itself helped
him in this.

Chapter Fourteen

THE LAST DAYS OF THE DUMA

No special justification was required for the dissolution of the
Duma; there were already reasons enough. It was clear to all that it
was impossible to continue the anarchy in the Duma without detriment
to the country, so the "appeal to the people" with which the Duma's
existence ended was, in reality, simply an excuse. Though it was
provocative in itself, it was a striking revelation of the gulf between
the Duma's pretensions and its actual accomplishments. By its
"appeal," the Duma struck a mortal blow at itself and hastened its
dissolution.

I shall recount how this happened.

On June 20 a government communication regarding the agrarian
question appeared in the Government Gazette. It was generally so
inoffensive that, at first, the Duma paid no attention to it. The government presented the main points of the bills it introduced for the
Duma's examination, intended to "improve the welfare of the land
peasantry, extend peasant landownership, and change the method of
land tenure on allotment lands." In addition to the bills that it already had introduced, the government pointed out some measures
that it proposed to adopt in administration, such as emigration and
assistance to the Peasant Bank.

Had the communication limited itself to this, even the pre-
tentious First Duma could hardly have objected to it. But the government used this announcement to object decisively to the "wide-spread
conviction among the peasants that land can belong only to those who
work on it; therefore, expropriation of all privately owned land must
be carried out."

In conclusion, the government reminded the peasants that the
improvement of their condition could be expected through peaceful
work rather than through confusion and violence, and reassured them
that their welfare was the tsar's constant concern.

That was the entire content of this notorious communication.
Now it seems surprising that the Duma should have been so indignant
about it and should have taken such violent exception to it. This reaction was illustrated in the speech of the first orator, Kuzmin-
Karavaev. He declared that when he read the government communication, though he was a moderate man and not a very young one, he

became violently angry. "Such a declaration simply calls for an uprising," he said. It is curious to note that in N. N. Lvov's memorandum to the tsar, which was being reviewed at that particular time, the
same Kuzmin-Karavaev was considered for a post in the Ministry of
Justice. His words were, of course, simply an excess of eloquence,
but why were the authors of the interpellation so disturbed? What
was unlawful or harmful about the government communication?

Had the Duma retained a shred of fairness, it would have recognized that the government had a moral right to its statement. Its
bills, mentioned in the communication, were ignored by the Duma,
whose elected Committee of Ninety-nine reviewed only the Duma's
bills, while the government's bills were not even sent to the committee as legislative "material." This was not all. The government presented the basic content of these bills in its declaration of
May 13, but the Duma asserted in its formula of transition that "the
government absolutely refuses to satisfy the popular demands for
and expectation of land." The government did disagree with the Duma about compulsory expropriation of private holdings, but the Duma
made it seem as though the government adamantly refused to satisfy
the desire for land. In view of such distortion of its intentions, the
government was within its rights in presenting its plans to the country.
Why blame it?

The Duma was indignant because the government communication
supposedly started a controversy with it, but this was jumping to conclusions and inaccurate as well. The communication took no exception to the Duma: it objected to the "conviction being spread
among the rural population," not necessarily by the Duma. Furthermore, the government announcement objected to the conviction that
"land must belong to those who work on it," which the Duma did not
say, but such a conviction did exist. It was even reflected in the
Duma, in the project of the thirty-three. As a matter of fact, the
Duma did not share this viewpoint and refused to send the proposal
to the committee, even "as material." So it is clearer than ever
that on this point the government did not object to the Duma. Therefore, the insistence that the government started a controversy with
the Duma was either a falsehood or an admission that the Duma
secretly aimed at the adoption of principles that it publicly rejected.
One inference is no better than the other.

The Duma's orators were also displeased because the communication mentioned the tsar's concern about the needs of the peasants and reminded them of what autocracy had done for them in its
day. This was regarded as intentional disparagement of the Duma.
Again, the tsar's concern was not contrasted with that of the Duma,
but with grasping revolutionary tendencies and the desire to settle
the question by force. Besides, why should His Majesty's government have been completely silent about the concern of the tsar?

Indeed, not a single law could go into force without his approval, and
all legislation, administration, and justice were carried on in the
name of the tsar. Why, then, should the mention of his name disparage the Duma, as though it alone governed the country?

Kuzmin-Karavaev gave a peculiar twist to the accusation by
protesting that the government announcement involved the tsar's name
in its own dispute. He said, "The impression is conveyed that the
announcement is expressing the will of the Tsar Emperor, the Highest Authority." It is true that he immediately added that this was
not "stated directly," but why discuss it in such a case? In the name
of justice he should have added that the communication stated something that was quite the contrary.

It began with these words: "Fulfilling the highest command of
the Tsar Emperor, about the immediate adoption of measures for the
improvement of the welfare of the land peasantry, the government
has introduced in the State Duma its proposals," and so on. Thus
the essence of the proposals was a matter of concern to the government; only the aim of these bills was the concern of the tsar, who
commanded that steps be taken immediately for the improvement of
the welfare of the peasantry. In fulfilling this command, the government acted on its own and introduced its bills to the Duma for examination. This did not in any way contradict the constitution.

What was the real cause of the Duma's genuine indignation?
This is not difficult to guess. For the Duma the entire agrarian
question was centered in its demagogic demand: confiscation of land
from the landowners. For the time being, it set aside everything
else: concern about regulation of land tenure on allotment lands,
deliverance of peasant owners from the heavy burdens suffered by
the peasant class, the conditions of land renting, and everything
else. In the address the Duma even declared itself in favor of indis-
criminate expropriation of privately-owned land, not realizing that
this would include peasant private land. The government announcement was quite different in character. It presented a program of
reforms about which the Duma did not think and with which the Duma
did not concern itself, but it rejected the expropriation of land. Certainly the government objected only to those who completely denied
rights to private land ownership, which could not apply to the Duma.
However, the Duma understood, and rightly so, that such a distinction was too fine for the popular masses, and it knew that many of
the government's conclusions were equally applicable to the bills
that had been presented to the Duma and were at the time studied
in the agrarian committee. The Duma could not tolerate even such
an indirect declaration of disagreement with it. Of course, the Duma
was itself to blame: in the desire to please everybody, the address
was so general that it could be interpreted to mean almost anything.
But since the Duma regarded itself as the spokesman of the sovereign

will of the people, it did not permit even sound objections. Hence its indignation. Psychologically it was quite comprehensible, but how could it be presented in the form of an interpellation? Difference of opinion between the government and the Duma was quite permissible under the constitution, and its expression was not considered irregular. So, in order to initiate an interpellation, the Duma resorted to subterfuge.

In its final form, after elaboration in the committee, the interpellation was formulated as follows:

1) On what basis did the ministry voice its proposals regarding the land question in the definite form of a government communication that may be considered by the people as an act of legislative character, emanating from the Supreme Authority?

2) What measures have been taken to ensure that all organs which published the communication make it quite clear that this announcement is simply a clarification by the ministry of legislative proposals they brought before the Duma for examination, which will not have any force or significance if they are rejected by the State Duma?

In this form the interpellation was not in earnest, because the Fundamental Laws decreed that "no law may be passed without the approval of the Imperial Council and the State Duma." Why, then, was it necessary to compel all publications to explain to the people this elementary fact that no one questioned? Besides, all this was already expressed in this manner in the government communication. In spite of the committee's efforts, the interpellation of the Duma proved completely pointless.

In the original wording of the interpellation there was another curious note, which the committee had the good sense to eliminate. The interpellation was expressed in this way:

1) On what basis is the aforementioned announcement made in the name of the government?

2) Have measures been taken to ensure that the aforementioned announcement, which does not emanate from the government, be immediately withdrawn from circulation and denied in publications that printed it?

It is impossible to understand this declaration without some explanation. In what way did this announcement not emanate from the government? A strange caprice of the chairman of the Duma was responsible for this accusation. In the session of May 24 in reply to

one deputy's demand that the government be asked to resign, the
chairman added this elucidation, as authoritative as it was incomprehensible: "The proposal was that the ministry, and not the government, resign. The State Duma is itself part of the government. The
government is the combination of state institutions embodying state
authority. "

Where did Muromtsev get this terminology, contradicting the
terminology of most western countries and the Manifesto of October
17? The chairman happened to forget that in the transition formula
of May 13, which was then under discussion, the ministry was called
the government. "The government absolutely refuses to satisfy the
popular demands...the government reveals an obvious disregard for
the true interests of the people"--all this was adopted by the Duma
without objections on the part of the chairman. Why Muromtsev later
confused the conceptions of government and state and maintained that
the Duma is part of the government remains a secret. But the Duma
obediently submitted to his demand and began to use the word "ministry" instead of "government. " However, the Duma's submission
to the caprice of its chairman was one thing, but accusing the government of being an impostor when it called itself the government
was something vastly different. The committee realized this and
excluded this ridiculous point.

This curious interpellation would have been forgotten along
with others like it and passed over without incident, had the Duma
not accompanied it by another unexpected gesture, the appeal to the
population. Its initiator was the same Kuzmin-Karavaev, who proposed it in quite a harmless form. Regretting that the Duma had not
yet adopted the proposals of the publishing committee concerning
circularization of the Duma's reports, which would have provided a
suitable procedure for the case now under discussion, he proposed
that: "The interpellation committee, or better still, the agrarian
committee, as the more competent one, be asked to work out a draft
for a reasoned resolution of the State Duma on a means of 'counter-
communication' that could be published in the name of the State
Duma. " So, on June 26, the Duma adopted two decisions: the interpellation to be handed over to the interpellation committee of thirty-
three to be edited, and the request for a project to deal with State
Duma communications, to be sent to the agrarian committee for
elaboration.

On June 27 the interpellation corrected as previously mentioned
was adopted by the Duma, and on July 4 the agrarian committee was
to present its report concerning the "appeal. " It is evident from the
stenographic reports that on June 26 the "decision" of the Duma was
imperceptibly changed into a "communication, " and by July 4 the
"communication" was renamed "an appeal. " This, in fact, became
the excuse for the dissolution of the Duma.

The manifesto dealing with the dissolution of the Duma named the appeal as one of the reasons for this action, stating that the Duma proceeded to "obviously unlawful activities, such as the personal appeal of the Duma to the people."

This conclusion about illegality is not convincing. The fifth chapter of the Duma Statute, dealing with the field of the Duma's competence, did not foresee, of course, "appeals to the people." This chapter enumerated matters in which the Duma had a share of state authority, but in an appeal to the people there is no evidence of authority. Anyone can make an appeal within the limits of general laws on freedom of the press and speech. Indeed, the Duma had the right to reply to greetings and to present an address to the tsar. In the very fact of appealing to the people there was nothing illegal.

But even if I do not see anything illegal in it, I cannot help considering it a very unfortunate political step, which, from various points of view, compromised the Duma and destroyed the last chance for a Cadet ministry.

In the session of July 4, explaining to the meeting the procedure that he proposed to follow in the discussion of the appeal, Muromtsev used an unfortunate expression: "I can compare this act with the act which the State Duma discussed at the very beginning of its activity, the address in reply to the speech from the throne." Apparently Muromtsev had nothing else in mind than the procedure to be followed in the discussion of the appeal. Yet this statement could easily be changed to imply harm to the monarchy. This attracted special attention at that time, since the prospect of the Cadets heading the ministry was being discussed. However, the comparison of these acts was correct and instructive from quite a different point of view.

The address was the first political act of the State Duma, the appeal was its last one. Both were the work of the Cadets, but how different was their fate! During the discussion of the address the Cadets were the leaders of the entire Duma; everyone accepted the address, even the eleven who disagreed and left the hall during the voting period. This was the reception accorded the first Cadet action.

After seventy days passed, the Cadets drew up an analogous act, an appeal to the people, which was attacked for three days both by the Right and by the Left. Only the Cadets defended it. Both the Right and the Left refrained from voting, and once more only Cadet voices were raised in its support--124 in number, a minority of the State Duma. All this was the natural consequence of Cadet tactics; they were paying for their first victory.

On May 4 the Cadets took pride in the unanimous adoption of the address. They, supposedly, succeeded in expressing the mood of the whole Duma and of all liberal society. That this was self-deception was revealed in the appeal. On July 4 Kuzmin-Karavaev, speaking as though it were common knowledge, stated: "The Duma is unanimous in everything that has to do with rejection, but there is no unanimity on positive action. Here our unanimity will inevitably vanish."

The address as a program of the Duma's work could not be based on rejection alone, but the apparent unanimity in the positive part of the program was reached by ambiguity. However, in the appeal, when it was necessary to come down to fundamentals and oppose the government on concrete questions, nothing remained of the vaunted unanimity.

The agrarian question gave further proof of the failure of Cadet tactics. The Duma would have liked to oppose the government communication on the agrarian question with a positive program of its own, but the Duma did not have one. In the address the Duma was united on the vague and ambiguous formula of "expropriation of private estates" only because it was vague and ambiguous. All three projects on this question, introduced in the Duma after the address, differed among themselves. It proved so difficult to carry on discussion in the agrarian committee that nothing was yet adopted by July 4 except the enumeration of categories of land that should be subject to expropriation. The chairman of the agrarian committee reported this to the Duma during the debate. With what could the Duma appeal to the people? Vagueness went so far that when the Duma felt the necessity for dispelling the apprehension, aroused by the publication of the address, that peasant lands would also be expropriated, (which from the first Stishinski and Gurko pointed out demagogically but quite correctly in their speeches and which the government communication of June 20 confirmed), it had to refute the address and refer to the "assumptions" of the agrarian committee. Now having decided to come forward with a shattering accusation, the Duma had nothing definite to offer. It did not even have any approved fundamental proposals on which it might have relied, had it followed the legal course in its legislative activity. But even these were nonexistent, since everything was thrown to the committee simply as "material." The Duma was indignant because the government questioned its promise of compulsory expropriation, but it really had no right to make a promise whose implementation did not depend on the Duma alone. The Duma could not pass anything positive by itself and had only the right to reject. The Duma could state in the address that it was working on a law about expropriation, and by this ambiguous phrase succeed in confusing the ignorant people. But now, when the "i's" had to be dotted, it could not repeat that the expropriation it was proposing would become law. This would have been a falsehood because it involved matters beyond the Duma's competence. What then remained to be said?

The Duma did say only what it could. Since the constitution gave it the right to reject all new bills that displeased it, a right no one questioned, the Duma decided to remind the people about this privilege. The appeal closed with these words: ''The State Duma will not retreat from these foundations of the new land law, and all proposals not in agreement with it will be rejected by the Duma.''

Did the Duma realize how its words might be construed? What did it want to say in general? There was much in the government communication that went beyond the question of expropriation. Its ten points referred to the purchase of new land by the peasants with the help of the state (a subject of insistent peasant demands), of the change-over from communal to personal ownership, of discontinuance of partition, of helping emigration, and of many other matters.

Thus the two programs were quite different. The Duma's program dealt only with expropriation, while the government's spoke of improving conditions on lands already belonging to the peasants, as well as extending the area of peasant land in the normal way, apart from expropriation. The two programs were not mutually exclusive, and some of the government projects were very desirable; should they have been threatened with rejection? What could the peasants think of such a muddle?

When the government promised to improve the mode of peasant land tenure on lands belonging to them now, by emigration of volunteers, elimination of cross-strips in allotments, and amalgamation of strips owned by individual peasants, was this in agreement with the Duma's project? And what of the proposed cooperation of a different kind in providing for voluntary purchases of land for peasants? This was not expropriation, but did it mean that these purchases were forbidden by the Duma? Because the Duma wished to pass its own law, which perhaps it might not succeed in doing, would it reject all other laws of benefit to the peasants? How would such a prospect be regarded, and what might the peasants think of it? This was expressed with simple clarity by the Octobrist, Prince N. S. Volkonski, who said:

> In the government communication the question is solved
> one way, and the very next day another solution appears
> from the Duma; thus the peasants conclude that the Duma
> and the ministers are quarreling and nothing more. What
> pacification can come of this? [Noise, laughter]... We
> have little to say [Noise, laughter] because we have not
> yet accomplished anything. Here, we say that the Duma
> will not retreat from its views, and the ministry states
> that it, too, will not retreat. If neither will retreat
> what will happen? [Laughter] It is quite clear where such
> action will lead. It seems to me that to take such a step

as a direct appeal to the people is by no means sound,
and it will not result in calming the people but will
excite passions even more.

All this was absolutely true. The Duma could say nothing because no unanimity on the agrarian question could be reached even
in the committee. Except for more confusion, no results could 'e
expected from the appeal. Why, then, was it necessary?

And here we come to the fundamental question: what actually
did the Duma wish to achieve by means of it?

During the discussion of the interpellation concerning the government communication, speakers maintained that it would provoke
disorders: first, because it disparaged the importance of the Duma,
the only institution in which the people had faith; and second, because
it denied compulsory expropriation of private estates which, supposedly, the whole nation demanded. The future showed how little
ground there was for the latter assertion. But if the reason for the
appeal to the people was apprehension of disorders and a desire to
prevent them, its content should have corresponded to this aim. If
the Duma actually were the sole authority in the country, its duty
was to call on the people to refrain from violence and let the Duma
defend their interests.

Indeed, many deputies wished to give the appeal such a character.
The stenographic report of the First State Duma concluded with the
session of July 4. There was no record of the last two sessions, and
although there were reports in the papers about them, it is difficult
to find them now. I remember some speeches made at these two
sessions, but I do not want to rely on my memory. I shall confine
myself, therefore, to the session of July 4, which was typical.

Once again the same two viewpoints clashed. Some wanted to
pacify the country with the appeal and prevent violent actions. Deputy
Gvozdev declared, "Let the Duma show that it represents not only
Bielostok[1] but all Russia; that it has been summoned to defend public
law and order no matter who violated it. Only the voice of the Duma,
respected by the peasants, can reassure those who have been deceived
by false instigations of outsiders." Cadet N. F. Ezerski said, "It
is absolutely clear that our appeal is directed against pogroms and
violence, which should not be tolerated in any civilized nations."
This was one point of view.

But there was also another, quite contradictory and unconcealed.
Zhilkin did not want tranquillity and did not consider this to be the aim
of the appeal. He declared:

I do not speak of pacification but of organized struggle
with the old order. "Peacefully and calmly" is an

equivocal expression. Did the State Duma come into being
because of the calm and peaceful flow of Russian life?
[applause]... We summon the people to struggle and say
to them: "No, do not remain quiet and calm, do not wait
peacefully until someday you shall get something from
above"... [and he concluded with these words:] when there
shall be restlessness in the land, in the broad revolutionary
sense, when there shall be organized support, when the
nation shall rally around the Duma, then there will be a
real land law as well as other laws [stormy applause].

Others expressed themselves even more definitely. Deputy Nikolaevski
announced: "The time has come when the State Duma must take over
executive authority into its own hands. I know that the people and half
the army are perplexed at the calm of the State Duma and await only...
[applause]."

These two mutually exclusive aims prevailed before the appeal
was issued. Though people of basically different political views
could vote unanimously for the address in May, which was self-deception, they could not adopt the appeal unanimously. Now a choice had
to be made: either to follow a constitutional course and advise the
people not to hamper it by unlawful actions; or, if the Duma lost
faith in constitutional methods, to stop playing guessing games, admit to the country that the Duma was powerless, and summon the
people to struggle against the government. There were supporters
of both points of view in the Duma and, as always, the decision depended on the Cadet choice. But the Cadets did not want to choose
between the two courses and tried to follow both at once.

The content of the appeal perplexed everyone and could not
have any quieting effect. While the government maintained that there
would be no expropriation, the Duma would not make up its mind and
declare that this was not true, and that expropriation would take place.
After two months' work, the people no longer had any faith in the Duma's omnipotence, yet the Duma was threatening to reject all laws
that were not in agreement with expropriation. Thus the Duma was
openly fighting the government. This, of course, would heighten the
revolutionary mood, but instead of pointing to an outlet for this revolutionary energy, the appeal concluded with these words: "The
State Duma hopes that the people will calmly and peacefully await
the completion of its work in passing such a law."

Considering the whole idea of the appeal, these words appeared
ridiculous. If the Duma really wanted peace and calm, why did it
exaggerate its conflict with the government before the people? But
if it wanted to be supported by the revolutionary forces of the people,
why did it express the hope that in spite of the appeal, the people

would wait patiently and peacefully? This was typical Cadet tactics, successful in reconciling the dissension in its own ranks and nothing more. So, in spite of differences of opinion among themselves, the Cadets once more voted unanimously, but they could not attract anyone else by this maneuver and remained alone in their ambiguous position.

There were other circumstances, too, which made the Cadet failure particularly clear. Debate was not yet ended when rumors began to circulate that the appeal was undermining the plan for a Cadet ministry. On July 5 Miliukov himself reported this to a meeting of Cadet deputies. Both contradictory trends were represented in the meeting, and the discord grew. Some proposed that the appeal be renounced, while the majority maintained their former stand. The controversy was settled in a typically Cadet manner. The revolutionary meaning of the project was left as it was, but the point about the peaceful conduct of the people was stressed somewhat. This was accomplished by transferring this idea from the last paragraph to the beginning of the appeal. This typical Cadet trick had an opposite effect. Having noticed the change, the left wing attacked the Cadets with even greater fervor. Vinaver testifies that the feeling of dissatisfaction found an outlet in various indignant speeches, stressing more than ever the split between the opposing groups and making the outcome of the vote ever more doubtful. This split always existed, but in the past it could be concealed; now former methods were useless and the gulf could no longer be bridged. It is unfortunate that no report of this session has been preserved. I remember the speech of Stakhovich who, unable to contain himself under the constant threat of a popular uprising, exclaimed with his customary passionate earnestness:

> If among the people there are voices which would decide
> this question by force, without taking anything into con-
> sideration, the Duma must say to such people: Be silent!
> This is an insane, criminal clamor. For a thousand
> years Russia was being created and built up with the sweat
> and blood of the people; Russia belongs to all, not merely
> to our tempestuous generation.

And when the Cadets adopted their appeal, after such impassioned speeches, with only the Cadets voting for it, Vinaver had this to say:

> It was not an act of all the popular representatives, impres-
> sive in its daring intent and in its unanimity and uplifted
> mood, but the exhausted product of the victory of one party,
> accompanied by the bitter indignation of some and the

morose silence of others. And what is most important,
by the process of its birth it revealed the inability of the
Duma as a whole to create, when necessary, a harmonious,
tightly-knit majority. The plan for a Duma ministry received its heaviest blow, and in the meanwhile a dilemma
had already been formulated: a Duma ministry or dissolution.

Miliukov alone remained satisfied, or tried to appear so. Here
is what he wrote:

> The consciousness of the importance of the step to be under-
> taken and the feeling of solidarity with the general work of
> the State Duma triumphed among the groups adjacent to the
> center. The voting that followed was unparalleled in the
> annals of the Duma, with 124 votes for the project. The
> victory of this majority was made possible by the action
> of the labor group and the Polish bloc. Neither of them
> wanted to support this project, but evidently they under-
> stood the political harm that could result from its defeat.
> Their decision to abstain from voting must be greeted as
> proof of the supreme unity that guaranteed the Duma its
> victory over the ministry under the most difficult circum-
> stances and in a time of critical decisions. After such a
> vote, the Duma fears nothing.

This was written on July 6, and on July 8 the Duma was dissolved.
The Duma's attitude toward constitutional legality, clearly revealed in the debate on the appeal, was another reason for hastening
the decision to put an end to the Duma. I pointed out elsewhere that
I did not consider the appeal an unlawful action of the Duma, but
others did not regard it in this light. What were they told in reply?
At the very beginning of the debate, Cadet Petrazhitski requested postponement of the discussion. He declared, "I am beginning to doubt whether we can make an announcement to the people
about the land question; whether we can appeal to them ... [noise,
voices: 'of course we can']. I consider that the appeal to the people
is so exceptional an action that I want to dispel this doubt."
The chairman interrupted him. As guardian of constitutional
legality in the Duma, he should have settled this question by means
of his prestige or even his authority. This, however, he did not do;
he simply prohibited it, saying: "I would ask you to speak only of
the subject on the order paper." Doubts about the constitutionality
of the appeal arose among others, too, but they were all silenced
by the single argument: we live in a revolutionary period when laws
may be disregarded. The Duma applauded enthusiastically. The

initiator himself, Kuzmin-Karavaev, admitted that "perhaps full
justification for this act might not be found in theoretical constitutionalism, but we live in such an exceptional period that necessity
compels, perhaps, a retreat from theory." Thus the constitution
was only a theory. This disregard of constitutional legality was expressed most clearly in the speech of Cadet Lednitski, who dotted the
"i's" and annoyed even the Cadets.

> We cannot help noticing that a certain change is taking
> place in the activity of the Duma; a new step is taken on
> a new road--a step which, perhaps, should have been
> taken earlier. There is no doubt whatever that the pro-
> posal which has been introduced is not justified from the
> point of view of the law or of form. However, we did not
> come here, in the name of form but in the name of demands
> of life, in the name of popular welfare, which brought us
> here and which we are trying to achieve. That is why
> I reject the formal objections that might be raised. Per-
> haps the Duma should already be engaged in the elabor-
> ation of the appeal, or even a manifesto to the people
> [stormy applause]; and in this manifesto describe the con-
> dition of the country, and point to the threatening anarchy
> and the efforts of the Duma to pacify the country after satis-
> fying the demands of the people [thunderous applause].

Such were the arguments that roused the enthusiasm of the Duma.
It was acting in an unconstitutional manner, but that was nothing to be
ashamed of; the chairman, by his silence, blessed this theory.
It is true that other speakers--Iakushkin, Kotliarevski and
Kokoshkin--tried to prove that there was nothing unlawful in the appeal; that it was wrong to attach to it the significance of a new step.
This was the correct basis for a constitutional institution to maintain,
but these words made no impression because the reverse was true
from the earliest days of the Duma. Not one of the speakers, least
of all the chairman, condemned an anti-constitutional approach or
stated that the Duma would not resort to it. No one said this because
it could not be said. Herein lay its fundamental fault. Some of the
deputies openly prepared for revolution, while others, though they
did not do so, did nothing to hinder it. The appeal brought all this
into the open. The tsar's plan to dismiss former ministers and entrust the government to a ministry of the Duma, in the hope that the
Cadets would be able to avert the revolution, was undermined in advance by the Duma itself. Dissolution became imperative and urgent.

Chapter Fifteen

DISSOLUTION OF THE DUMA

AND THE VIBORG APPEAL

The prelude to the dissolution of the Duma makes it clear that there was no intention of repealing the constitution. On the contrary, the Duma distorted the constitution, which could be saved only at the price of dissolution, as sometimes the aim of a Palace revolution may be the stablization of the monarchy. No wonder the chief culprit of the dissolution, Stolypin, tried to set up a liberal ministry under Shipov to handle this matter as delicately as possible. Perhaps Stolypin did not understand our society, but this attempt showed what his real intentions were. No one would expect Shipov to agree to betray the constitution for a portfolio. Neither would anyone think that of N. N. Lvov, who approved Stolypin's plan. The circumstances of the dissolution confirmed this interpretation. If the Duma were dissolved and all former ministers dismissed at the same time, it meant that the ministry did not triumph. Furthermore, the enemy of the constitution, Goremykin, was replaced by a constitutionalist, Stolypin, who would not become a second Goremykin when he assumed the post of premier. Once more Stolypin approached Shipov, and as Shipov himself told us, when they met, Stolypin's first words were, "Well, D. N., the dissolution of the Duma has taken place; what is your attitude towards this fact now?" To Shipov's reply that he still held his former convictions, Stolypin said, "I appeal to you both [N. N. Lvov was also present] to enter a cabinet which I will form and assist in the realization of the constitutional principles announced in the Manifesto of October 17. " These words were sufficiently clear; they showed that dissolution was not a blow at the constitution, nor a plot against it.

Outside the Duma everything was done to leave no doubt about it. In the ukase about the dissolution, in conformity with the Fundamental Laws and in spite of the unusual but easily explained period between the Dumas, the exact date of the convocation of the next Duma was stated. The manifesto confirmed the tsar's decision not to violate the constitution. It read:

Dissolving the present State Duma, We confirm at the same
time Our unchanged intention of retaining in effect the same
law concerning the establishment of this institution, and
according to this Our Ukase this July 8, We instructed the
Governing Senate to set the time of the Duma's new convocation for February 20, 1907.

Everything remained as before, as in the October Manifesto; the
government continued the struggle against revolutionary violence while
pursuing a course of liberal reforms. The dissolution manifesto
stated:

But let Our subjects remember that a permanent improvement of national welfare is possible only under absolute
order and tranquillity. Let it be known that We will not
permit any high-handedness or lawlessness, and will use
all the strength of the state power to bring disobedient
persons to the subordination of Our Royal Will.

The struggle against revolution did not presuppose either the
abolition of the Duma or refusal to continue the restoration of Russia.
The manifesto stated this clearly: "With firm faith in God's mercy
and the wisdom of the Russian people, We shall await from the new
State Duma the realization of Our expectations and the introduction
of legislation corresponding to the needs of the new Russia."
Such were the intentions of the government at that time. So
when the Cadets imagined that dissolution repealed the constitution
and it had to be saved, and that they actually did save it by the Viborg
Manifesto, such ideas revealed the atmosphere of self-deception in
which they lived at that time. That was why nothing positive could
be accomplished. When this falsehood is repeated even now, however,
the motive is a political one.
The untimely dissolution of parliament is always an exceptional
event, but it is foreseen by all constitutions and is not considered
catastrophic. However, as Stolypin warned, the dissolution of the
First Duma was regarded as a state upheaval and was a shock indeed. Everyone believed that the country must reply immediately,
as though it had met some challenge. The First Duma self-confidently predicted all along that the country awaited only a signal to
depose the powerless government, and if any encroachment should
be made on the Duma, nothing would be left of the government. "The
dissolution of the Duma," wrote Miliukov confidently on July 6,
"is the equivalent of civil war." Then dissolution came, and to
everyone's amazement, the country remained calm.

Sensitive people could not grasp this passive acceptance. The wise and matter-of-fact Vinaver, whose admiration of the Duma diminished his customary far-sightedness, could not believe his eyes after the dissolution. He tells about that morning as follows: "On my way to Petrunkevich I looked about me; searched in people's faces and in inanimate stones for the reflection of our disaster. Sleepy pedestrians, sleepy horses, a sleepy sun; desolation; no life, no signs of movement. I wanted to scream in anguish and horror."

Though I was in the country at the time, fifty versts from Moscow, I remember distinctly the impression of that day. A telegram delivered in the morning stated: "The Duma dissolved. Stolypin premier." That there was nothing resembling agitation among the peasants was quite understandable. But toward evening--it was a holiday--many visitors came from Moscow. All who came from the center were amazed at the imperturbable calm of the city, for we had not forgotten the stormy reaction to lesser events: the general strike and the barricades. We expected at least a railway stoppage, agitation, and excitement in the streets, but everything was calm. This seemed so improbable that we continued to hope; we waited not for the superficial simmer in the thin layer of the intelligentsia but for the profound, elemental upheaval. It tarried but it was still awaited. On July 16 Miliukov consoled his adherents in Speech: "The very calm and tranquillity which followed July 9 should have frightened most people connected with the coup d'état more than the most striking public demonstrations. The mood has not calmed down; it has only withdrawn inwardly." On July 18 Miliukov predicted in Speech:

> Unwilling to yield to the demands of the popular representatives, the government will be compelled, at the last minute, to bow to more extensive demands, which will be presented by the new revolutionary wave. A glance at the calendar of our popular movements will show that all this will happen before February 20. July is an uneventful month, but in a month's time the upheaval will begin and towards winter the popular movement will be at its height.

On July 19 the unexpected happened at Sveaborg. Miliukov was triumphant:

> Events are unfolding faster than could have been foreseen.... It was thought that the signal had to come from the country, and working class and army support would be contingent upon the success of the agrarian movement. Unexpectedly, the explosion came from the opposite side. From a Finnish newspaper we learned today about a series of astounding events... Fortress Sveaborg is in the hands

of a rebel garrison. Since Sveaborg dominates Helsing-
fors, whoever controls this stronghold controls Finland,
a firm military base. The sympathy of the Finnish Red
Army and railway workers for the newly-started movement is apparently assured, and the movement of Russian
troops across the border will be made difficult by the interruption of railway communications.

This is how events were represented. The country was awak-
ening at last. But the illusion did not last long. The people remained
indifferent, and neither heroic military revolts nor the terrible terrorist act on Aptekar Island moved them. All inflamatory sparks
fell on damp powder. I was told by military people who put down the
uprising how unexpectedly easy it was to crush it. After the preliminary success the rebels understood that they were alone and defended themselves without enthusiasm. No revolutionary dynamic
was found in the country, or else it was so weak that Stolypin's police
measures proved stronger. Yet the tactics of the First Duma were
determined by its reliance on an invincible revolutionary uprising,
which was even considered the duty of the country. Much later, at
a congress summoned to implement the Viborg Appeal, I reproached
D. I. Shakhovski, half-jokingly saying that this appeal deprived us
of an excellent platform for the elections. He replied earnestly,
"If after the dissolution of the Duma nothing except a few military
revolts occurs in the country, it means that the country deserved
dissolution."
Thus the Cadets transferred responsibility to the country,
which supposedly failed them when they expected defense and assistance from its elemental upheaval. Yet at this time the country had
an even greater right to expect advice and guidance from the Duma.
"The country awaits direction from the center," wrote Miliukov on
July 16, and in this he was right. It was given from Viborg.
But before proceeding to the famous manifesto, we must understand clearly what was expected of a popular movement. For the
representatives of destructive revolutionary upheaval this posed no
problem; an attack on the Duma by the government had to precede
the events of 1917, which they greeted with delight even in wartime.
But what was the aim of the Cadet party, which two weeks before
had considered itself capable of forming a Cadet Ministry and
counted on a majority in the Duma? What did it expect of elemental
popular upheavals?
Miliukov answered this question in an article in Speech on
July 19. He wrote:

Now the success of the slogan "the return of the old
Duma" may be considered more probable.... It must be

admitted that in spite of the singularity and peculiarity of
this demand from the strictly constitutional point of view,
in reality the repeal of the ukase of July 9 and restoration
of the plenary powers of the deputies of the old Duma would
be the simplest and most practical way out of a difficult
situation in which the government has placed itself. Actually, the strictest lawyer could deny the legal force of this
ukase with a clear conscience because of the formal errors found in its publication. The annulment of the ukase
of July 9 could be of tremendous benefit to the government and the whole country. The fierce hurricane, whose
first signs appeared yesterday, would then pass by; peace
would be restored to the land, and further upheavals,
whose extent it is difficult to determine, would be avoided.

I was not close enough to the center of party leadership to know
whether this was the personal opinion of a Cadet leader or the policy
of the leadership core, but one might involuntarily ask, was this
naiveté or cunning? Or even to use historic words, was this "stupid-
ity or betrayal?"

From the point of view of the triumph of revolution, such an
outcome, of course, must have been desirable. In fact, it would
have meant revolution, for the constitution would have been trampled
by the government itself, and the deputies returned to Taurida Palace
with unlimited sovereignty as conquerors. It would have been a
repetition of June 23, 1789, when to Mirabeau's words, "Allez dire à
votre maître (Go tell you master)," Louis XVI good-naturedly replied "Si ces messieurs ne veulent pas s'en aller, qu'ils restent (If
these gentlemen do not want to go away, let them stay)." By doing
so he consecrated revolution.

It was possible to want revolution and to declare this openly,
but what blindness or cunning could offer this advice to the government as a means of escaping revolution, or ask for the support of
the newly-formed Party of Peaceful Restoration, which broke away
from the Cadets because it did not want to violate the constitution?
And yet Miliukov, who recently ridiculed and rebuked this new party,
now appealed to it as follows:

Citizens, peaceful reformers, now you can show you really
appreciate conditions under which "peaceful struggle" is
possible in Russia. It is up to you now. You can either
prolong the crisis, or by withdrawing from the scene,
bring about a speedy dénouement. Only remember that if
you prolong the crisis, the consequences will be appalling,
and all the blood of the victims of civil war will be upon

your hands. Be sagacious for once in your life; admit
that your time has not yet come; the Thermidorian reaction has not yet started.

These were the arguments with which Miliukov tried to tempt
the Peaceful Restoration party. Their time, he assured them, the
time of reaction, had not come yet. Therefore they should help the
coming of revolution. He recommended to them what the French
call "la politique de Gribouille (the politics of Confusion)."
There was one more "legal" argument in the tirade quoted
above. Dissolution was, supposedly, unlawful, and so much so that
even the strictest lawyer could deny the legal force of the manifesto
with a clear conscience. The argument might have been settled by
the saying that "paper tolerates everything." All sorts of things
were written at that time. But such an explanation would have been
too simple. It is interesting to note that this curious conclusion was
shared by able jurists, and this was a serious matter. I have in
mind Kokoshkin's speech at the Viborg trial. He spoke to the judges
and to posterity. What did he say about this vital matter of the illegality of dissolution?
He argued that the date for the coming elections was not stated
in the act on the dissolution of the Duma. But Article 105 of the Fundamental Laws did not require this. It read as follows: "By the same
ukase new elections to the Duma and the date for its summons are
fixed." The date for the summons was set by the ukase, and it was
unnecessary and even impossible to set the date for the elections,
because there could no no such procedure under a constitution where
elections were held in several stages.
It was charged that the act was not "countersigned." However
Kokoshkin himself admitted that it was countersigned, but as the
countersignature was not published this led him to conclude that it
was printed in a modified form rather than in the original. Yet Article 24 of the Fundamental Laws, which requires the countersignature
of the Highest Command and imposes on the Senate the duty of pro-
claiming royal instructions and orders, does not mention publication
of the countersignature. This omission, of course, does not prohibit
publication, but the article does not prescribe it. There is another
Article, 91, which forbids the Senate to publish a law if the method
of its publication does not correspond to the regulations of the Fundamental Laws. The fact of the publication of the ukase should have
been considered proof that the countersignature was there. One must
admit that it would have been desirable to have published the countersignature together with the order, as was actually done later. But
to conclude from the omission of the countersignature that the ukase
was published in modified form is simply a play on words. The
Act of June 8, 1906, in no way resembled that of June 3, 1907.

Finally, the only really worthwhile argument was that the budget could not be examined and approved in time because of the too distant date for the summons of the Duma. Petrunkevich was particularly insistent on this point. This was, of course, the inconvenient aspect of a prolonged break, but there was nothing illegal about it. The law demanded one thing only: annual convocation of the Duma. The consequences of failure to examine the budget within the prescribed time limit were indicated in the law itself--Article 14, Budget Rules. So there was nothing illegal about this either.

Thus all of Kokoshkin's arguments about the illegality of the dissolution of the Duma were strikingly worthless, even if they were sincere, but it was puzzling that the Cadets in particular resorted to such arguments. This would have been the logical course had they shown themselves pedants of constitutional legality. But they considered the promulgated constitution "coercion of the people" and more than once questioned the "necessity of lawfulness in the existing revolutionary period." Yet, while arguing by chicanery the unconstitutionality of dissolution, they still found the simplest and most practical way out of the situation, the re-establishment of the plenary powers of the dismissed Duma, an obvious and crude violation of the constitution. Politics permits even greater contradictions, but why speak of "the clear conscience of a strict lawyer?" It would have been better to remain silent.

All these arguments and advice show clearly that the Cadets had no practical plan to propose to the government after the dissolution of the Duma was accomplished. They did not know themselves what could be demanded of the government, since all their cards were mixed up by the dissolution. In fact, they might have kept their advice to themselves, for the government no longer had any faith in them; but what did they say to the people who had a right to expect instructions from them?

Though the Duma was prepared for dissolution, it was still caught by surprise. The Cadets had decided long ago that if it happened they would not disperse. Once, when the question of a summer recess arose, the Cadet party determined by a majority vote that the Duma would not submit. On May 13 the most moderate M. M. Kovalevski triumphantly announced from the Duma's tribune that "the Duma would not cease its legislative activity, and only brute force would drive us from here." This was the way they talked, but no one thought beforehand how this would be accomplished. In his History of the Viborg Appeal, Vinaver, rather embarrassed, admitted that everyone was sure that the ukase about dissolution would certainly be proclaimed in a session of the Duma, for which they were prepared. At the Viborg trial, Kokoshkin even argued that only such a procedure of dissolution was constitutional, and he painted an idyllic picture of the way this should have been done. "The ukase on dissolution is read from the tribune to the popular representatives by the person authorized by the head of the state, who is greeted with cheers in honor of the monarch...." It seems that Kokoshkin forgot the nature of the Duma in question, for this Duma, in case of dissolution, threatened a popular uprising and declared openly that it would submit only to force and would not disperse of its free will. What kind of cheers of loyalty could be expected of it? It was naive to expect that, knowing the Duma's mood and intentions, the government would prepare for it a situation appropriate for nonsubmission. What did the Duma take Stolypin for? He did not play at parliament and had an important job to do. And who but revolutionaries might have desired to witness scenes of violence, perhaps even bloodshed, in the Taurida Palace? However, even this might not have been sufficient for a flare-up, since the dissolution itself proved inadequate. Furthermore, the majestic spectacle that the deputies pictured could have a reverse side: it could be a picture of fear in the face of brute force, and shameful flight. It is only one step from the sublime to the ridiculous. We saw this ten years later in the dissolution of the Constituent Assembly. Praised be Stolypin for saving Russia from this ordeal, and for not hindering the deputies from leaving for Viborg in order to speak freely to the country.

Rank imposes obligations. Had the Duma been an ordinary Duma acting within the framework set for it by the constitution, no instructions to the people telling them what to do would have been expected of it. But in the light of its recent conduct, the Duma could not die silently and submissively; something had to be done in its name.

In this tragic moment the Duma's "opposition majority" placed itself once more, without question, under Cadet leadership. Vinaver describes vividly the symbolic meeting with the Trudoviki:

> At one of the turns at the intersection of Nadezhdinski and Znamenski, we met a group of Trudoviki wandering rather despondently. I. V. Zhilkin stood out in the whole group, not only by reason of stature but also by his sorrowful facial expression. He shook hands with us and kept repeating, "Well, now we'll be with you as one. Lead us."

And so the Cadets led. The Viborg Appeal was the third and last act of their initiative, following the "address" and the "agrarian appeal." The agrarian appeal and the Viborg Manifesto resembled each other in many ways and suffered from the same organic defect, only in the Viborg Manifesto this stood out in sharper relief. The situation was, of course, a difficult one. The deputies were a powerful force in the country, so long as the government recognized their Duma; so long as they occupied the Palace, managed state funds, and had the rights granted them by the constitution, they were the center of attention and possessed exceptional influence. All this disappeared

when they were left on their own, no longer backed by the state, despite their former talents, energy, and great names. In Viborg they
were surrounded only by newspapermen and sensation seekers. Life
already passed them by, and they were regarded with open curiosity
and sometimes with malicious joy. Now new heroes received the
ovations and old Bren's saying came true: "Woe to the conquered!"

The Duma might at least have died with dignity and with sincerity and not attempted to wriggle out. But how could this be done
without a split and without deviation from the former party line? For
people who accepted the basis of a constitutional order, no matter
how difficult dissolution was, it presented no tragic problem. The
dissolution of the Duma was the constitutional prerogative of the monarch, and such action did not imply withdrawal or violation of the
constitution won with such difficulty.

The Duma is dead, long live the Duma! It was now necessary
to prepare for elections to the new Duma. Under the best of circumstances, according to some famous historic precedents, it might
have been possible to change the elections into a plebiscite for the
old Duma and instead of a platform propose the reelection of the former deputies. This is what happened in France in 1830 and 1877. In
this sense, the Duma could issue in its name the last appeal to the
people. New avenues of action could be explored, and new, more
natural electoral combinations devised as they learned to distinguish
friends from foes. All this would have been a constitutional reply
to dissolution.

But the former attitude of the Duma and of the Cadets prevented
such a normal outcome. All along the Duma considered itself above
the law, the spokesman of the sovereign will of the people, the legislative authority. Having attempted to implement such a policy, could
the Cadets recall the constitution that they rejected and offer to submit to it loyally? After their former declarations such conduct would
appear cowardly.

Not only did the Cadets themselves refuse to follow a constitutional course, but their leaders, too, did not permit others to do so.
When the small party of Peaceful Restoration was formed after the
Duma's dissolution and came forth with such a loyal appeal, Miliukov
attacked it fiercely. At the Viborg trial Kokoshkin spoke of this
party as follows: "There appeared in the Duma a small group of
people, which turned to the nation with a special appeal. In this proclamation the people were asked to await calmly the next elections...
I know that this group went astray in good faith and I think that it
now regrets its fallacy." Such is the strength of prejudice! To regret such action after the Viborg Manifesto failed!

To be consistent, rejection of the constitutional course should
have meant a call for revolutionary insurrection. If the earlier
threat of such an uprising had been in earnest and the revolt was now

actually awaited, if it was sincerely believed that the constitution was
violated and destoyed, then whoever thought so should have considered
himself duty-bound to stop at nothing and share in the coming struggle
the fate of those who revolted. There are times when this becomes a
duty even when there is no hope of success. On December 2, 1851, a
dissolved assembly called its supporters to the barricades, and
Baudin, who fell there, is remembered to this day.

The Cadets neither wanted to pursue a revolutionay course themselves nor dared to advise others to do so, and consequently they had
nothing with which to appeal to the people. They could say nothing
useful and spoke only so as not to remain silent. Besides, they were
again sitting on both sides of the fence, confusing two contradictory
courses.

The Viborg Manifesto did not attempt to soothe the people; on
the contrary, it recommended "a firm stand for the violated rights
of the popular representatives." The Cadets maintained that "the
government would have seven months to obtain an obedient, complai-
sant Duma, and if the government should succeed in crushing the
popular movement altogether, it would not summon any kind of Duma
at all."

Thus the manifesto of the tsar promising not to violate the constitution was declared to be a lie by reason of the appeal which advocated a popular movement, assuring the people that Russia must not
remain a single day without popular representation.

How was this to be achieved, and what form should the popular
movement take? The Duma, in complete contradiction between the
task to be accomplished and the means to be employed, recommended
the precedent that learned lawyers dug up from Prussian or Hungarian
history, to which they attached the bombastic name "passive resistance." The appeal advised the following: "Until the popular representatives are summoned, do not pay a penny to the treasury and stand
up for your rights as one man; no power can withstand the united and
unbending will of the people. In this struggle, forced upon us but
inevitable, your elected representatives will be with you."

Now, in truth, "the mountains have brought forth a mouse."
What could the people make of these bombastic words? What were
they advised to do now that their rights had been violated? If the
country were not to remain a single day without representation, wherein lay the struggle if it were postponed to November until the elections
were held?

The Viborg Manifesto obliges us to recall that less tragic attempt
at appealing to the people, the Duma's agrarian appeal. Then, too, it
was impossible to understand what the Duma wanted of the people, and
why it turned to them empty-handed has remained a mystery.

How much stronger and more striking did this incongruity appear in the appeal to the people from Viborg! I remember distinctly

my impressions. I learned of the dissolution of the Duma while I
was in the country; there, too, the first responses to the appeal
reached me. N. N. Bazhenov, who managed to contact many party
comrades in Moscow, reported their reactions when he saw me.
There was general perplexity. What did the appeal mean? Why was
this done? Before long I was in Moscow, on my way to St. Petersburg to a session of the Central Committee. The impression of general perplexity had become stronger. I saw Iollos in the editorial
office of Russkiia Viedomosti (Russian News); he merely laughed
at the appeal. Kotliarevski phoned me in great indignation and asked
me to condemn it in the Central Committee, and yet they were members of the Duma who signed the appeal.

I say nothing of the others. It was approved only by the extreme
left wing as an attempt to pursue a different course, but even they
did not understand its uselessness. When I arrived in St. Petersburg
for the meeting of the Central Committee, I expected to find the members disconcerted by the rash action at Viborg, but here the atmosphere was different. Miliukov, reporting on the situation, considered
that it had improved, as fortunately the Viborg Appeal had been
signed. I remember that I protested and spoke of the Moscow mood
in this regard. Everyone attacked me. Vinaver, who regarded my
"reactionary views" in a benevolent manner, demanded, with un-
accustomed anger, that the Central Committee's attitude toward my
statements be determined by a vote. It was Miliukov who quieted
him and prevented the incident from developing into something serious.

S. A. Muromtsev, recently one of the most prominent persons
in the country, sat on ⌐ sofa in the adjoining room, sad but dignified
as ever. I was ashamᵤ now of the harshness of my objections, and
wanting to moderate them, I said to him that "I am still not altogether
in agreement with the appeal." He answered mysteriously: "Quite
a number of those who signed it are altogether not in agreement with
it."

Only distortion could result from efforts to unite those who disagreed, but this time it was most curious that all arguments about
the Viborg Appeal went on only among the Cadets. I do not speak of
the right wing who were consistent in refusing to protest the dissolution and did not go to Viborg. The left wing submitted to the Cadets
this time, so heated arguments went on only in the Cadet circles,
while the left-wing parties waited obediently until the Cadet arguments
should end. These arguments clearly revealed the irreconcilable
duality of the party, which no one was willing to admit either before
or afterwards.

In his History of the Viborg Appeal, Vinaver is astonished not
only by the fervency of these arguments but particularly by the excitement and ardor of the opponents of the appeal, as exemplified by
such usually well-balanced people as Petrazhitski, Hertsenshtein,

and Iollos. This amazed him. He supposed that "here, for the first
time, there came to the surface those differences of opinion that
always divided us into two almost equal groups until the final moment,
and who knows, perhaps divide us into two such groups even now."
He was mistaken in only one thing. The sharp cleavage of the Cadets
into two almost equal groups existed openly from the moment the
party was formed. A difference of two ideologies, the constitutional
and the revolutionary, divided the whole country, and the Cadets were
at the junction of the two trends with the line of demarcation passing
through them. All the Cadets, of course, were for the constitution,
but some of them considered that, for the time being, it was still
necessary to follow a revolutionary course until all objectives should
have been gained; then would come the time for the constitution. Herein lay the irreconcilable discord between the two streams. The Cadet
leadership contrived to conceal this and postpone a split till a more
favorable time. By the irony of fate the split occurred abroad; but
at that time, in the Belvedere Hotel, when everyone expected the
revolution, when the party had to decide on the choice of a definite
course of action, no one was deceived by the ambiguous formula, invented by the party leaders, the notorious "passive resistance"--
where there was no resistance because it was "passive" and no submission to the constitution because "resistance" was recommended.

The split might have occurred there and then, but the day was
saved by deus ex machina, the unexpected intervention of the Viborg
Governor-general, who demanded that Muromtsev break up the Congress, stressing particularly "the inevitability of ruinous consequences
for Finland, which gave the Duma asylum, if the meeting were not
immediately dispersed." Muromtsev, speaking for himself, gave
his word that he would not continue the meeting, and left saying that
it was a matter of honor as far as he was concerned.

This unexpected development saved the situation. The opponents
of the appeal, Petrazhitski, Hertsenshtein, and Iollos, though their
views remained unchanged, declared that they no longer opposed the
appeal and would sign it. It was then adopted unanimously. Vinaver
describes the closing scene as follows:

> Enthusiastic, radiant faces, happy voices, handshakes,
> nowhere a sign of dissatisfaction, nowhere any doubt.
> Hearts were lighter. The fruit of torment and painful
> wavering was ripe. The First Duma did not disperse
> without a trace. It was once more forged into a united
> whole and left the people a posthumous legacy of strug-
> gle for violated rights.

This mood, which Vinaver described so eloquently and vividly,
did provide the ill-fated atmosphere that explains the blunders of the

Duma. Our intellectuals went into raptures over trifles because they
did not understand either the difficulty of the task that lay before
them or their responsibility to their native land, like those madmen
who in 1914 blithely started the war, "fraîche et joyeuse (carefree
and gay)." Why did these thoughtless politicians in Belvedere rejoice? What was this fruit of "torment and wavering?" What was
there to be proud of in the soap bubble that the Duma left for the
edification of the people? How characteristic all this was! Russia
was forgotten for the time being, as though the entire country fitted
into the hotel hall. They were victorious, discord was concealed
once more, and thus, supposedly, something was gained for Russia,
too.

Thus ended the ill-fated Appeal; they made a gesture, removed
the responsibility from their shoulders, and remained content with
themselves. But before long they had to face the task of implementing
this absurdity.

I remember the Cadet conference near Moscow, at the estate
of V. V. Przhevalski, where this question was discussed and decided.
Communications from various local centers were definite and to the
point: no practical success could be expected from the appeal. This
did not, however, embarrass the Cadets and everything was taken
care of in the classical manner, since their leaders were masters
in the art of conciliatory formulas. The appeal was approved in principle, but at the same time the Cadets pointed out that it had already
attained its goal and the Duma would be summoned on the date set.
Therefore there was no need to implement the Appeal, and refusal of
tax payments and compulsory military service was unnecessary. The
party again appeared united and tightly-knit, and even fifteen years
later, in 1921, writing in Three Attempts, Miliukov was for some
reason seriously suggesting to his readers that the Viborg Appeal
attained its goal. Supposedly because of it, the Duma was summoned.
According to Miliukov, "The Viborg Manifesto lost its political significance and obviously could only be the signal for persecution of individual victims. Thus, instead of continuing militant demonstrations,
the members of the party began to prepare for elections to the Second
State Duma." This is the way legends are preserved, but who was
being deceived by this in 1921?

But the matter did not end there. Another difficult ordeal lay
in store. The deputies who signed the Appeal were called to account
and prohibited from participating in the elections. Because of this,
the First Duma disappeared forever from political life and lesser
Cadet lights appeared in the Duma. In 1907, in quite a different
atmosphere, the members of the First Duma were brought to public
trial.

The legal defense of the deputies who signed the Appeal was not
left to them alone but was in the hands of able lawyers who had good

grounds for a case. The activities of the defendants did not come under
Article 129, under which it was proposed to try them, since they were
guilty only of writing the Appeal--which could, of course, be considered criminal--but not of disseminating it. From the legal point of
view there was a vast difference between these; the defendants accused only of writing the Appeal could not be deprived of their political rights. In this argument the moral victory was won by the lawyers, though they did not convince the judges. Eloquent proof of this
took place at the trial. The court, yielding to the defense, had to
change the formulation of questions three times, and even after the
third time objections could not be avoided. But it was impossible
to confine oneself to the legal aspect of this case. For a few days
the First Duma, which could and had to justify before society and history the strange instruction that it had given to the people, appeared
to have been reborn. It even acted like the First Duma: when
Muromtsev rose, all the defendants rose, and even did so several
times, not noticing that this was quite ridiculous. The first explanations of the defendants were given in the name of all, by the three
great political figures: Petrunkevich, Kokoshkin, and Nabokov. They
were allowed to say all they wished without any interruption and could
express themselves freely. Suddenly a new note rang false in the
speeches of the Cadet orators. Petrunkevich and Kokoshkin, in their
preliminary explanations, and clearest of all, Muromtsev, in his
concluding words, conveyed the impression that the aim of the Viborg
Appeal was to restrain the masses from a revolutionary uprising.

It is impossible to suppose that these words were insincere,
spoken to win over the judges to their side. The Viborg defendants
did not conduct themselves at the trial as did the Peasant Union later
on. But their words were characteristic as an illustration of self-
suggestion. People have a natural tendency, by backdating, to ascribe
to themselves foresight of the unexpected because they do not like to
admit mistakes. This new explanation of the manifesto was elaborated
when the Viborg Appeal failed as fruitlessly as the armed uprisings
which were predicted earlier, and which were expected to succeed.
It became tempting to say to themselves, and later to others, that
even this failure was in reality only a new Cadet victory. It is useless to try to find out who invented this legend or who believed it.
Undoubtedly no one thought of such an aim at Viborg, because at that
time it was the indifference of the population, not its excesses, that
was feared, and the aim of the Appeal was to excite, not soothe. People already in a revolutionary mood could not be attracted by the
Viborg Appeal for it gave them no way out, and it could not inflame
indifferent people because the instructions emanating from this high
source were so meaningless. The Appeal could only dampen enthusiasm, and indeed it did. It was therefore only a new Cadet mistake. But to claim that this cooling off was the aim of the Appeal

and that was why it was written was merely pretense at infallibility,
and those who were not ashamed to explain it this way did not understand the awkwardness of their position. I well remember the pain-
ful impression this assertion made at the trial. To begin with it
aroused the indignation of the revolutionary parties that submitted
to Cadet leadership after the dissolution and signed the Appeal without debate. They were hurt to learn that the aim of the Appeal was
to prevent the revolution. It was even more shameful that the people
were to be deceived by participating in the Appeal. The Trudoviki
(Lukin) and the Social-Democrats (Ramishvili) disavowed the Cadet
explanations. Ramishvili did this particularly clearly. He admitted
that the Viborg Appeal was a weak, ineffective protest, but "that was
not my aim when I signed the Appeal." He concluded sorrowfully,
"It is clear that what we had done did not feed the flame of revolt."
Neither the conceited cunning of the Cadets nor their later boasting
added much to their fame.

    The dissolution of the Duma was the work of Stolypin and it
brought him to the forefront. His plan might have succeeded. In
politics everything is quickly forgotten and former enemies can work
together later. Liberal society, personified by the Cadets, could
forget the collapse of the Cadet ministry, the dissolution of their Duma, and much else. But in spite of all his talents there was much
that Stolypin did not understand; he had no conception of the fact that
the victor must make his peace with the vanquished, if he cannot
destroy him. He repeated the error of the First Duma when the latter considered itself the victor. His program came to be based on
contradictions. No matter how mistaken the Cadets' tactics were in
the Duma, it was impossible to implement liberal reforms and establish a liberal regime while simultaneously carrying on a merciless
struggle against the Cadets; this simply restored them to their former popularity. Stolypin failed to understand that a policy of strife
strengthened only the extreme flanks and deprived his liberal policy
of a firm foundation. His policy created the completely left-wing
Second Duma, and after its dissolution, it pushed Stolypin into the
hands of the right wing. But this is already beyond the scope of this
book.

CONCLUSION

There comes a time in the life of a person, or of a whole country, which seems to determine all future existence. The meeting of the First Duma seemed to be such a moment. This may be only the self-delusion of contemporaries, and with the passage of time, a different point of view may prevail. Even the downfall of Old Russia finally may be regarded as only a minor episode in history, when everything has been re-evaluated. But when events of catastrophic significance occur, contemporaries cannot be indifferent. What pushed Russia on this road of destruction?

In his Reminiscences[1] Miliukov quotes Witte's words, which he regards as flattery: "It is too bad that I did not know you well; perhaps things might have turned out differently." After 1917 similar admissions were made from even more unexpected quarters. But there is some truth in Witte's statement. It is, of course, not a matter of the personalities of Miliukov and Witte, but they are symbols, and it was most unfortunate that they could not have worked together in 1906. Witte regretted it because he understood how helpful Miliukov could have been to him. Witte could have been of even more help to Miliukov, but Miliukov did not understand this.

Witte was one of the best representatives of the old state authority. He favored reform, not merely the preservation of the old order. But as a practical man trying to get results, he always took into consideration the realities of the situation and the benefits that could be derived from it by the government as well as by the people. He knew that inertia must be overcome by patience, not violence, and his opinions were shared by other members of the bureaucracy. There were more forward-looking men among them than people believed, but they suffered from the usual failings of "practical people": they were insufficiently educated theoretically. "Educated" people superciliously called them "talented by nature," "self-learners," etc. Better acquaintance with Miliukov would therefore have been useful in correcting Witte's one-sided upbringing.

But in what way was Miliukov also a symbol? In Three Attempts he wrote of Kokoshkin: "In the Moscow circle of friends only Kokoshkin showed the promise of a true politician." Miliukov himself was such a "real politician." Practical liberal workers were to be found in various spheres of social and state life. They engaged in a constant

233

struggle with the existing authority, but they did not reject it, nor did they refuse to collaborate with it.

The Liberation Movement created quite a different kind of liberal fighters and raised a new banner of combat. It was invented by those who came to be called "real politicians," rich in theoretical knowledge rather than in political experience. The stubbornness of the government exhausted the patience of liberal workers, and the theoreticians directed their attention to the source of evil, the autocracy. The conviction that "there will be no improvement in Russia as long as the autocracy exists" came to be the simple solution for all difficulties. Instead of the former struggle for "reforms," the battle for "reform," for a constitution, began.

These "real politicians"--learned men, writers, etc.--naturally became the leaders of this movement, and left their imprint upon it. To the question of what would replace autocracy, the new leaders sought an answer in the institutions of more advanced states. In their opinion, not evolution but rejection of the old order had to become the foundation of the new one; in their aloofness from reality they saw the best proof of their perfection. Miliukov was a good representative of such "politicians." He was not a "practical worker"[2] and his prestige in politics came mostly from his profession as a writer and his authority as a man of learning.

While the Liberation Movement continued, Witte could not be useful to Miliukov, as they would not have found any common ground. Witte could not have understood either the necessity for immediate destruction of the autocracy, or the indifference of theoreticians to practical improvements of life. But the Liberation Movement could not win otherwise. The sin of the autocracy lay in creating it, but once the movement began, victory was impossible to attain in any other way. It became, therefore, the victory of "real politicians," of whom Miliukov was a symbol.

But when the autocracy granted the constitution, the task changed. By classical comparison, instead of erecting a new edifice, the old one could be thoroughly renovated. A choice had to be made: either to disregard the concession of the government and to continue the former struggle till complete victory was won; or to be satisfied with the constitution as it was and on that basis to conclude an agreement with the government.

In case of such an agreement, Witte was indispensable to Miliukov. He was the symbol of all that was wholesome in the old order. If Miliukov could best outline the goals to be attained, Witte could much more skillfully determine the methods and tempo by which these could be realized. The qualities that gave "real politicians" superiority in wartime put them at a disadvantage when the country had to be calmed and reeducated on a new basis. The

practical wisdom of the "politician" and his superiority over the
"theoretician" consists of his ability to do that. To ensure the victory
of 1905 therefore, collaboration of idealists and practical men, wise
propagators of the new and the best representatives of the old, was
necessary.

But the "real politicians" did not want to surrender their pre-
eminent position. Compromise and gradual achievement were regarded as "lowering the flag;" everything was to be achieved at once.
Of course, the ideal of liberalism in 1906, constitutional monarchy,
was quite attainable, but it could not be fully realized immediately.
Considering the country's lack of preparedness for them, a transitional
period was necessary before establishing in Russia the "four-tail,"
the single chamber, and a responsible ministry.

The impatience of the doctrinaires was most evident in the matter of "theoretical assertions and principles," which were the chief
baggage of the theoreticians. Concessions in such matters were regarded as betrayal. This gave rise to the unrealistic and harmful
attitude of Cadet "politicians" toward the position of the monarchy in
Russia.

According to the ideology of "theoreticians," the basis of state
authority was the "sovereignty of the people," which in Russia's
immature state was simplified to a scheme involving the absolute
authority of popular representation. The monarchy, considered a
survival of backward political customs, was no longer necessary.
Therefore only a Constituent Assembly had the right to draft a constitution. This assertion, made as far back as 1905 in the name of the
Congress of Zemstvos, was conveyed to Witte. In 1921, in Three
Attempts, Miliukov confirmed that this was the only theoretically
correct course. Such an approach is an abuse of the prestige of
theory. The science of government teaches us that the value of state
forms is relative. When a permanent state order is being established,
it is necessary to consider not what is theoretically correct, but
what is best suited to the particular people concerned; what they can
understand and accept. A nation does not live by theories. Governments often stay in power on irrational foundations: recognition of
inequality, submission of the government to "Divine Providence,"
respect for elders, and many other "backward" justifications. Recognition of authority is a question of psychology, like the basis of mor-
als, rights, or religion. These are not the same for everyone. The
intelligentsia did not regard the prestige of state authority in the
same way as did the unenlightened masses, which were the predomi-
nant group in Russia. In 1906 these masses regarded the authority
of the monarch not only as the customary but also as the only lawful authority, resting on general popular acceptance. There could
be dissatisfaction with its actions, as there could be grumbling even

against God; but the monarch's right to be the governing authority was
not subject to any doubt. Had the monarchy fallen in 1906, making it
necessary to establish a new governing force, it is doubtful whether
the country would have submitted to the rule of a "four-tail" election.

Fortunately for Russia, the government was not toppled and
this question did not arise in 1906. The customary, lawful authority
of the tsar, blessed by the church and ancient tradition, was not
denied by anyone. The tsar introduced a new constitutional order in
Russia, and in this origin lay its chief strength, but theoretically this
superiority was not desirable. The theoreticians could not understand that, at that time, the people would not accept the "independent"
authority of the Constituent Assembly, or the Duma; to them these
would be the master's plaything.

It was in the interests of Russia to make use of the prestige of
the monarchy, not to reject it, and to combine the demands of "theory"
with the realistic force of popular consciousness. This was better
served by a constitution designed by the monarchy than one drafted
by the Constituent Assembly. The gradual evolution of the constitutional monarchy was the best means of leading the country to complete
popular sovereignty. The unity of Russia and its state interests were,
until now, personified by the monarch. Undermining his authority,
and entering into conflict with him, was harmful and beyond the strength
of the Duma. It was impossible to introduce the constitutional order
by humiliating the monarch, subordinating him to the Duma, and trying to inspire the country by a scheme of parliamentarianism in
which the monarch had no authority; such a scheme was not quite
comprehensible even to the intellectual élite. This road could lead
only to revolution; the monarchy protected Russia from it. This was
recognized later even by the "real politicians," as was demonstrated
in 1917 when Miliukov, though the monarchy's prestige had been undermined by war, still urged Michael not to reject the throne. But
this was not thought of in the irresponsible year 1906.

The Cadet position was ambiguous, as always. They did not
wage war on the monarchy, declaring themselves "republicans"
only when the monarchy disappeared; they did not employ any impolite words in the address, and even included terms of respect in
it. But at the same time they did not hesitate to debase the prestige
of the monarchy in the eyes of the people at every opportunity. They
declared the proposed constitution to be a "violation of the will of
the people," and claimed that the wishes of the Duma were above the
law. "In the name of the people" they demanded a system of government that the people did not understand. Even if the intellectual
élite did not need the monarchy, and was prepared for a parliamentary republic, the masses of the people regarded the prestige of the
monarch above the prestige of the newly-created Duma. When the

Fundamental Laws gave both forces (the old and the new) the opportunity of working together, they provided the best solution for Russia's
problems.

Not only was collaboration the best solution; it also conformed
to the psychology of the liberal workers themselves. They were not,
by nature, uncompromisingly hostile to the government; rather they
suffered from the opposite extreme. Their existence in the midst of
a hostile state apparatus cultivated in them caution, compliance, and
fear of sharp protests. But the government was not the only thing the
liberals had to fear; equally dangerous was the impatience of the people whom they tried to serve, and who reproached them for moderation and indecision. This stereotyped reproach was levelled mainly
against liberals of note like N. Miliutin, A. Saburov, M. Loris-
Melikov, and others. However, the same reproaches became the
lot of numberless obscure workers who followed the same course.
Our literature has preserved some of these accusations in the work
of the lyric poet N. A. Nekrasov, who forever vacillated in his ap-
praisal, both of himself and others, between criticism of "caution"
and the realization that a useful existence is often a more difficult
feat than a dramatic but useless catastrophe. Compromise with the
government was frequently evidence of true heroism of Russian
liberalism.

The promulgation of the constitution and convocation of the Duma opened to people of this type hitherto unheard-of opportunities
for action, which were at the same time in conformity with their
habit of working together with the government, within the framework
of law. But when this occurred in 1906, the old liberalism had come
under the leadership of the "real politicians," people of a new type,
who had passed through the school of the Liberation Movement in
alliance with the revolutionaries, and who were infected by their
psychology and methods. Little by little they drew away from the
former peaceful, gradual reform activity, mesmerized by the victories and fireworks of "revolutionary epochs," which they emulated.
Criticism of revolutions and recognition of their weaknesses came
to be considered a betrayal of "liberal principles." The revolution
was described as the "heroic period," which supposedly reveals the
best qualities of the human soul and quickly leads to a glorious future.
If it brings in its wake much injustice, baseness, and brutality, this
is only deserved retribution for the iniquities of the past. Besides,
the sufferings of individuals are insignificant compared to the benefits that the people as a whole derive from revolution. Revolutionary
housecleaning leads to the goal faster and more surely than gradual
reforms.

Such an unnatural cult of "revolution" among the supporters
of a legal order and liberal ideas had its counterpart in the cult of

"war," in the opposite political camp. Here war, instead of revolution, provided the great opportunities for talent, heroism, and self-
sacrifice, considered man's best instincts. And here, too, the inevitable sacrifices were repaid a hundredfold by the victory and its
glorious results. How dull and colorless, compared to war, seemed
peaceful "bourgeois life"!

Those who survived present-day wars and revolutions do not
understand these cults. In the first place, both these phenomena have
become familiar to us in their true light, and not as they are painted
in battle pictures and cheap popular literature, so that much of their
fascination has disappeared. Second, we can see clearly that to resort to preponderant force in the hope of obtaining permanent social
improvements is self-deception. That is why war and revolution
are always disastrous in themselves; either they are unnecessary or
they solve nothing.

Let us take war. The rare benefits that it may bring can always
be won more gradually by peaceful means. Present-day national interests are so interwoven that a temporary preponderance of one
power cannot be regarded as a permanent condition. Instability can
be concealed by acrobatics only for a short time, and international
equilibrium is always gradually restored with the passage of time.
We witnessed this in World War I.

The same may be said of revolution. We Russians experienced
several great events in the twentieth century, among them two revolutions. It is instructive to trace through them the correlation between liberal reforms and "revolutionary conquests."

The first of these events, the Liberation Movement, had no
revolutionary goals. In fact, many of its leaders strove for the introduction of a constitutional order to protect Russia from the menace
of revolution. The reforms demanded by the Liberation Movement
could be a direct continuation of the Epoch of Great Reforms. The
connection of the Liberation Movement with revolution was a temporary anomaly, born of the blindness of the old order and the impatience of our political leaders. The latter felt that the autocracy
would not return to the path of liberal reforms and was more harmful than the revolution. So autocracy became enemy number one.
During the Russo-Japanese War, the periodical Liberation claimed
that Pleve was more dangerous than Japan. Liberal leaders no
longer believed that the evolution of the autocracy was possible.

This was a two-fold error. With all its failings, the autocracy
was still immeasurably preferable to revolution. Besides, it did
prove capable of correcting itself, and even of changing over to a
constitutional order. But victors are not judged, and the "politicians"
were victorious. They won the constitution without a revolution.

This was a brilliant victory for liberalism, and the way lay
open before it. But though the revolutionaries lost their best opportunity as a result of the concession of October 17, they still would

not surrender. The constitution itself became the object of their
attacks and the Cadets their most dangerous enemies. This attitude
was consistent, but it is difficult to understand why the Cadets, under
such circumstances, tried to maintain their ties with the revolutionaries and to keep them "in reserve." Neither alliance with revolutionaries, nor a Constituent Assembly, nor conflict with the monarchy
was now necessary to introduce further liberal reforms. Political
freedom and social justice were now attainable by the simple implementation of the new order. And yet the Cadets, together with the
revolutionaries, continued to rock the constitution. They refused to
observe its rules until they attained full popular sovereignty, a single
Chamber, an impotent monarch, party government, and party domination. To achieve this goal they thoughtlessly pushed the country
toward an unnecessary revolution.

    Fortunately the government proved sufficiently strong to prevent
revolution in 1906, and the constitutional interlude (1906-17) began.
It did not save Russia, however, and ten years later the revolution
came anyway. Neither liberal society nor the revolutionary parties
provoked it. Rather, it was brought on by the unbearable burden of
war and the mistakes of the government, which lost its head. Only
the October Revolution was the work of revolutionaries, who began
to work for the seizure of power in February, 1917. Their attitude
toward the Provisional Government resembled that of the First Duma
toward the tsarist régime in 1906, only the Bolsheviks were more
consistent and so they were victorious.

    The Bolshevik Revolution was harmful because its goals did not
correspond to Russia's needs. Achieved by force, such a victory
could not bring beneficial results. So far, nothing that the October
Revolution promised has actually been achieved: neither popular
sovereignty nor equality, neither the domination of workers nor
communism. On the contrary, all the sores of the old order have
reappeared in an uglier form--personal authority, privileged classes,
a new all-powerful bureaucracy and the defenselessness of the individual. Of course, the commanding heights are now in the hands
of a different group; a new aristocracy has arisen, a new court with
its officialdom; the workers have become complete outcasts; and
ambitious persons have become the new bureaucracy dominating the
people. The new masters may, perhaps, be pleased with their personal fate, but these were not the tasks set by the revolution, and so
it did not win. Only a few benefited from the common misfortune.
The same thing happens in war, but that is not why wars are fought
and revolutions acclaimed.

    In this history, February occupies a special place. It is in-
structive for liberal society, which won its revolution in February.
The Cadet dream of a union of liberalism with revolutionary idealists
was resurrected. The new government announced the very same
program that was proposed in 1906. All the old slogans were there:

a sovereign Constituent Assembly, "the four-tail," abolition of the
death penalty, the repeal of the Exceptional Regulations, respect for
the rights of the individual, and expropriation of private land. All that
the First Duma tried to attain was announced in the first declaration of
the revolution. In February the First Duma had its revenge, and its
veteran, Vinaver, identified and hailed the Duma's original policy in
the proposals of the Provisional Government. Perhaps he was right.

But a liberal program was unable to control the Acheront. Such
a program might have been implemented in 1906, gradually and in
agreement with the existing authority, which would have been a guarantee of its permanence. But to introduce it at once, by means of revolution, was "squaring the circle." The liberal February Revolution,
which dreamed of doing this, was destined to failure at its birth.

The position of the Provisional Government was, of course,
exceptionally difficult, but the difficulty did not lie in the fact that it
had simultaneously to reform the state order and continue the war.
The government was not deposed by a foreign enemy but by the Bolsheviks, who from the first understood, deceived, and used the
Acheront, and then silenced it with a brutal hand.

The February Government should not have disputed with the
Acheront but should have fought against it; yet, since it sincerely
believed in liberal principles, it did not want to govern by force.
Nevertheless revolutionary achievements can be confirmed only in
this way. When former authority is destroyed, stability can be restored in the troubled state only by despotic, not by liberal measures.
That is why victorious revolutions are always hostile to human rights
and lead to dictatorships. Without the dictatorship of the Jacobins,
France would have been crushed by a foreign coalition. France could
not have put down the revolution in Spain without brutality, and the
Spanish Republicans could not have fought for three years without
similar cruelties. To try to achieve liberal ideals through revolution
is to start a hopeless contest. Failure to understand this, coupled
with the desire to make the revolution not only great but also blood-
less, and to make it the triumph of liberal principles, was the cause
of the collapse of the Provisional Government, but it also gave a
peculiar fascination to the February period.

In the early days of the revolution, I was invited to Karabchevski's
home, to a meeting of lawyers. Kerenski asked us to help him "to
put Russian justice on an unrivalled plane," and the meeting enthusiastically undertook this task. I did not participate in this fruitless
effort because I considered that the revolution, which was in reality
the violation of law and rights, was not an appropriate time for improving justice. I was attacked for my pessimism, particularly by
Karabchevski. The cream of the intelligentsia were there, and they
were convinced that the revolution would regard law and rights with
respect and "would put Russian justice on an unrivalled plane." In

conformity with this delusion, Muraviev's Commission was set up to
bring to justice former ministers for violation of laws that were repealed by the revolution judging them.   This Commission, with its
contradictory task, became the symbol of this period.

The people who had to control the revolution in 1917 were not
suited to the task of restoring the order that the revolution destroyed.
They did not have the necessary capacity for violence and ruthless-
ness, and were too sincerely devoted to the principles of freedom and
justice.   No wonder they did not want revolution in 1917 and did not
try to gain the power that was thrust upon them against their will.
But this cannot be said of their adherents and predecessors, the members of the First Duma.   They were equally incompetent to control
the revolution, but disregarding this, they voluntarily rejected the
opportunity of realizing their aims peacefully and steered a revolutionary course.   Yet they only had to be true to themselves to carry
on peaceful work; they were born for this.   The Duma had to realize
that it was not the whole country, that it was not above the law and
needed the constitution, and that the monarchy was a beneficial force.
Liberal society had to develop the consciousness that its collaboration
with the traditional authority would be more useful than the continuation of its aggressive alliance with the Acheront.   No greater sin could
be committed against liberal ideas than to provoke the revolution at
that moment.   But in this regard liberalism actually saw eye to eye
with the revolutionaries, and in so doing not only repudiated itself,
but also paved the way for the events of 1917.

After October 17 the leaders of the revolutionary movement,
realizing that the Cadets were not their fellow-travelers, deserted
them, but the Cadets still did not want to lose their contact with the
revolution.   "We knew," said Miliukov,[3] "that this collaboration
would still be useful."   This expectation of two fronts made open
Cadet agreement with the government impossible and their efforts
at a behind-the-scenes agreement insincere.   The Cadets rejected
coöperation with the government, kept the revolution "in reserve,"
and as a result, remained isolated from support in the country.

And the question remains: how could the clever people who led
the First Duma prefer such tactics to an honest attempt at implementing the constitutional order?

Whatever way we regard the concrete mistakes made at that
time, the root of them all lay in the phenomenon common to all such
circumstances, the defeat inherent in every victory.   In the normal
evolution of life changes must not be represented as victories.   Too
often victors consider their temporary advantage as a permanent
condition; they usually exaggerate their strength and the enemy's
weakness, and so lose their victory.   Thus in 1919 the Allies were
convinced that they had crushed Germany forever.   In 1936 the Front
Populaire, believing it would never lose power because it had defenders,

acted in accordance with these illusions. The same thing happened in
Russia in 1906. The Duma did not deign to be a loyal parliament and
could not be a full-fledged representative assembly. It proved to be
a monstrosity.

All legislative activity is the adaptation of external forms of
life to internal social forces. Real statesmen visualize this growth
in advance and progress is made in good time, imperceptibly. But
if this adaptation is not made in time and the equilibrium is disturbed,
convulsing upheavals and "epochs of reform" occur. Social achievements made under such difficult conditions are remembered as great
reforms. If, however, the state apparatus continues to oppose the
changes, the destructive forces of the revolutionary storm rush into
the struggle and mercilessly smash the obsolete apparatus: this is
the cause and the significance of revolutions. Revolutionary leaders
are brought to the forefront by their destructive dynamic, for their
constructive plan is always utopian and in its utopianism lies its revolutionary strength. When the task of the revolution is fulfilled, revolutionary statesmen appear on the scene. Their former supporters
consider them traitors, for they forsake the utopias for which the revolution was fought and try to combine the old and the new to restore
peace on some new basis. This reconciliation indicates the end of
the revolution.

Russia had both these: statesmen of high caliber and revolutionaries of great destructive force. But what did liberal society,
personified by the Cadets, achieve in the period of the First Duma?
It proved capable only of hampering both the revolutionaries and the
reformers. It had no destructive force and so could not lead a revolution. Nor did it give scope to its statesmen, for its creative force
could be exercised only in collaboration with traditional authority,
which the Cadets rejected. They held the belief that the deposed
authority would not rise again and the revolutionaries would submit
to them, and they would accomplish everything singlehanded. Life
by-passed these childish pretensions.

The leaders of the Cadet party destroyed it by this shortsighted tactic, their play at revolution. All periods of upheaval, of
course, whether they be in the time of Peter the Great or Konvent,
foster a revolutionary mood and methods. The normal development
of life is then generally disturbed; former orderly customs lose
their force; and then liberalism loses its chief support. We were
going through such an epoch of upheaval when, under pressure of
the Liberation Movement, the ancient citadel of autocracy was shaken.
The old order lost its prestige, but the stormy period should have
ended on October 17, 1905, and the task of the Duma in 1906 was a
constructive one: the reconciliation of the old and the new. But the
Cadet leaders could not understand this task, or perhaps they

refused to face it. Their talents were directed toward a false and
harmful goal.

The inglorious end was hastened by another factor. Epochs of
upheaval created the particularly unhealthy atmosphere which Miliukov sympathetically called "the enthusiasm arising from the broad
scope of events." He reproached me for not realizing it, but he was
mistaken, I did.[4] This malady of all brilliant epochs can result in
great harm if we regard it as a healthy sign, for it furnishes a favorable ground for human weaknesses. Interdependence is a vital characteristic of social life, and modest people contribute as much to the
common welfare as do great public figures. But governing the state
is the business of professionals. In ancient times it was the sole right
of the state authority; in our democratic age this monopoly has been
taken over by politicians. This is a sound procedure, but in an epoch
of "enthusiasm" this, too, is changed. Then everyone wants to be a
politician, regarding with contempt the ordinary citizens who are
busy with their personal affairs; the air is filled with notions that "a
cook can rule the state" and government is a simple matter. In 1917
V. V. Shulgin quipped: "Autocracy--an orchestra is playing but the
public dares neither to boo nor applaud; Constitution--the public wins
the right to express its opinion about the orchestra; Revolution--the
public has driven out the musicians and grabbed the instruments helter-
skelter." This is the result of "enthusiasms arising from the broad
scope of events." The evil lies not in the fact that the public grabs
the instruments, for it will soon realize its error. A worse evil
results when the musicians fear the loss of their popularity. Instead
of opposing the childish enthusiasm of the public, they surrender and
praise its inexperience as maturity.

The First Duma met in such an unhealthy atmosphere. The recent victory of the Liberation Movement created all the temptations
typical of such a period. The most placid people lost their heads; the
leaders did not have the courage to swim against the current, and
forgetting their wisdom, they were swept into the common flood. The
Cadet leaders rejected that which constituted the essence of liberalism:
voluntary submission to a legal order, work within the framework of
the law, and respect for the rights of others. This explains the false
course followed by the First Duma. It is useless and even unfair to
criticize them, for this is a universal phenomenon. But there can be
no greater mistake than to try, for some reason, to conceal this.
Who will be deceived now? The First Duma passed through history
with flashing brilliance, but it was completely fruitless. It wasted
an opportunity which never came again and which if taken might have
changed history. Its members deserved to accomplish more than
their unfortunate tactics permitted them to do. Others had to take
up the task where the Duma left off. But as I said, this is beyond
the scope of this book.

NOTES

Introduction

1. <u>Posledniia</u> <u>Novosti</u> (<u>Latest</u> <u>News</u>), May 28 and 30, 1937.

2. <u>Latest</u> <u>News</u>, June 16, 1939, printed Miliukov's speech in connection with the fifteenth anniversary of R. D. O. [The United Democratic Republicans, a group formed by P. N. Miliukov consisting of emigré liberals and Cadets in Paris in the mid 1920's. It became part of a national committee of "Russians outside Russia."--M. B.] He says of himself, "I was not a dictator, or leader in the specific sense of the word; we mutually arrived at certain decisions which I considered correct." This was in reference to R. D. O., but the man always remained himself.

3. Muromtsev believed this and spoke in this manner.

4. I mentioned the Cadet "Star Chamber" in the reminiscences of later Duma existence, but Miliukov speaks of the same thing during the existence of the First Duma, <u>Russkiia</u> <u>Zapiski</u> (<u>Russian</u> <u>Memoirs</u>), p. 113. "Though Petrunkevich, as patriarch, stood above us all and enjoyed the greatest respect, he was unable to bear the burden of the extremely strenuous daily work of the Duma. Former party leaders-- Kokoshkin, Vinaver, and I--naturally came to the forefront in positions of responsibility." And regarding relations with the peasants: "Their leaders proved to be three left wingers--Aladin, Anikin, and Zhilkin. They were in contact with us three--Kokoshkin, Vinaver, and myself."

5. <u>Latest</u> <u>News</u>, July 16, 1939. Miliukov accused me "of failing to correct my views of his personal role, even after his reminiscences were published." I do not understand what I am supposed to correct. Previously he accused me of considering him personally "chiefly responsible" for party actions. He now reiterates that my criticism of the party is a criticism of personalities. This is a misunderstanding on his part; I do not consider him chiefly responsible. He did not lead the party. But at the close of the same article, he formulates the accusation differently, and he accuses me and Professor Pares "of confusing Miliukov with the party." But how does he want us to distinguish between them? Miliukov never permitted himself any deviations from the general party line. Even when he disagreed, he felt duty-bound, as leader, to acclaim party actions.

245

Herein lay his strength in the party; he was always its spokesman.
How, then, can he complain of being confused with the party? To
prevent such confusion, he should have, at least now, pointed out
the issues on which he disagreed with the party, and what were the
mistakes it made. But then he would be doing the same thing for
which he condemns me, but with this difference: I speak of general
party errors, not excluding myself, and he would have had to exclude
himself. Leaders as well as rank and file members must not resent
being called to account for their party's actions. This is the reverse
side of the benefits they have gained from the party.

      6. Russian Memoirs, March, 1939, p. 102.

Chapter One

      1. Vinaver, Nedavnee (Recently), p. 81.
      2. Vinaver, Recently, p. 262.
      3. Miliukov, P. N., Tri Popytki (Three Attempts), p. 25.
      4. That the tsar did not like to use the word "constitution" is
unquestionable and understandable. But it is just as certain that he
understood that he did promise a constitution on October 17. Writing
to his mother on April 19, he did not avoid this word. He wrote, "I
could follow a different course--grant the population civil rights,
freedom of speech, press, assembly, and unions, inviolability of the
person, and the Duma's consent for new laws, in a word, a constitution." But using the term in writing to his mother does not necessarily mean that he should have used it publicly, too.
      5. The Bulygin Duma Statute states: Legislative proposals
rejected by a majority in a general meeting of the State Duma and the
Imperial Council are not presented for Sovereign examination, but
are returned to the minister concerned, or the head of the department
affected, for further elaboration.
      6. Shipov, Vospominaniia I Dumy (Memoirs and the Dumas),
p. 234.
      7. Kryzhanovsky, S. E., Vospominaniia (Memoirs), p. 183.
      8. Kokovtsev, Count, V. N., Iz Moego Proshlago (Out of My
Past), p. 168.
      9. Miliukov, P. N., Russian Memoirs, May. Even Miliukov
admits that the policy of the period was based on a mistaken conception of Witte's resignation and Goremykin's appointment.
      10. Grusenberg, O., Vchera (Yesterday). The author revealed
certain facts in Shcheglovitov's defense, but noting his later moral
downfall, he says there was nothing gradual about it, it was a land-
slide. This observation, suggesting some mysterious catastrophe,
may or may not be acceptable. The drama of Shcheglovitov remained
a riddle, but there are reasons to believe that something exceptional
did influence him.
      11. Miliukov, P. N., Three Attempts, p. 12.

Chapter Two

1. A club for community leaders which I described in detail in my first book. Vlast i Obshchestvennost na Zakatie Staroi Rossii (Government and Society in the Period of Decline of Old Russia), p. 291.
2. The stenographic report of this session was not published after the dissolution of the Duma.
3. The list is taken from Ezerski's book, Pervaia Duma (The First Duma).
4. Lokot, The First Duma.
5. Lokot, The First Duma, p. 142.
6. Lokot, The First Duma, p. 118.
7. Vinaver, Konflikty V Pervoi Dumie (Conflicts in the First Duma), p. 9.

Chapter Three

1. Izvolsky, A. P., Au Service de la Russie (In Russia's Service), letter dated May 3-6, 1906.
2. Miliukov, P. N., Speech, April 28, 1906.
3. Miliukov, P. N., Speech, April 28, 1906.

Chapter Four

1. Vinaver, Konflikty (Conflicts).
2. Lokot, The First Duma, p. 163.
3. Iollos, G. B., Russkiia Viedomosti (Russian News).
4. Speech, May 3.
5. Conflicts, pp. 41, 42.

Chapter Five

1. Vinaver, Recently, p. 191. This proposal made by Vinaver aroused Shershenevich's enthusiasm. He dashed through the lobby, eyes shining, and shook Vinaver's hand while he exclaimed, "a stroke of genius, a stroke of genius. You have saved us..." This was the result of Cadet policy in the State Duma. They deserved something better.
2. Regarding partiality for the word "demand" I recall this incident. Cadet H. H. Shchepkin defeated the Octobrist candidate in the Moscow primaries, and a banquet was held in his honor in the Arts Club. Speaking of the forthcoming work of the Duma, the guest of honor said: "The winner of the primaries will not request, he will demand." His words met with stormy applause. Such is the significance of loud words in a meeting. Where is the force of the word "demand" if there is nothing with which to back it up? Such is the power of words over wisdom.

3. Miliukov, P. N. Russian Memoirs, July. The attitude has changed now. In his Memoirs it was not difficult for Miliukov to say that the address "included a request for complete amnesty." But this is not exact. The words "petition, request," were very carefully avoided and never mentioned.

Chapter Six

1. Miliukov, P. N. Russian Memoirs, July. Miliukov mentions the tsar's desire to reply in person. It is most surprising that he considers this "the continuation of the peculiar playing at parliament." Controversy with the tsar over the Duma's address would be the negation of parliamentarianism. This assertion of Miliukov is a reflection of the existing conception of comparing the Duma to the National Assembly of the French Revolution. During the revolution the king made a personal appearance on June 23, followed by Mirabeau's famous reply. But Miliukov forgot that at that time France had no parliament and no constitution.

2. Kokovtsev, Memoirs, pp. 183, 184.

3. Vinaver, Conflicts, p. 62.

4. Miliukov, P. N., Russian Memoirs, July. Miliukov contends that Count Heiden, supposedly, proved the "unconstitutionality" of the declaration. This is absolutely incorrect, and it may be seen from the stenographic report of his speech. He did not and could not do anything of the kind.

5. Who was the author of the declaration? Kokovtsev claims that it was written by Stolypin and Shcheglovitov only edited it (Memoirs, p. 184). Miliukov maintains (Russian Memoirs, July) that its author was that reactionary Gurko. This is unimportant, but what is surprising is that Miliukov, even now, considers it a weak and poorly motivated message to the Duma, aggressive in spirit. Apparently there is difficulty in judging impartially a matter which concerns one. Reading the declaration now could enable one to judge the fairness of this evaluation.

Chapter Seven

1. Miliukov, P. N., Russian Memoirs, July. Miliukov said that after this session of the Duma the idyll ended. The Duma's attack on the government and on the constitution was an idyll in his eyes.

2. Vinaver, Conflicts. (Quotation from Nasha Zhizn (Our Life), no. 445.) "This was the first, and to give credit where credit is due, possibly the most brilliant speech. This seemed to be the general consensus of opinion, and it impressed me as such."

3. I am speaking, of course, of the Duma, that is the address adopted by the Duma, and not the individual speeches; the government was replying only to the address.

4. Lednitski, May 3. Speaking during the debate on the address, Lednitski spoke especially about the Polish question. But the address did not mention it.

5. Miliukov, P. N., Russian Memoirs, June. Miliukov admits that he "intentionally influenced the meeting to adopt the formula proposed by the Trudoviki." He does not explain the reason for doing that.

Chapter Eight

1. Kokovtsev, V. N., Memoirs, pp. 183, 184. Kryzhanovski, S. E., Memoirs, p. 66.

Chapter Nine

1. This was in accordance with the constitution, Article 57 of the Statute of the Duma.

2. This formulation corresponds to Articles 56 and 57 of the Statute of the Duma, not in their present form but in the new one proposed on May 23.

Chapter Ten

1. The government was definitely not approaching the solution of this problem by abolition of capital punishment. That is why Muromtsev explained that the Duma is itself "part of the government." Apparently the introduction of the Duma's bill was regarded as the government's approach to the repeal of the death sentence.

Chapter Twelve

1. Vinaver, Recently, p. 137.

Chapter Thirteen

1. Count Kokovtsev, V. N., Memoirs, p. 176.

2. Miliukov, P. N., Russian Memoirs. Miliukov introduces unexpected information as though Trepov agreed to the Cadet plan for expropriation on condition that this reform come from the tsar without the Duma's participation. I do not know who could have given Trepov authority for such an illegal action under the existing constitution, but there is one characteristic and instructive feature in it. In the

program of the Cadets and indeed in the whole Duma, expropriation
became a tactical maneuver, a weapon to attract peasant sympathy
to the Duma, not an agrarian reform for the benefit of the peasants.
This gave Trepov an opportunity to use it to promote political aims,
to win support for the monarch. The sin of the Cadet agrarian project lay in the fact that it disavowed the country's interests for considerations of this kind. Trepov only followed their example.

3. Russian Memoirs, July. In the July issue of Russian
Memoirs, the last one I was able to read before publishing my book,
Miliukov concludes his Memoirs with this expression: "...the question of the dissolution of the Duma entered the last decisive phase.
What became of the plans for a 'ministry enjoying the confidence of
the Duma' we shall see later on." This conforms to his idea that
later negotiations were a continuation of the previous ones with Trepov about a parliamentary ministry. In this mistaken conception lay
the source of later misunderstandings. Miliukov has not renounced
this idea even in his latest memoirs.

4. Izvolski, A. P., Memoirs, 1923, p. 197.

5. Miliukov, Three Attempts. Shipov, D. N., Memoirs and the
Dumas. Shipov recorded Stolypin's story of his conversation with
Miliukov. The latter adds some comments to it, thus the fact is in-
disputable.

6. Probably to soften the abruptness, amusing when the real
attitudes of the participants is known, Miliukov adds that he referred
to Shipov. This is an incorrect allusion, for Shipov did not say anything like this to Stolypin. Miliukov was confused: Shipov spoke of
this to Muromtsev, not to Stolypin, when they discussed a Cadet, not
a coalition, cabinet under his chairmanship. In the conversation with
Stolypin, Shipov mentioned no ministerial portfolios.

7. Miliukov, P. N. He emphasizes this even more categorically in Memoirs.

Chapter Fourteen

1. Simultaneously with this debate, the Duma was engaged in
the discussion of the Bielostok Jewish pogrom and sent authorized
agents to investigate this pogrom on the spot.

Conclusion

1. Miliukov, P. N., Russian Memoirs, February, 1939.

2. Poliakov-Litovtsev: "On n'est trahi que par les siens."
It is curious that this fault of Miliukov was regarded as a merit.
During the jubilee celebrations one of his admirers wrote: "On
thinking it over, one comes to the conclusion that Miliukov was the

only real politician in the period of the four Dumas. There were social politicians, industrial politicians, professor politicians, lawyer
politicians, landlord politicians, but Miliukov alone was just a politician, though he was a learned historian and professor."

3. Russian Memoirs, March, 1931.

4. Miliukov, P. N., Latest News, May 30, 1937. Miliukov
stated that I proved unable to evaluate the "deep faith of the Cadet
leaders in the principles they defended, and the enthusiasm aroused
by the broad scope of events."

RUSSIAN AND EAST EUROPEAN SERIES

Russian and East European Institute
Indiana University

VOLUMES IN PRINT

All correspondence should be addressed to the

INDIANA UNIVERSITY PRESS
TENTH AND MORTON STREETS
BLOOMINGTON, INDIANA